The Postcolonial Cl

Theory, Culture & Society

Theory, Culture & Society caters for the resurgence of interest in culture within contemporary social science and the humanities. Building on the heritage of classical social theory, the book series examines ways in which this tradition has been reshaped by a new generation of theorists. It also publishes theoretically informed analyses of everyday life, popular culture, and new intellectual movements.

EDITOR: Mike Featherstone, *Nottingham Trent University*

SERIES EDITORIAL BOARD
Roy Boyne, *University of Durham*
Mike Hepworth, *University of Aberdeen*
Scott Lash, *Goldsmiths College, University of London*
Roland Robertson, *University of Aberdeen*
Bryan S. Turner, *University of Singapore*

THE TCS CENTRE
The *Theory, Culture & Society* book series, the journals *Theory, Culture & Society* and *Body & Society*, and related conference, seminar and postgraduate programmes operate from the TCS Centre at Nottingham Trent University. For further details of the TCS Centre's activities please contact:

Centre Administrator
The TCS Centre, Room 175
Faculty of Humanities
Nottingham Trent University
Clifton Lane, Nottingham, NG11 8NS, UK
e-mail: tcs@ntu.ac.uk
web: http://www.tcs.ntu.ac.uk

Recent volumes include:

The Body in Culture, Technology and Society
Chris Shilling

Globalization and Belonging
Mike Savage, Gaynor Bagnall, Brian Longhurst

The Sport Star
Barry Smart

Diaspora and Hybridity
Kalra, Kaur and Hutnyk

The Postcolonial Challenge

Towards Alternative Worlds

Couze Venn

SAGE Publications

London ● Thousand Oaks ● New Delhi

© Couze Venn 2006

First published 2006

Published in association with Theory, Culture & Society,
Nottingham Trent University

Apart from any fair dealing for the purposes of research or
private study, or criticism or review, as permitted under the
Copyright, Designs and Patents Act, 1988, this publication
may be reproduced, stored or transmitted in any form, or by
any means, only with the prior permission in writing of the
publishers, or in the case of reprographic reproduction, in
accordance with the terms of licenses issued by the
Copyright Licensing Agency. Inquiries concerning reproduction
outside those terms should be sent to the publishers.

SAGE Publications Ltd
1 Oliver's Yard
55 City Road
London EC1Y 1SP

SAGE Publications Inc.
2455 Teller Road
Thousand Oaks, California 91320

SAGE Publications India Pvt Ltd
B-42, Panchsheel Enclave
Post Box 4109
New Delhi 110 017

British Library Cataloguing in Publication data

A catalogue record for this book is available from the
British Library

ISBN: 978-07619-7162-7

Library of Congress control number available

Typeset by C&M Digitals (P) Ltd., Chennai, India

For Hari Ashurst-Venn

Contents

Acknowledgements

I have been lucky to have known so many interesting colleagues and students over the years, generous with their time and ideas, with whom I have been able to discuss and develop much of what appears in this book. These exchanges have ranged across disciplinary boundaries so that they have somehow become fused in a mixture of theory and friendships that has shaped my writing. The following people have read and commented on the whole or parts of early drafts or engaged in exchanges that have provided insights and arguments without which this book would be more inadequate than it is: Pal Ahluwalia, Roy Boyne, Neal Curtis, Mike Featherstone, Julian Henriques, Matt Merefield, Scott Lash, Tina Papoulias, Bobby Sayyid, Scarlett Thomas Patrick Williams. Particular thanks are due to Matt, Scarlett and Neal who surveyed the work as it progressed and whose keen eye for lame arguments and insipid prose has saved me from some pitfalls. A constant source of inspiration has been the research seminars held at the Nottingham Trent University that I organized for the Theory, Culture & Society Centre. Through their ideas and their work the participants have enriched my understanding of the wider issues that are addressed in the book, and I have the following to thank: Roger Bromley, Steve Brown, Elizabeth Burrell, Sokho Choe, Neal Curtis, Mike Featherstone, Anders Hog Hansen, Richard Johnson, Kenichi Kawasaki, Gulshan Khan, Joost van Loon, Kevin Love, Sonia Melo, Matt Merefield, John Phillips, Inga Scharf, Tomoko Tamari, John Tomlinson, Neil Turnbull, Sally Waddingham, Patrick Williams, Andreas Wittel. They of course bear no responsibility for any inadequacy that may remain in the book. I must thank also a number of anonymous readers whose critical comments have encouraged some much needed rewriting. My editors at Sage, Chris Rojek, Kay Bridger and Mila Steele have been amazingly patient and supportive, often making suggestions that have made my task easier. I am indebted to my family, Francesca, Scarlett, Sam, Hari, who inspire me to write and have given constant support and encouragement.

1

Rethinking the Scope of the Postcolonial

Postcoloniality and the 'new world order'

This book begins with the recognition that new forms of colonization are at work in transforming the world today, more insidious and totalizing than previous forms. It intervenes in this moment of danger at the theoretical and methodological levels, interrogating the present conjuncture through a reconceptualization of problems ranging from issues of modernization and identity to the problem of establishing a political economy of **postmodern** times that could open up new grounds for imagining alternative worlds. In doing so, it develops a critical **postcolonial** standpoint that extends the focus and terrain of postcolonial theory, drawing still on the discursive formations with which it has been in solidarity, such as feminism, race studies, cultural and development studies, but equally on positions in the social studies of science and technology and in critical phenomenology in order to interrogate the material cultures and the complex character of the apparatuses that constitute the plural lifeworlds of today. The re-orientation in approach is, of course, sustained by the vocabulary and lessons that postcolonial studies has already established in its critical engagement with European colonization and its legacy at the material and discursive levels, for example, the conviction that the relationships between the present and the past, the local and the global, the vernacular and the cosmopolitan, the postcolonial and the postmodern are much more intertwined and of longer duration than appears in many accounts in the social sciences. In challenging established boundaries, disciplinary or otherwise, and in seeking to overcome the limitations posed by the dualities of north–south, developed–developing, modern–traditional, centre–periphery, it is concerned not so much with showing their interrelatedness and mutual dependencies, something already accomplished in postcolonial work, but with the underlying problem of opening critical spaces for new narratives of becoming and emancipation. The orientation of this questioning is transmodern, that is, properly postcolonial and post-occidental.

The intervention which this book makes is shadowed by the global 'war on terrorism', 'regime change' in Afghanistan, Iraq and elsewhere and homicidal fundamentalism that clearly illuminate what is at stake in the new world order which is being put into place. We can now see more starkly the alignment of forces in establishing or resisting the new machineries of what Hardt and Negri (2000) have called Empire. But it does not follow that one therefore knows what is to be done, for it is not a matter of a simple option between existing parties, for instance, between the kind of globalization from above advocated by the Davos World Economic Forum and its tributary organizations, and countervailing fundamentalisms founded in revisionist religious doctrines. We are now living in a time of the clash of fundamentalisms – religious, ethnic, neo-liberal – and the simultaneous archaic and postmodern terrors they inflict. Aligned against such forces, one finds the broad church of the 'globalization from below' as evidenced in the great gathering of oppositional movements at Porto Allegre in 2001 and 2002, and Mumbai in 2004 under the banner of the World Social Forum (WSF). The latter has brought together an uneven and disparate combination of a variety of counter-hegemonic social movements committed to resist or challenge in one way or another the ravages and dispossessions produced by existing forms of exploitation based upon gender, capital or race (Fisher and Ponniah, 2003).

Foremost among the forces of subjugating power, one would single out neo-liberalism and its project of establishing the sovereignty, if not **hegemony** of a postmodern totalizing form of capitalism. Mentioned *ad nauseam* in every debate, it must nevertheless, like capitalism, be kept in sight in any analysis of postcoloniality. As Fisher and Ponniah put it:

> Neoliberal globalization is not simply economic domination of the world but also the imposition of a monolithic thought that consolidates vertical forms of difference and prohibits the public from imagining diversity in egalitarian, horizontal terms. Capitalism, imperialism, monoculturalism, patriarchy, white suprematicism, and the domination of biodiversity have coalesced under the current form of globalization. (2003: 10)

There is a lot to unpack here, and to examine critically, as I shall do in Chapter 4, but the thrust of the argument is to highlight the emergence of a new form of colonization, totalizing in its scope, since it invests every sphere of life, including temporalities of the lived, and leaves no space for alternatives.[1] Hardt and Negri (2003) see in the WSF the expression of an anti-capitalist transnationalism in search of 'a new democratic cosmopolitanism', being established through linkages and networks that are concerned with 'finding what is common in our differences and expanding that commonality while our differences proliferate' (ibid.: xvii).

As Young (2001, 2003) shows, these differences and commonalities have a history that encompasses colonial struggles of liberation and socialist struggles, as well as the divergences regarding the particularities of locality. These are echoed in differences at the level of theory addressing the wider problems of the analysis of globalization and problems to do with what is to be done politically. One important aspect of these differences appears in the underlying tensions between universalism and particularism that runs through the issues that have surfaced time and again in the history of emancipatory struggles. Mbembe (2001), addressing the problem from the point of view of postcolonial theory, highlights the inadequacy of two kinds of lexicons, generated by the tension between universalist theory and particularist contentions, that have emerged to make sense of Africa as a project of development of the nation. One lexicon is located in the discourse of social theory elaborated within the conceptual framework of Western modernity that tried to understand Africa 'solely through conceptual structures and fictional representations used precisely to deny African societies any historical depth and to define them as radically *other*, as all that the West is not' (ibid.: 11; original emphasis). The other approach can be detected in the discourses that challenge the colonial denigration of the African subject and that seek to validate the memory of a misunderstood Africa and rediscover the assumed 'essence' or distinctive genius of the black 'race', as, for instance, in the Negritude movement and the more recent black essentialist position. Echoing du Bois' ([1903] 1989) analysis of double consciousness and Fanon's (1967) explorations of the splittings of identity arising from the othering of the colonized, Mbembe argues that the scene upon which was played out the tension between universalism and particularism, emancipation and assimilation, has ended in an 'inner twoness' or doubleness for colonial subjectivity, and 'an endless interrogation of the possibility, for the African subject, of achieving a balance between his/her total identification with "traditional" (in the philosophies of authenticity) African life, and his/her merging with, and subsequent loss in, modernity (in the discourse of alienation)' (2001: 12). The recognition of the historical dimension in these struggles and their theorizations, and the recognition of the co-existing 'multiple temporalities' – the linear, fast time of modernity and the slower recurrent time of 'tradition', and the home or the domus – in which real subjects find themselves in concrete situations everywhere is a lesson that postcolonial theory must keep on its agenda. The point, however, is that if postcolonial critique is about redrawing the diagrams of possible worlds, one must now abandon these spatial and temporal dichotomies and the political divisions they support and move towards a view of the commonalities that offer the possibility of properly dismantling **colonialism** in its various forms.

This means that it must break with the narratives of 'development' and 'modernization' that support the idea of Western modernity, or rather occidentalism (Venn, 2000), as the model of social advancement. Postcolonial critique therefore continues and seeks to complete the work of decolonization. It develops an oppositional analytical standpoint that targets the conditions, the narratives, the relations of power that, in their combined effects, support the iniquitous forms of sociality and the varieties of pauperizations that characterize the current world order. These forms include 'traditional' and customary socialities that inscribe gender and communalist ethnic oppressions. Postcolonial interrogation takes for granted the argument that the forces that established the Western form of colonialism and imperialism continue to operate, often in altered forms, through mutations in local circumstances, and through different apparatuses, to constitute what Mbembe

(2001) has called the postcolony. The latter concept, though applying more strikingly to Africa in Mbembe's argument, is marked, first, by the co-existence in the concrete postcolonial world of displacements and entwine-ments arising from the multiple temporalities 'made up of discontinuities, reversals, inertias, and swings that overlay one another, interpenetrate one another, and envelope one another: an entanglement' (ibid.: 14), and, second, by the mutation of the form of governance and sovereignty that operated in colonial conditions into a form of commandment that now rules on the basis largely of the violent production of insecurity and scarcity. It is crucial to point out, in relation to this history, the fact that the process of decoloniza-tion has been distorted by the intervention of the cold war, or Third World War, which enlisted countries of the 'Third World' on one side or the other and derailed their own alternative projects of development.

It follows that the prefix in postcoloniality is not meant to signal the end of the previous period but to stand for the sign of an emancipatory project, that is, it announces a goal yet to be realized: that of dismantling the economic, political and social structures and values, the attitudes and ideas that appeared with European colonialism and its complex combination with capitalism and Western modernity, and it is important to add, with pre-existing forms of exploitation. Postcolonial critique is thus a counter-occidentalism as well as an emancipatory task. A longer and complex history underlies this standpoint about postcolonialism, aligning it with the history of anti-colonial struggles, itself already

> a diasporic production, a revolutionary mixture of the indigenous and the cos-mopolitan, a complex constellation of situated local knowledges combined with radical, universal political principles ... and widespread political contacts between different revolutionary organizations that generated common practi-cal information and material support as well as spreading radical political and intellectual ideas. (Young, 2001: 2)

This view adds to the understanding of anti-colonial struggles as the activities that subvert, disrupt and contest the strategies towards the homogenization and privileging of a centre or an origin or a sovereignty or a world-view which is at the heart of every form of colonization or subjugation, past and existing. In this book colonialism is understood in terms of forms of dispossession sup-ported by these forms of homogenization, often acting in combination. It will be clear also that the point of view of diaspora that I am elaborating under-mines the grounds of the discourse of colonialism.

This is the wider theoretical and political frame and the broader spatio-temporal space, or **longue durée**, that circumscribe the arguments in the book. Yet we know too that when we divert attention from the 'big picture', we have to recognize the enormous differences that exist if we were to contrast the everyday lives of people in a village, say, in the Sind province of Pakistan with what happens in a village in England, or in a town in the Midwest of the USA or in Brazil. Indeed, the difference between the same Pakistani village and Karachi is just as striking at the level of technology, customs, laws, the spatial disposition of the material world and the temporal flow of daily life. However, in postcolonial times, all have come under the scrutiny of the new surveillance, intensifying the gaze of the multitude of organizations – governments, NGOs, transnational corporations, experts and researchers – that have for some time taken these places to be the object of their interest. In the 'informational turn' of regulatory bodies like the International Monetary Fund, they figure in reports about economic development, health, demographic composition, education, technology, crime, poverty, natural resources, and so on that are used in the strategic calculations of disciplinary forces. In these circumstances one may well ask: where and what is the postcolonial? Once, in the days of the 'cold war', and after the Bandung Conference in 1955 of 'non-aligned', 'tri-continental' nations' (i.e. from Asia, Africa, Latin America), it was possible to imagine what was called the 'Third World' as a space in which the post-independence countries could detach themselves from the legacy of imperialism and the territorial and ideological investment to which the world was being subjected, and thus determine their own destiny. The wars fought across the territories of the ex-colonies in the name of the cold war, together with the strategic interventions of globalizing organizations such as the World Bank, the International Monetary Fund, UN bodies and trade associations have dispelled the illusion of independence or autonomy. Furthermore, differences at the local level have become open to transnational and transregional processes and systems that delimit what is possible at the practical level of social action.

These processes, clearly, relate to globalization; they direct attention to the flows and turbulences and networks in the circulation of goods, peoples, cultures, technologies, and ideas that have come to characterize the global. These flows and networks establish mobile and complex relationships between what Appadurai calls 'scapes', that is, the flow of people, communication forms and practices, technology, money, ideologies that can be thought of in terms of ethnoscapes, mediascapes, technoscapes, finanscapes and ideoscapes – to which one should add an infoscape, though it is implied in all these categories. They constitute the 'building blocks' for 'imagined worlds'; they are 'the multiple worlds which are constituted by the historically situated imaginations of persons and groups spread around the world' affecting everything from clothing styles to the working of capital (Appadurai, 1993: 328, 329). I would emphasize the processual co-articulation between these scapes, as I establish in the rest of the book, and particularly in Chapter 4. This heightened sense that the inter-connectedness between the local and the global at these different levels establishes a complex and mobile organism is one element that has led me to look for ways of establishing at the analytical level clearer or more explicit links between postcolonial studies and cognate fields such as cultural studies, political economy, gender studies, the social studies of the technosciences and the theorization of subjectivity. They overlap on the terrain of cultural theory, itself an eclectic bundle of concepts and theories from semiotics, literary studies, philosophy, ethnography, sociology, history, psychoanalysis assembled in opposition to conventional or authoritative protocols for describing the socio-cultural world. This theoretical apparatus is sketched in the methodological section below, and put to work in the postcolonial analysis of modernity, identity and political economy that I go on to develop.

The standpoint it constructs has been directed in this book into an interrogation of modernity and modernization from the point of view of its **genealogy** and its constitutive relation with capitalism and colonialism (Chapter 2), a complex I have called occidentalism (Venn, 2000, see below), and the analysis of postcolonial identity from the point of view of the **imaginary** institution of the social world (Castoriadis, 1987), conscious of the fractured or disjointed temporalities and signifying practices that make up the experiential reality of that world (see Chapter 3). Colonialism, of course, attempts to subsume the different temporalities, thus literally the different lifeworlds, within the timeframe of the subjugating power. The chapter on modernity attempts to make visible the peculiarities of modernity as a period, arguing that a genealogy shows that postcolonial thought must be attentive to both the taken-for-granted aspects of modernity buried in the minds of people everywhere – as in the positive evaluations, say, about science and technology – inscribed in the concept and in the process of modernization, as well as the unexamined features of modernity that continue to have effects precisely because they are invisible, for instance, the basis for individualism in the presupposition of the unitary, rational, self-centred, autonomous character of the modern subject. This resilient relay concept is still central in law and in the social sciences; we find it in psychological accounts of every aspect of human behaviour; in judgements about rights and responsibilities and culpabilities take it for granted; it can be detected in interpretations of new technology and research in cybernetics in relation to the human and to artificial intelligence; it is posited as a given in the technologies of new (increasingly neo-liberal) governance that takes the individual to be the primary focus of all its regulatory and disciplinary machinery; it reappears in the form of the ego-centric ideology sustaining consumer culture; it lives on in the efforts to redraw the map of equitable redistribution and capabilities that some radical liberal thinkers like Nussbaum and Sen have been making (see Chapter 4) and, it goes without saying, it has become essentialized in the foundation of neo-liberalism.

There is no doubt that the task of making sense of this complex set of interrelated problems is a difficult one. The comprehensive scope of the book comes up against the hazards inherent in any project that attempts to combine in a coherent way apparently quite disparate areas and interests. The solution proposed here has been to organize the material in terms of key themes that have surfaced both in the literature on postcoloniality and in the 'globalization from below' movement exemplified in the concerns of the World Social Forum. This organization of the material is clarified in what follows.

A methodological assemblage for postcolonial critique

I must emphasize that the critical ambitions of the book would not have been possible without the many fine Introductions[2] to 'postcolonialism' and postcolonial theory that already clarify the conceptual ground upon which postcolonial critique has been established so far. They provide the detailed accounts of the key texts and authors, and explanations of the main disciplinary approaches, sufficient to enable the reader to tackle the complex theoretical apparatuses, such as poststructuralism and Marxism, that are deployed in the field; they help to make sense of the debates and disputes that have enlivened postcolonial studies, for instance, regarding issues to do with the when, what, where, which and whose of postcoloniality (see Childs and Williams, 1997; Stuart Hall, 1996); they point to the political and theoretical stakes fought out through these debates. They make it unnecessary for me to repeat these arguments, except where they enable me to try and relocate critique in the wake of the kinds of developments that I have indicated and that have conjoined to determine the context in which the postcolonial as a field of study needs now to be reconsidered. This context is marked, as I noted at the beginning, by the profound changes that are reshaping the world at the level of culture and knowledge, and by the increase in the scale and intensity of exploitation and violence across the world, exceeding even that experienced in the period of the European colonial enterprise of subjugation. The two periods are clearly not unconnected; indeed, the continuities as well as discontinuities emerge as soon as one examines the conditions for the current conflicts in any particular region, from the Congo to the Philippines to Israel/Palestine.

In this book, the linkages are constructed through analytical threads that run through the different chapters and are relayed in terms of several reconstituted problematics common to them, regarding respectively modernity, subjectivity and agency, political economy. Among the analytical threads, I will highlight the following: (1) occidentalism; (2) **genealogy** and critical phenomenology; (3) subjectivity, **diaspora** and **creolization**; and (4) disciplinary societies and militarism. They are combined on the basis of a methodological **assemblage** that I elaborate below.

Occidentalism

The centrality of modernity, as a period and as a discourse (or rather a matrix of discourses) for the analysis of postcoloniality can be understood by reference to what I have called occidentalism (Venn, 1993, 2000). I propose this term to designate the correlation of a conceptual space, a global, world-transforming project and a world order. It is the result of the co-articulation of these three developments that together have instituted the world as it exists today, namely, the emergence of a technocratic modernity as dominant at the level of thought and practice, rational capitalism and its global

7

implantation, and the Western form of colonialism. It is also the conceptual and historical space of the becoming-West of Europe and the becoming-modern of the world. Critical postcolonial studies targets that conceptual and imaginative space, rethinking in the process the fundamental principles that legitimate and ground it. That is why it must address modernity as a period: its foundational narratives, the functioning of colonialism and capitalism in its emergence and development; equally, it involves dealing with issues of universality, difference, plurality, emancipatory narratives, and in the background the underlying ethical question of what it means 'to live well with and for others in just institutions' (Ricoeur, 1992: 330).

The conceptual framework of occidentalism is circumscribed by the following propositions. First, the idea that the distinguishing feature of modernity is that it understands itself in the form of a project, that is, as an idea to be realized. The idea of project inscribes a drive for constant change towards desired ends, that is, it advocates linear historical progress through the renewed rejection of the past in favour of a better future achieved through human action. This linear temporal dimension is aligned with a narrative of the becoming of the subject, and with the goal of the transformation of society towards an ideal of sociality to be realized, guided by master narratives that function as the ultimate foundation legitimating the project (Lyotard, [1976] 1984). It is important to point out that other projects and master narratives have existed in all cultures, mostly by reference to religious doctrines that define the ideal community and seek its realization. In order to locate the specificity of modernity I will start with the claim that every period and every major culture have been framed by the specific answers that each provides to some basic questions about human existence, questions that one can group by reference to concepts of truth, the good, beauty, and, I should add, the way human temporality is understood and lived. Religious discourses ground such concepts in a theology, while philosophies establish their foundation in the discourses of epistemology, ethics, and aesthetics. The conceptual framework or, rather, **episteme**, of every major period determines the relationship between them. The significant aspect that I want to highlight is that notions of truth and so on have to be grounded in principles and ideas that function as foundation for them. Until modernity, that foundation was sought in a religious or quasi-religious discourse, and therefore by reference to a sacred dimension, usually by reference to an idea of God, and an after-life, that is, on the basis of a transcendent Being or a transcendent domain or state (Heaven, Nirvana) which is placed outside any doubt and outside of human-time. Typically, this religious and/or theological or philosophical foundational discourse addresses very general issues that inscribe universal principles, with implications or lessons for how every subject is to judge his or her own actions, that is to say, it is made to relate to an ethos and to a way of life by being applied to every individual, instructing each one as to his or her conduct; one finds it in its most elaborate form in monotheisms and in varieties of Buddhism. So, correlated to every foundational discourse, whether it is religious or secular (as in the discourse of modernity), we find a **problematic** about the subject, or rather about being, inscribing the narratives and concepts that give a content and meaning to ideas of truth, beauty, the good, a content that can be attested to at the level of the culture and of individual lives. This is not surprising, given that religious and foundational discourses in the last instance arise from existential experiences and realities, specifically, the recognition of finitude and death, the experience of suffering, loss, and fragility, the recognition of a liminal or spiritual dimension to the experiential that exceeds representation (for example, the experience of the sublime), and, crucially, the recognition of temporality itself (see Chapter 2).

One of the characteristics of modernity as a period, then, is that it imagined it would bring into existence a particular concept of the subject, namely, the subject as (ideally) the unitary, rational, autonomous, self-sufficient, masculine, and European agent of the history of humanity. This notion of the subject, sometimes referred to as the logocentric subject, is located in the discourse of modernity as at once a project, that is, something to be realized, and the agency of that project; it is correlated to the idea of the advancement or progress of 'humanity', that is, the idea of the linear development in time – as History and its teleological thrust – both of civilizations and of the subject. Part of my approach in understanding postcoloniality is that the discourse of modernity, as well as the process of the institution of modernity throughout the world, through colonialism and in the form of modernization, has introduced this narrative of the subject that appears to have become hegemonic in the social and human sciences and in technologies of formation of subjects, though it usually competes with religious and 'traditional' narratives when it comes to the reality of how people actually live their lives. The development of such a view of subjective becoming alongside colonialism has meant that its dominant form as Eurocentric and masculine has been over-determined. As I shall establish in the next chapter, the whole of Western metaphysics, classical ontology and modern epistemology find their expression and relay in that conceptualization of the subject. The latter is the distinguishing mark of the difference from non-Western, nonmodern forms of the subject; the dominant form has been positioned as the privileged model against which, in the discourse of Western modernity, other forms are declared defective and underdeveloped, or even arrested in time at some primordial primitive stage, lagging behind. The notion of civilization itself, and therefore of differences in civilization, can be rethought in terms of the particular and different narratives of the subject that are proposed as desirable or ideal and appropriate in different foundational discourses for determining the worthwhile life. The implication is that the postcolonial as much as the postmodern is concerned with visions of the future that implicate the transfiguration of this subject of modernity.

The peculiarity of the philosophical or theoretical discourse of modernity that I am highlighting is precisely the fact that it is grounded in secular principles and that it invents the idea of temporality as linear progression towards an anticipated future. By contrast, religious or theological discourses propose an ordained established order in the world present in the everyday and in an explicit metaphysics that vests that order in a transcendent realm known to God alone. In this way, the cosmological and the experiential are thought to reflect each other – for instance, in the idea of a homologous or symmetrical relation between the microcosm and the macrocosm – while the human being is assigned a determined but relatively insignificant place as an element of the system. One finds this world-view in religious doctrine, say, Christianity, just before the emergence of modernity from the sixteenth century when it had established a conceptual system for understanding both the universe as a whole and the human being: it functioned as the basis for the production and distribution of wealth; it determined the principles regulating government and the exercise of power; it was the basis for law, while knowledge was produced within its epistemological framework; and it incited the production of every kind of artistic work. Within its conceptual framework it was impossible to think of human subjects as autonomous agents of history. The difference is striking when we consider that the liberal version of the project of modernity claims that the history of 'humanity' is a process of advancement directed by the agency of the rational, self-sufficient, autonomous subject and the instrumentality of the rational sciences. This radical difference in foundation marks out modernity from all other narratives that address the key or 'big' questions about the meaning of human existence. I should point out here that the force of religious or spiritual narratives of being have not significantly declined, despite (sociology's) claims that associate modernization with the secularization of beliefs, claims that now appear wishful. Indeed, in the context of the postmodern loss of faith in the project of modernity – bound up with the failures of democracy and the epistemological, ontological and ethical violences associated with occidentalist modernization – these narratives have acquired renewed force in guiding people regarding their conduct, or in functioning as ideology authorizing ways of being or in shaping social policy, for example, about abortion. Religious and 'spiritual' master narratives have become more, rather than less, important.

For reasons that I shall explain in Chapter 2, the instrumental and technocratic dimension of the project of modernity gradually came to dominate the process of modernization and the criteria used to determine and legitimate its course of action (Adorno and Horkheimer, 1979; Habermas, 1983; Lyotard, [1976] 1984). The ethical and emancipatory goals and values of social development were gradually replaced or converted into those of efficiency and economic growth, though they survived in the radical discourses that also emerged with modernity; the ideal of the good society became identified with the goal of prosperity and orderliness. Indeed, in postmodern times, the distinction between what is just and what is true has been dissolved in the criterion of good performativity, that is, the maximization of input–output ratios in practices that allocate lives to the growth of power, the legitimation of which 'is based on its optimising the system's performance – efficiency' (Lyotard, [1976] 1984: xxiv). This privilege of the instrumental-bureaucratic dimension and the value of efficiency is what I call positivist or technocratic modernity.

The hegemony of technocratic rationality can be related conceptually to the second proposition regarding occidentalism, namely, the claim that rational capitalism, as a mode of production, operates on the basis of concepts and practices that fundamentally dehumanize the human being and are indifferent to human suffering. Its logic motivates a tendency to colonize modes of thinking and lifeworlds, converting everything into commodities, from human beings and objects of consumption to the arts and knowledge, to be bought and sold as abstract entities made equivalent through money as the prime determinant and measure of value. This tendency of capitalism is congruent with a totalizing and universalizing impulse.

The third aspect of occidentalism is the idea that the European model of colonialism is distinct from other models in that its form of appropriation-as-dispossession is overlaid with a discourse that locates the colonized as 'Other', not just the stranger or the different, but as fundamentally and ontologically inferior beings to be brought under either the tutelage or the ban of the West (itself constituted within the logic of the West and its 'other'). The violence characteristic of this form of colonialism combines physical violence (common to all colonizations) with epistemic violence, that is, the denial of the authority and validity of the knowledge of the colonized; ontological violence, namely, the refusal to recognize the (non-assimilated) colonized subject as a fellow human being; and symbolic and psychic violence, the silencing of the voice of the colonized, the denial of the latter's ability to tell his or her story. This form of colonialism, particularly its denial of the humanity and agency of the colonized, is congruent with the dehumanizing spirit of capitalism and the technocratic reason of positivist modernity. The co-emergence and co-articulation of these three aspects of occidentalism have meant that they have shaped each other in the course of the history of modernity and its implantation or its translation in other cultures. The genealogy (see below) of these effects passes through the reconstruction of the world-view framed by occidentalism and the reconstruction of the apparatuses that were pragmatically put into place to constitute the material world of modernity and modern forms of sociality. A central part of the postcolonial standpoint I am proposing is the claim that the effects of these developments abide, albeit unevenly, at all levels of thought and of the material world globally (but see the case of Japan in the next chapter). Furthermore, an important element of the analytical framework shaping the book is the view that the situation noted at the beginning of this chapter is a development in keeping with the logic of occidentalism, perhaps even its completion. It follows that the postcolonial as post-occidental critique aims to make visible the mechanisms at work in the making of this reality, including the task of showing the interrelations at the level of theory between postcolonial studies and that reality.

Genealogy and critical phenomenology

The concept of genealogy is used in this book to indicate the recognition of the historicity of the present, that is, the sense that the present inscribes and is conditioned by the historical past in the very material reality of the everyday world and in the accretion of meanings attaching to its every aspect. The constitutive presence of the past in the present, and the indeterminate, contingent mobility of its effects are a reality that postcolonial studies cannot ignore. In his work, Foucault (1975, 1976) applied the concept of genealogy more specifically to the history of concepts, for instance, the concept of discipline or that of sexuality, when he retraced the conditions of possibility that in the course of the development of the particular concept determined its mutations and its material effects. Genealogy is used in Foucault to counter the idea of continuities in history that are supposed to be stable and to follow logical paths of development from some clear origin, as in the conventional history of the sciences. Foucault here relies on the work of Canguilhem and Bachelard who elaborated approaches critical to conventional histories of science in their development of an epistemological history and an historical epistemology respectively; these approaches reject the idea that there are logical lines of progression from an early state or stage of knowledge to the later state, a progress that a 'history of ideas' was meant to trace through the search for precursors in specific discipline. This work emphasizes instead the positivity of scientific activity, the constructed, 'materially normed' character of concepts, the constant interrogation of knowledge, the historicity of concepts and discontinuities in the history of the sciences (Bachelard, 1949, 1951, [1938] 1972; Canguilhem, 1966, 1975; see Venn, 1982, for an elaboration). Located against this polemical background, genealogy shows that these neat lines of progression appear so only retrospectively, and is thus a simple reiteration of the internalist **paradigm** operating in the history of ideas. Instead it draws attention to contingency and disruption in history (whether of the concept or of practice), to conditions of possibility that include cultural and historical factors outside particular disciplines, and so to the constructed character of concepts. The approach I am signalling assumes that the writing of history proceeds in terms of an archaeological search for the hidden and for what every narration erases in its telling, including, symptomatically, a history of errors. Equally, the secret life of the concept reveals the unexpected and the often invisible but ever present effects of power. It is possible to reconstruct different genealogies, since the decision on conditions of possibility depends not only on attention to a broad canvas but also to the interests that guide the judgement of effects, for example, in a genealogy of the World Bank or Bollywood that would differ according to, say, a feminist instead of a liberal economic standpoint. Genealogies are not neutral: as histories of the present, they construct a specific gaze, thus offering a specific orientation on the past and the future. The application of genealogy to the emergence of modernity in Chapter 2 enables one to reconstruct the complex effects of the colonization of the New World on the self-representation of Europe, on the recasting of discourses about nature and culture, on the disruption of the foundations that supported the hegemony of Christian doctrine and Greek science, on the central role allocated to the modern subject in the discourse of modernity. Thus, the history of European colonialism and European encounters with the rest of the world is revealed to have been a constitutive factor in capitalism and modernity (Goonatilake 1984; Nandy, 1990), both at the level of historical development and change as well as at the level of the discourses and knowledges that emerged and have come to be seen as the mark of modernity; there are serious implications for how one is to envisage the transmodern/transcolonial world to come.

My extension of the idea of genealogy supplements it with approaches developed within the social studies of the technosciences and their application to the analysis of practices of constitution of the social. The main components are: in addition to the epistemological history/historical epistemology that I have indicated earlier, the approaches in the social studies of science and technology that reject internalist explanations of their emergence and development in favour of situated and culturally embedded knowledges and the idea of a compossible relation between technology, or technics, and culture (Canguilhem, 1975; Haraway, 1991; Knorr-Cetina, 1981, 2002; Latour, 1993, 1997, 1999; Needham, 1969; Stengers, 1997; Venn, 1982, from a long list); postcolonial critiques of Eurocentric narratives of civilization and the development of Western sciences and technology that show the non-European provenance of key concepts and findings and make visible the borrowings and the dynamic transcultural interactions that have determined their development (Goonatilake, 1984; Harding, 1998); alternative approaches in the social sciences and humanities that emphasize complexity, co-articulation, heterogeneity, reciprocal conditioning among socio-cultural and economic factors (indicatively: Tarde, Castoriadis, de Certeau, Hall); philosophical reflections that elaborate the implications for the critique of occidentalism of alternative ontologies and epistemologies that break with Cartesianism and logocentrism that I began to develop in Venn (2000) (see also Heidegger, 1962; Ricoeur, 1992; Arendt, 1959; Derrida, 1982; Levinas, 1969). These diverse departures often ignore each other; in this book their combination is analytically organized in terms of a critical phenomenology that puts emphasis on two interrelated features: the technically and conceptually normed character of the world we encounter, and the constructed and historical character of that world from the standpoint of the existential, durable and meaning-constituting space in which subjects live. The following are examples of the cumulative, pragmatic, deliberative, polyglot, inter-subjective, structured-structurizing (if indeterminate) action and interchanges between human and material actors and actants: social structures such as the family, the state of knowledge at any particular point in time and its form of authorization, as in the idea of science, practices of production of material life and the discourses that have been invented to describe and regulate them, the inventive and renewed institution of communities or socialities through acting in common, in pursuing common goals, and institutions of all kinds that have gradually been put into place, as assemblages, as part of the conditions of existence of specific communities.

An example from Bachelard (1951) will allow me to clarify the relationship between genealogy and this critical phenomenology. Talking about the technical, and technically normed, apparatus that makes a world available for us to know, he stresses the fact that, for instance, the biologist sees what the microscope sees. Clearly, it is also the case that the microscope sees nothing, since it has neither a conceptual apparatus nor the sense of a questioning to direct its gaze. Besides, the biologist sees according to the coordination of the technical apparatus – the microscope – together with a conceptual apparatus and an orientation to the world inscribed in a paradigm (say, about the biochemistry of enzymes). Such coordination is achieved through an apprenticeship, that is, through a formation as biologist, with implications for cognitive and subjective location. Thus, when one looks at the technical means that one has at one's disposal, one must recognize that they have been developed over years under specific conditions, and are the product of previous knowledges and techniques and ways of acting upon the world; they function as extensors and prosthetic devices that amplify, but equally, structure what we are able to know about that world. In any case it is not a raw world, but one always-already worked upon and categorized by previous theoretical and technical knowledges and action. Furthermore, extending the scope of the example, one could argue that these extensors, props, artifices, prosthetic tools – works, in Arendt's (1959) sense, or equipment in the Heideggerian (1977) sense, or generative mechanisms as I would call them – are the scaffolding and the assemblages that insert the human into a world, so that one knows according to them. Assemblages are ordered, organized combinations of tools, knowledges, operating rules, techniques put into place in the form of interconnecting networks, ready to be set into motion to achieve goals specified by a practice (see also Deleuze and Guattari, 1988); thus, the stock exchange, the car, and the body can be considered as different kinds of assemblages.[3] The human cognitive process relies upon their framing and mediating function and has developed in a dynamic relation with them; they function not only as generative devices, but equally as threshold and as a tissue that connects the human and the natural (see also Haraway, 1991), and as memory devices that encode and archive the enduring history of human accomplishment.

One implication is that technologies and knowledges are profoundly social and cultural, to be understood within the scope of the historicity of lifeworlds and the intentionality of actors. If one bears in mind Foucault's insistence on examining the conditions of possibility of practices and discourses as part of constructing genealogies, then one must recognize that knowledges and technologies limit and circumscribe as much as they produce and reveal a world. Power is inscribed in the way they are operationalized, for instance, today in the functioning of what Derrida (2002) describes as the 'tele-techno-media-scientific, capitalistic, and politico-economic' complex instituting globality, discussed in Chapter 4. It is worth juxtaposing Heidegger's (1977) analysis of technology here (without developing it, and without the technophobic inclinations it betrays) since it tries to go beyond the 'instrumental and anthropological definition of technology' (ibid.: 5) so as to draw attention to the ability of a techne to bring forth, to 'unconceal', to unlock, and bring to presence. The calculations that people make in the everyday as well as in expert practices are framed by it. Techne combines the art of making with a creative capability so that newness may emerge, as the realization of possibilities immanent in a situation and as a way of bringing to presence the unprecedented. Furthermore, technology thus defined would be allied to the artwork when the latter is understood as the imaginative and expressive opening up of the world to the questioning of being and to the possibility of an historical becoming. The artwork thus understood nourishes the principle of hope and the promise of joy. The important link to culture and to the idea of project, thus to the idea of being as potentiality (Ricoeur, 1992), that is, to the possibility of the realization of an unprecedented state of being, is indicated in this line of reasoning.

I apply the analytical apparatus that I am sketching in my postcolonial account of the emergence of modernity in Chapter 2, in the problematic of postcolonial subjectivity and identity in Chapter 3, and in rethinking the elements of a postcolonial political economy in Chapter 4. For instance, concerning the economy, it can be argued that it is the result of the functioning of assemblages – in the active and purposive combination of specific technologies of production, institutions like banks, knowledges, human personnel, geographies, built environments, objects of the world – put into place over the years to accomplish the goals relating to the production and distribution of the means of existence at determinate points in time and place. These assemblages and apparatuses enframe economic practice. Many are *ad hoc* devices invented in response to specific conditions and goals, for instance, banks in the mid-seventeenth century. They work for pragmatic reasons and through constant adjustments, in accordance with the substantive logics hard-wired into the know-hows and regimes of familiarity conditioning practice, and not because of the kind of rational necessity that the physical sciences take for granted about natural phenomena (see also Latour, 1991). Cultural factors such as ideologies, values, and ways of being play their part in determining what kinds of devices work and in what conditions (see also Boltanski and Thevenot, 1991). Yet economic theory assumes necessary relationships and invariant correlations, much as Newtonian physics does. In other words, it assumes that it is legitimate to proceed through the logic of abstraction that characterizes conventional Western science, as if the economy operated according to laws that would be inherent in its nature, and not according to humanly constituted and variable practices that work under quite specific conditions that are equally subject to human manipulation. Indeed, a recent disputed tendency in economic theory is to rely on sophisticated mathematics to describe and solve problems, on the presupposition that law-like regularities, however complex, determine the behaviour of the system. In effect, it theorizes a virtual world, that it is possible to imagine as a theoretical construct, but which is not actualized in real economic practice. Economic theory nevertheless has real effects, namely, in legitimating the kind of practices it naturalizes in its claims, and in constituting subjects for it. Its principal function is thus that of ideology, that is, as a theory that authorizes a specific organization of the social. The question for postcolonial theory is the construction of a political economy that would break with such a model, a problem I elaborate in the last chapter.

For now, I would note that my approach means that the calculations one makes about the appropriateness of ends and means are conditioned by living history and directed by our insertion in the world as beings: that is, the history existing in the techno-material world and in the culture and language. People think and act as beings who are coupled to a world and who operate as subjects who have been constituted as members of particular epistemic and existential communities. We are born, indeed, thrown, into already constituted worlds, that are the material and mental sedimentation and result of action performed by previous generations and that we encounter in the form of the givenness of our world. Bodies, objects, tools, organisms, knowledges co-mingle in the reiteration of the complex web of the world as well as in its inventive creation and modification (see also Stengers, 1997). We learn to act upon and within that world and relate to other actants at the same time as we learn to be particular selves. This means that inside and outside are intertwined so that being-in-the-world and world-in-being can be thought of as the two sides of the coin of being. I am trying to say that although world and being are ontologically distinct, they are existentially co-variant and non-hierarchical, that is, they form a chiasm in Merleau-Ponty's (1968) sense, suggesting the relationship of the curve to its hollow (see Venn, 2000). The human being is a node and a recursive loop in a complex system of interchanges and assemblages and flows. Turbulences within these processes attest both to the fact of resistance and to their indeterminacy (which is a feature of complexity). Today, all these mechanisms and devices, through their inscription in cultures – that is, their inscription and encryption, and thus their imbrication in the space of becoming as 'lieux de mémoire' (Nora, 1984–93; Radstone and Hodgkin, 2003) – increasingly operate across national, geographical and cultural borders. This means, among other things, that the analysis of cultures and identities must be located at the points of intersection-translation of the local and the global, the indigenous or vernacular and the cosmopolitan, producing 'vernacular cosmopolitanisms' (Hall, 1999).

Language is fundamental in all this. Its emergence in the course of human evolution has led to the development of the kind of complex, reflexive, cumulative, collective mechanisms and processes I am describing. This is because, as I have explained elsewhere (Venn, 2000), language was necessary for two co-articulated developments that are the defining characteristics of human beings: the emergence of consciousness, particularly, the consciousness of time and of humans as beings in time, and the emergence of the mechanisms that made possible the increasing complexity of social systems, and, related to it, reflexivity and autopoiesis in the evolution of cultures (see also Maturana and Varela, 1980). Language enabled the consciousness of time as movement or passage to be given expression in signs and speech, and narrative, and thus for the process of the exchange and keeping of memories to instantiate the fundamentally plural and heterogeneous character both of subjectivity and of culture. Through language, as a signifying practice, the experience and knowledge acquired by one generation could be transmitted to the next as a memory and a stock of capabilities so that each generation did not have to start from zero or be condemned to repeat the conditions of existence. That is to say, language is central not merely for communication, but because it has been essential for the development of mental capability from the beginning of human history and as the alloplastic cognitive technology inserting the human being as a link in the web of the world. Language functions as the adaptive extensor of human capability as well as the affective and communicative medium that binds subjects into inter-subjective and reflexive networks through action between people by way of objects of the world, whether real or imagined. It thus also binds the inside and the outside (see Henriques et al., 1984; Ricoeur, 1988; Vološinov, 1973). This is the sense in which I mean that we are coupled to a world, a world which is at once material and discursive, such that external space and interior space are co-articulated in the lifeworld and in consciousness. This recognition enables one to anchor the idea of the temporality and historicity of the subject in the existential flux of being-in-the-world and being-with, and to give a sense of the material conditions and practical limits within which we all operate (regarding theory as well as practice, the material as much as the mental conditions of existence).

As I explain below, this is translated into a different approach to the analysis of postcoloniality (and sociality generally). It includes, among other things, the construction of a new kind of archive that brings together theoretical and historical material alongside accounts of events and everyday practices so that a whole way of life is gathered in its diffused and lived aspect and made available for analysis. The intention is to counter the tendency of theory in the human sciences to subtract itself from these conditions. Thus, Chapters 3 and 4 start with concrete examples, concerning identity and economic activity, to ground theory in 'thick descriptions' (Geertz, 1973) of the everyday and to counter the abstract claims that are made in the social sciences because of the assumption of the detached objectivity and scientificity of theory, for instance in economic theory as I have noted, or because of the privilege of the problematic of representation and discourse in the analysis of subjectivity and sociality. The point of view of the historicity and polyglot character of knowledges and cultures has important implications for the relation of theory to practice, and for the analysis of actually existing postcolonial/postmodern worlds.

Identity, subjectivity, diaspora, creolization

The third thread of my assemblage running through the analysis is the centrality of identity and subjectivity as organizing concepts. The concept of the subject acts as a node through which master narratives about the 'big questions' pass – ontological, epistemological, and ethical. It is the core concept in relation to which the analysis in the book makes sense of issues about identity, about the theorization of otherness and alterity, about problems of agency, and the question of change. I have already indicated an aspect of the centrality of subjectivity and the notion of the subject when arguing for the importance of locating the postcolonial by reference to a history of modernity and modernization. I develop these aspects in Chapters 2 and 3.

A concept linking subjectivity and the postcolonial is that of diaspora around which questions about hybridity, mestizaje and creolization can be reorganized. There is now a vast literature about diaspora in relation to the 'uprootings and regroundings' (Ahmed, 2003) that chart the massive displacements of people both within the nation-state and across borders. I indicate a number of salient features in the Glossary; here I will focus on the methodological departures that the topic has provoked. An indicative and familiar position about the polyglot character of cultures is expressed by Said when he says that 'all cultures are involved in one another; none is single and pure, all are hybrid, heterogeneous, extraordinarily differentiated, and unmonolithic' (1993: xxix). It is an argument against the policing of cultures by dogmas of purity and authenticity: 'Far from being unitary or monolithic or autonomous things, cultures actually assume more "foreign" elements, alterities, differences, than they consciously exclude' (ibid.: 15). Processes that are described using terms like diaspora, hybridity, transculturation, syncretism, creolization, mestizaje are not new; they have been at work in the mutation and transmutation of cultures from time immemorial (see Walsh, 2003). The restless movement of peoples and cultures is more prevalent in history than is recognized in conventional accounts of culture, especially those that are framed within the problematic of the nation-state and the modern form of the state as a territorialized, bounded homogenous entity. Besides, as Clifford argues, 'practices of displacement might emerge as constitutive of cultural meanings rather than as their simple transfer or extension' (1988: 3).

As an example, especially given the present geo-political circumstance, I will point to the diasporic cultures and identities that developed around the Mediterranean from the end of the Roman era and in the wake of Arab expansion throughout that area (and beyond). One cannot underestimate the importance of the exchanges between the Arab world, Byzantium, India and China – in the domain of philosophy, mathematics, medicine, agriculture, technologies of all kinds – for the emergence of European Renaissance later. Given their network across continents, and their systematic search for knowledge from other cultures, the Arabs were key to the mutations and advancements that occurred and that have functioned as conditions of possibility for Renaissance thought (see Chapter 2). The physical evidence that remains, for example, in Spain and Sicily, and the ancient texts, attest to the diasporic character of Mediterranean culture and their mutation in response to underlying forces.

Equally, one could point to music as a striking case, witness the travels of instruments and styles, their appropriation through the dialogue of cultures, the subtle blendings that tell the story of travelling cultures; more: the enrichment of existence through the building of common expressive worlds, as the history of jazz and blues and rock today illustrates. The history of languages is an exemplary place to detect the processes of diaspora and hybridity at work, say, the Indo-European languages, and English language itself as an exemplar, made up over time of elements from Anglo-Saxon, Viking, French, Celt. The same processes punctuate the genealogy of empires – for example, the Roman, the Chinese, Ottoman, Mughal Empires – and the mutations in religions, whether concerning the Semitic or Abrahamic religions – Judaism, Islam, Christianity – or the variation in Buddhism in its translations from India to other regions such as Sri Lanka, China, Korea and Japan. In more recent times, the intertwining of cultures and peoples has been played out in the similarities and differences that 'contrapuntally' (Said, 1993) reconstitute modernities and identities throughout the world, postcolonial and otherwise (see also Ahmed, 2003), as my contrasting examples of Japanese and Indian modernities show in the next chapter.

At the level of theorization, I extend the concept of creolization from its regional application (in parts of French and Spanish colonies) to account for the process of translation across cultures and the process of appropriation and recombination of elements from different cultures in the formation of new lifeworlds and forms of expression (see Enwesor et al., 2002, 2003); cultures are all recombinant cultures. This goes beyond the inventive and playful borrowing and mixing of elements and practices from a diversity of fields in the making of the new, that is, beyond 'bricolage' (Lévi-Strauss, 1962). The processes of mixing and recombining that are variously described as creolization, hybridization, transculturation, marking the formation of diasporas, often take place in conflictual situations in which groups of unequal power and unequal access to the means of legitimization of ways of being attempt to establish liveable spaces and identities without surrendering forms of constituting the community that preserves core elements of the original (or subaltern) cultures (see also Isaac Julien, 2003). At their core, they inscribe relations of power, and are therefore fundamentally political. Language is central here, given its historical functioning for domestication and subjection by modern forces of occupation – for example, the English in Ireland, the Japanese in Korea, the French in the Antilles. I shall examine in Chapter 3 the effects for the 'disorder of identity' arising from the lived experience of 'belonging to a language which is not one's own' (Derrida, 1998; Khatibi, 1990).

Disciplinary societies and militarism

A final thread weaving its way through the conceptual apparatus is the idea that in the course of the mutations of colonialism and capitalism, a form of discipline correlated to modern militarism (Clausewitz, [1832] 1976) came to dominate strategic and instrumental calculation and decision-making, operating at the level of economic, technological, administrative and regulative thought, establishing a kind of mindset: ubiquitous, powerful, unnoticed. This is not simply the recognition that military strategy and economic and/or administrative interests tend to support and refer to one another, for this is an aspect of the use of force that one finds in all colonial and imperial rule. It is here about the interpenetration of several developments in the course of the history of modernity:

First, the deployment of a new form of power that begins to emerge with modernity and that constitutes 'disciplinary societies' (Foucault, 1975). This power is also a power over life, a biopolitics operating through bodies considered as machines capable of a disciplined formation. It is about the amplification of capabilities, the sensitizing of conduct to particular temporal regimes: learning to keep to standardized time, working or operating within specified timeframes, coordinating activities across geographical boundaries, it is about subjecting oneself to norms and values that are established within technologies of production and of the social, and of course it is about being able to trade one's body in the form of standardized labour-time.

Second, the emergence of rational capitalism that reduces relations between people to relations between things and objectifies the economy in the language of abstract processes and agents: the market, money, labour, the possessive individual, property, all now expressed in the accounting abstractions of (neo)liberal political economy. My argument is that with corporate capitalism, economic strategy has become militarized; elements and sectors of the economy operate as hinges and relays (Bishop and Phillips, 2002) between the economy, state planning and the military apparatus.

Third, the gradual supplanting of the ethical goals inscribed in the ideals of radical Enlightenment thought by the instrumental calculations of regulative systems governed by the logic of rationalizing projects. I should note that the convergence of these three developments was forged in the crucible of colonial subjugation, relayed by the conceptualization of **the other** as 'Other'; at the limit that other is reduced to the status of chattel and the remnant, and can be killed as an expression of the sovereign will of the ruler/master (Agamben, 1998). An associated concept is the Protestant (Lutheran) rejection of the principle that the love of God entailed the love of God's creatures, including one's fellows, and the support this different othering of the other has given to a solipsistic and individualist morality, legitimating capitalist exploitative practice. It has mutated into the Evangelical fundamentalism that today legitimates neo-liberal ideology.

Fourth, the effects of these values in the emergence of the form of rule I call imperial governmentality, which is elaborated in the next chapter. Core elements of this governmentality determine the mode of operation prevailing in businesses and public institutions, in particular, the insecuritization of the everyday, the institutionalization of intimidation, the deployment of disciplinary agencies in the formation of subjectivities, the constitution of new imaginaries and subjectivities through teletechnologies, the operationalization of the ground rules of modern warfare in the language and conduct of agents in administrative and social institutions, and increasingly in government.

Fifth, the convergence and consolidation of militarist and colonial and management values in a vocabulary of action and a discourse of legitimation that is becoming normalized and normalizing through the homogenization of practice across apparatuses of state and business.

Sixth, related to the last aspect, one finds the production of knowledge within the enframing constituted by the military-industrial-educational-informational complex, privileging instrumental knowledge of the kind that consolidates existing relations of power rather than the emancipatory goal of knowledge as understood in radical Enlightenment thought and in many philosophies such as Buddhism, where knowledge is in solidarity with wisdom and a liberatory freedom. Today, corporate capitalism and neo-liberal discourse are perfecting the militarization of life; it is being universalized in the name of the 'new world order'. Counter-hegemonic movements, such as those represented at the WSF, may arrest this form of total colonialism.

Mapping the territory

One starting point for the exploration I am elaborating is the recognition that because colonialism, capitalism and modernity are entangled with one another in quite complex ways, the major problem for thinking about the postcolonial is that modernity and capitalism constantly erupt as central factors clamouring for attention. The fact is that the period from the end of the fifteenth century, marked by European expansion in the New World, coincided with the gradual emergence of modernity and of capitalism; 1492 was an event, presaging the epochal transformations that mark the history of the present. One may think that this coincidence is purely accidental. However, their co-emergence has affected the history of all three elements to such an extent that it is difficult to disentangle the one from the other when it comes to constructing an account of, say, the Caribbean states or France over the past five hundred years. These reciprocal effects have been locally specific, with the result that variations and mutations in modernity and capitalism have taken place, producing vernacular forms, inflected by the specific local conditions and histories of colonialism. For example, although we may categorize India and Latin America as postcolonial when speaking in general terms, important differences appear when we address the problem of the effects and legacy of the implantation of capitalism and modernity, or the effects of religion, in these two vast and historically complicated regions. What does this mean?

Let us take the example of a minor colony like Mauritius in the nineteenth century, and, to be perverse, England in the same period. In the former case, one would note, at the general level of changes, the emergence and modernization of the sugar cane industry, the massive immigration of workers as indentured labourers from India, adding to the Creole descendants of East African slaves and French settlers and to the smaller Chinese community, with all that this implied from the point of view of the 'hybridization' or creolization of culture, and the emergence of apparatuses of administration and regulation that derive greatly from the models then developing as part of what Foucault has described as the sciences and technologies of the social (see Chapter 3). So, modernity and modernization in the nineteenth century for the colony meant the introduction from the outside of changes at the level of the economy and the land, technology, the state, the population, culture such that as soon as one considers the (mainly capitalist, but mixed) economy one would need to relate it to the colonial and imperial goals of England (and France), the administrative and legal systems and the commercial and trade institutions put in place to achieve them, and what they made possible in that period – the new labour force and its composition, roughly divided along ethnic lines, the laws and the social mechanisms for relaying the one to the other, the bilingual, and, among migrants, multilingual character of communication in the everyday, the wider international order of empire that located Mauritius as strategic port and regulated trade. The lived dimension of these changes is the dimension in which the intertwining of modernity, capitalism, colonialism in the midst of vernacular cultures is most concretely accomplished, inscribed in the practices of the everyday shaped by a creolization affecting all levels of the society: the language, everyday activities like cooking and shopping, leisure activities, education, the emergence of diasporic identities, and so on. Importantly, these changes were mediated by local circumstances and factors, so that the beliefs and practices of the different cultural and ethnic groups thrown together in the diaspora of colonial Mauritius unevenly mixed according to the disjointed histories of migrations, the division of labour, the proximities arising from these circumstances, the solidarities that were necessary for constituting liveable spaces, the separations and exclusions dictated by the relations of power and by religious and ethnic affiliations. The result is that elements from the different communities – the Creoles, the Hindus, Muslims and Tamils from India, a small Chinese community, a number of British administrators, and the descendants of the French settlers (who held effective economic and political power for centuries until a few decades ago) – combined to produce a vernacular modernity. The result is that today one sees amalgams of the most modern technologies of production together with 'advanced' or bureaucratic forms and mechanisms of administration and regulation operating alongside 'traditional' and customary practices regarding, say, illnesses or births or marriages. Meanings about daily life are generated out of this diaspora that cannot be understood either as reiterations of previous lifestyles or as instances of a stereotyped Westernization. In Mauritius as elsewhere, colonialism introduced a new scale, evident at all levels of society, that conventional sociological theorizations about the reality of modernity have yet to fathom, for instance, about the resilience of religion and custom, or about the complex mechanisms of the appropriation and translation of cultures in forming and reforming liveable spaces, social imaginaries and identities, and the political stakes fought over through these processes.

In England in the same period, by contrast, the further development of the industrial revolution went hand in hand with the consolidation of capitalism and colonialism as part of nation building and as part of the emergence of a properly imperial state, as I shall examine in Chapter 2. Modernity and modernization in England in the nineteenth century involved the development of new technologies such as steam power, new discoveries in chemistry, advances in civil engineering, later, the emergence of the electrical and the petroleum industry as part of the second industrial revolution; it saw changes in transport and communication technology, and what they made possible – altering cities and countryside, transforming the lived experience of time and space; it included the emergence of a new public culture in places such as clubs, libraries, educational institutions and public archives of all kinds – museums, zoos, collections; the emergence of radical organizations like the trade unions and new political demands in the wake of the brutal exploitation of the propertyless or, rather, the pauperized; one should add to the list the emergence of Enlightenment ideas about the progress of 'humanity', and, inflected by such projects, the French and American Revolutions and their repercussions; one should note too the spread of the novel and new artistic forms like photography. All of this participated in transforming what people could envisage of themselves, how they perceived English society, how they located their personal relations in the context of England as a growing imperial power. If the visibility of empire was relatively occluded in representations of the English, say, in the novel, its centrality for the whole culture was in no doubt. Postcolonial re-readings of these representations have demonstrated this symptomatically unmarked presence, for example, in David Dabydeen's (1985) interpretations of painting or in Catherine Hall's (2002) exploration of the constitutive role of empire in the formation of Englishness and in Edward Said's work, *Culture and Imperialism*, as I have noted. Thus, historical and postcolonial work now reveals the mechanisms that in England made possible the correlation of modernity with colonialism and the growth of capitalism at every level of the economy, culture, politics and thought. In his admirable analysis of Jane Austen's *Mansfield Park*, Said has this to say about the intimate relations between culture and England's imperial order:

> Austen here synchronizes domestic with international authority, making it plain that the values associated with such higher things as ordination, law, and propriety must be grounded firmly in actual rule over and possession of territory.

> She sees clearly that to hold and to rule Mansfield Park is to hold and rule an imperial estate in close, not to say inevitable association with it. What assures the domestic tranquillity and attractive harmony of the one is the productivity and regulated discipline of the other. (1993: 104)

These two examples illustrate the dynamic character of the changes that have occurred and the *longue durée* against which the present makes sense as the constituted world that postcolonial critique takes to be its object. We find in the examples the complex mingling in the everyday processes and events that the social sciences and humanities disaggregate and analyze separately through the wide variety of disciplines that constitute their own objects of enquiry, and that often ignore each other. I have argued instead for the co-articulation of structural, subjective, psychic, discursive and material dimensions in the making of the world we encounter. The relationship between the theoretical/cognitive, the material/embodied and the meaningful must be thought of in terms of a mutually productive dynamic, that is, a compossibility.

So, how does postcolonial critique sets about its tasks? How does one make sense of the mass of diverse histories and practices and cultures? What does one include and exclude? On what basis? Take, for example, India today, a democratic state made up of such a range of cultures and religions and ethnic communities that one encounters problems as soon as one attempts to talk about them in terms of the singular name: India. Or, consider East Timor, still in the throes of establishing itself as an independent state, suffering the disruptions of wars and diverse colonizations. Or, indeed, Canada: can one call Canada postcolonial, on the grounds that it was part of the British Empire, administered as a colonial country, without opening up the term to a vagueness that disarms analysis or without introducing asymmetries that undermine the standpoint of postcoloniality? Or, does the inclusion of Canada as a postcolonial country oblige analysis to start by taking nothing for granted? Does it not also make us think of dates and the process of decolonization itself? For example, it could be argued, depending on one's political perspective, that Canada didn't really fight for independence or wasn't a proper colony in the first place; or that its colonial experience is too far into the past, as in the case of the USA which was a colony, and did fight for independence. But then, the Inuit people or the French Canadians have different reasons for thinking of their experience as in some important ways (post)colonial. Along a different track, we find many Australians and New Zealanders who have turned to postcolonial theory in order to address their experience of the legacy of empire as expressed in writings (Adam and Tiffin, 1993; Ashcroft et al., 1998), or films (*Once Were Warriors*, dir. Lee Tamahori, 1995), and history (Merefield, 2001, 2004). Increasingly, many Native and migrant Americans whose experience of subalternity and/or diaspora is recent, apply the term postcolonial to address some of the problems associated with that experience or produce writings that may qualify as 'postcolonial' (Alexie, 1998; Cao, 1998; Lahiri, 2003; Madsen, 2003; Mohanty, 1993). For the moment, it is important not to allow existing dichotomies and what is at stake in them to delimit in advance the disengagement of a terrain for postcolonial analysis. As I have pointed out and as will become clear in subsequent chapters, my analysis tries to take the postcolonial out of the ghetto of sub-disciplinary particularism, and realign it with thinking about what is to come after modernity and occidentalism, a broader project.

It becomes clear, then, that the 'what' of postcoloniality is related to the question of the 'when' and of the 'why' of postcoloniality. To be perverse, one could ask: why does the postcolonial not include England or the USA? For, in a sense, hardly any country has not been at some point a colony, say, parts of what became England, which had at various points in history been Roman, Viking, Norman, and so on, with an interesting history of the 'English' as a diasporic and creole culture yet to be written. Or Korea, which has been a colony of China and Japan. Indeed, it has been argued that a place like Wales in the nineteenth century can in some important aspects be considered to have been an 'internal colony' (Roberts, 1996). The approach I have described earlier, in highlighting the point of view of the correlation of modernity, capitalism and colonialism, and the specificity of the European form of colonialism, provides some criteria for answering these questions, though a problem remains when we consider a case such as that of Korea in the modern period.

I point to the problem of periodization in order to reiterate the fact that colonization is a process that has been decisive for transformations in cultures for a considerable time, so that almost no culture can claim the kind of homogenous purity and authenticity that ethnic fundamentalism and racism today phantasize: 'hybridization' and syncretism, or what I prefer to call creolization, are age-old processes, historically endemic to cultures.

Now, although the postcolonial question is not an issue that emerges out of a question about the nature or history of colonization in general, I think it is interesting to try and compare, say, Roman or Egyptian colonization with European colonization, not as an academic exercise, but as a way of thinking through an issue central for understanding the postcolonial. And this issue is this: what has been specific to European colonization compared to other forms? What has characterized and differentiated it? What was different about it that has made the problem of what is to come after it, or, indeed, the problem of surviving colonialism and imperialism such a central one for theory as well as for everyday living in 'postmodern' times? Thus, the question of time and temporality arises too, concretized in terms of the recognition of the different, often disjointed or discrepant temporalities, and problems of transitions, that are appropriate to different regions and periods. As my reference to Mbembe (2001) indicated, the standpoint of the 'postcolony' draws attention to the continuity of disjunctures – of culture, beliefs, technologies and so on – in the everyday, the 'entanglement' of different *durées* in the lifeworld that are experientially actualized in everyday living. Indeed, it can be argued that what appears as 'disjunctures' are so only from the point of view of a normalizing power and discourse. In other words, the co-habitation of different temporalities and spatialities is in fact a characteristic of the normal situation, especially in cities, and now much more visibly in mega-cities in Africa and elsewhere (Bishop et al., 2003; Simone, 2001).

I want to signal three historical aspects of European colonization that will be explored in greater detail as part of getting a hold on the questions of the what and the when and the why of postcoloniality. First, the break which announced the violent birth of Europe's colonies also inserted them into the linear temporality of modernity. This insertion at first took the form of evangelization and 'civilization', before modernization proper is instituted, after the development of modernity itself had become aligned with the progress of 'humanity' and the elaboration of a universal project, led by Europe. I will argue in the chapter on modernity that colonialism was necessary for the emergence of this discourse of modernity, so that colonization is seen not as something outside Europe or the West, or that happened elsewhere, but as an event productive of modernity as a historical period, that must be re-inscribed into its discourse.

The conceptualization of the colonized as 'Other' that I discussed earlier triggers a question about the forms of othering that underlie all forms of systematic exploitation, given that in order for a group to inflict persistent suffering upon another group, as has happened throughout history, and as persists today in all cultures, a distancing, an estrangement must take place that removes the other from the sphere of one's concern or ethical responsibility; it is a homicidal estrangement. Concepts of the ethne, class, caste, gender, nation, race, religious affiliation have variously functioned as metonymic substitutes in this discourse of othering. With European colonization, an othering that derived from the combination of the logic of monotheism together with the rationalizations of exploitation, developed into the assertion of ontological differences at the level of legitimating discourses and institutional practices, converting difference into pathology and fundamental lack. In practice, of course, relations between colonizer and colonized have been simultaneously both genocidal – witness Tasmania – and ambivalent as with members of the Indian ruling elite, while the messiness of everyday interaction allowed for innumerable instances of transcultural exchanges and dialogue, witness the history of cricket. Nevertheless, the systematic denigration of the other in colonial discourse and the long period of what Spivak (1988) calls subalternization has left a legacy buried in the psyche and at the level of cognitive grasp of the world that continues to have effects for the problem of (postcolonial) identity (Trinh, 1989). They are reiterated in the difficulties involved in breaking away from the hold of occidentalist categories, for instance in the conceptualization of development and modernization. As I shall examine in Chapter 3 by reference to the colonial disorders of identity, there is too often a tendency to unconsciously defer to the 'West' or to Western authoritative discourses, or else to misrecognize one's own location in relation to subalternity.

A further important feature of modern colonization concerns the way that capitalism, allied to modern technology from the seventeenth century, re-constitutes a world for it: the colonies are drawn into the orbit of its activities and gradually become integrated within the system at the economic, cultural, epistemological, and political levels. One could cite the 'Triangular Trade' as the exemplar of the complex exchanges of people and goods and income that altered the lifeworld in all the places invested by capitalism: in Africa, in the Americas, in Europe, indeed, irrevocably inter-mingling their destinies. This trade, more extensive and transformative than other practices of slavery at the time, involved the exchange of goods and services between West Africa, England and the Americas/New World that by the eighteenth century had established clear directions of flows and relations of power. Slaves were brought from the West Coast of Africa – revealingly and appropriately called the Gold Coast by Europeans – transported to the Americas where they were sold; their produce (sugar, cotton, tobacco) were brought by the same ships to England to fuel industrial production and the expansion of consumption; goods manufactured in England were transported to Africa and sold there to complete the cycle (Fryer, 1984). Profits were made by the shippers and traders at every stage of the trade, and it directly contributed to industrialization and the growth of imperial economic and military power; it also made possible the world peopled by the characters described in *Jane Eyre*, as Said (1993) has demonstrated. Another example is the planned goal of transforming some colonies into monocultures, for example, the 'banana republics', that has ensured not only the lop-sided character of their economy and their dependence on trade with the 'developed' world, but also the remaking of the physical space and the transformation of daily life to fit in with these changes. Interestingly, the importance of sugar and tobacco in Cuba, and by-products like rum and cigars, is not just economic but, because people's lives are organized around its production and use, and because the whole landscape is altered to constitute the living matter for such a way of life, it constitutes social relations and the culture and enters into the psyche. In the worlding of the (post)colony, as in other worldings, the exterior spatiality of productive and consuming activity and the interior landscape of identity, memory and sociality mutually condition each other (see Kraniauskas, 2000).

The plural spaces of the postcolonial

Let us pick a number of countries that are, from one point of view or another, 'postcolonial', and begin an exploration that will illustrate some of the elements I have been highlighting and clear the ground to enable the issues to properly appear. India, Algeria, and Vietnam will provide sufficient contrast and common ground for a first exercise.

The obvious common ground is that they have all been colonies of Europe and been transformed in significant ways as a result. In particular, in the period of imperialism, they were all under the administrative control of the major European imperial states, England and France, their economies had gradually been modified to fit in with the interests of the metropolitan economy, the system of governance inside these countries had also been adapted to suit the administrative and regulative system of the imperial states. They also share the fact that they have all had to fight for independence, with consequences for the formation of the notion of nation and for what has occurred after decolonization. In particular, there are the effects and responses to globalization. They all have long histories of sophisticated cultures which have been subject to significant change over the years. For instance, all three have themselves been colonizers.

The differences concern the length of occupation by European powers, the reach of colonialism, the religious distribution of the populations, the geographical location, the profile of the natural resources of the regions, and ethnic particularisms. Equally important are the different histories of colonization relating to the differences between French and British colonial policies, the circumstances regarding the struggle for independence, developments after independence, for instance, the specific economic, cultural and political relationship that they maintain with the old 'centres', and the locally specific effects of globalization.

If we look more closely at Indian colonization, one can pick out a number of salient markers of its surface history, precisely the surface that genealogy excavates to uncover underlying or written-over features of colonialism. Thus, one can note at that superficial level the gradual extension of mainly commercial arrangements established through the East India Company, backed by military force when necessary, supported by the British government. The collusion of economic and military interest is explicit here. Interestingly, diplomatic moves retained an important role, in that agreements with Indian reigning monarchs and with the elite were consistently sought, and often necessary for commercial and trading ventures to be successful at all. Annexation proper happened in part after the failure of the East India Company to deal on its own with growing rebellion (1857) and to cope with the complexity of the networks that had been put into place. Although the British government had major contributions to make to the administration of various states in India from 1619, India became an imperial colony after the transfer of power to the Crown, with a British governor-general and the definition of Indian citizens as British subjects, that is, with sovereignty judicially passing into the hands of the British state, although collaborating princes were able to exercise significant local power. Specific state policies organized through the Colonial Office regarding education, the formation of an administrative and military cadre, and the determination of an overall strategy of governance, and so on, logically followed.

On the ground, of course, matters do not quite follow the script of official history. For instance, studies carried out by the Subaltern Studies Group have shown that the elite narrative of the history of India has to be countered by the prose of insurgency. The latter shows the extent to which the events surrounding key uprisings can be understood only if one takes seriously the calculations of neglected groups and local circumstances, including the power relations and cultural stakes that motivated people outside elite strategies and shaped the political action of indigenous groups. The point of view of the interests of the elite and the rulers is insufficient in accounting for the realities of resistance and the process of mobilization of insurgency. Studies of uprisings such as the Basarat (1831), the Santal (1855) reveal that they were the result of conscious and planned action, typically taking the form of stages in a strategy of negotiation and dissent, with uprising as last resort; they do not conform to the elite narrative of spontaneous and undisciplined action by peasants. This means that one has to pay attention to the dynamism of cultural factors having effects in a field of forces, for instance, the religious beliefs inscribed in everyday practices and relationships, particularly relating to the economy, that determined, depending on circumstances, the political options of particular groups in a given community.

Viswanathan's (1989) analysis of the functioning of literary study as part of the strategy for establishing the cultural conditions conducive to imperial rule points to the less visible elements that operated to try and constitute hegemony. The problem for the exercise of power is about authority, and thus about the means for countering a countervailing local discourse of authority. The standpoint of hegemony immediately brings to light the ideological and strategic calculations that motivated specific policies. Viswanathan argues that the introduction of English was a response to complex and changing political and historical pressures arising from conflicts of interest involving the English Parliament, the East India Company, missionaries and the Indian ruling elite. The study of English was seen as the instrument for transforming sectors of the Indian population into a less rebellious, more docile and receptive body for imperial rule. However, the stereotypes, the misconceptions and misreadings, the disavowals, the interests of a new emergent form of governmentality, and resistance to English rule all contributed to the failure by administrators and historians alike to understand how the implantation of English was actually received. The tools of postcolonial theory – if one may appropriate Viswanathan's study in this way – have made visible the complex forces at work, and, importantly, pointed to the agency of the subaltern/the subjugated in determining the outcome of the new strategies of governmentality in India, and by extension, elsewhere, from the nineteenth century.

Bhabha's (1994) interrogation of the location of the Bible in the narratives of the cultural transformation of India by the British throws further light on the question of authority and of resistance. His interest lies in showing the ambivalences and the fractures in the imaginary of English cultural authority. He selects a scene in Delhi in 1817, relating to the introduction of the Bible among the Indians, that has become emblematic in colonial discourse's retelling of the inaugural moment of the English cultural subjugation of India. The Book, in its combination of the ethical and truth, stands for the alliance of Europe's civilizing mission with the project of the salvation of the non-West. (A similar mythical inaugural moment can be read in Columbus' description of the first landing in the New World and encounter with the indigenous people of the Caribs, see Chapter 2.) Imperial authority, and this imperial gaze, derive from these epistemological and ontological foundations; to be saved necessitated the recognition of that authority and, thus, the acceptance of Europe's tutelage. Yet, the story told demonstrates clearly the stratagems of displacement and deferral, of acquiescence and resistance that enabled the subjugated to defer to real imperial power while differing in the address of that power's authority. For the natives acknowledge the superiority of the doctrines of the Bible, but do not agree to accept the Sacrament, for 'Europeans eat cow's flesh' which cannot be accepted. Baptism must therefore be deferred until all of India agrees to receive the Sacrament (Bhabha, 1994: 102–5). And, as the story goes, it is pointed out that the demands of the harvest beckon and cannot be adjourned: the 'ruses of the weak' find ways of opening up get-out clauses. In India under imperial rule, as elsewhere, the practices of everyday life, as de Certeau (1988) has shown, contain the cultural stratagems for protecting uncolonized spaces from complete investment by a subjugating authority. They relay and re-articulate the agonistic spaces of power. The conceptualization of the other as 'same but not quite', and the slippages in the colonial 'Manichaean aesthetics' (JanMohamed, 1986) whereby the presumed otherness of the other is nevertheless assumed to be amenable to a 'civilization' into sameness produce ambivalences and disjunctures in the process of recognition and difference and in the structure of authorizing narratives such that authority is undermined from within and from the difference that escapes its hold. Bhabha says:

> Colonial presence is always ambivalent, split between its appearance as original and authoritative and its articulation as repetition and difference. It is a disjunction produced within the act of enunciation as a specifically colonial articulation of those two disproportionate sites of colonial discourse and power: the colonial scene as the invention of historicity, mastery, mimesis or as the 'other scene' of Entstellung [distortion as in dream-work, the displaced register of its inscription of affect], displacement, fantasy, psychic defence, and an 'open' textuality. Such a display of difference produces a mode of authority that is agonistic (rather than antagonistic). (1994: 107, 108)

Although the emphasis in Bhabha's argument is on the point of view of ambivalence, hence the point about its agonistic character, the antagonistic dimension in the exercise of power should remain central, as my discussion of imperial governmentality in the next chapter shows. Indeed, he goes on to note the effects of power in examining the presence of coloniality beyond the text, for the 'immediate presence of the English' inflects the system of address, directing the gaze of the colonizer which is oriented towards the establishment of authority. Thus, colonial authority cannot work simply in terms of the enunciations in the authorizing discourse of the colonizer; its address betrays the veiled presence of power in the split between the subject of the enunciation and the addressee, for the latter is positioned as different, lesser, consigned to an otherness that the universalizing discourse both constitutes and disavows. I should point out that historically the dividing strategies of colonial power are amplified and modified because of the fact of indigenous relations of power, as the analyses undertaken by the Subaltern Studies Group have shown. Furthermore, as Suleri has argued, the binarisms of colonial discourse do not sufficiently recognize the 'intimacies' and the 'mutual narratives of complicities' (1992: 2) that structure the texts of the colonizer and the colonized. Read against the grain of conventional cultural critique, the production of the colonial imaginary, in counter-cultural as well as in the narrative of empire, returns us to the reality of migrancy, and the reality of a colonial diaspora that messed with identities and chronologies and cultural categories to an extent that challenges easy binarisms. The question of nationalism is thus problematized by reference to assumptions of unitariness or wholeness and the temporality of an evolutionary logic, with implications for contemporary politics and for the postcolonial rewriting of (post)modernity (see also Chakrabarty, 2000; Chatterjee, 1993).

A postcolonial position would have to add the following points of view to the analysis of the Indian situation: the economy, for instance, a critique of the 'Asiatic mode of production' thesis and the analysis of the effects of global corporate capitalism; the materiality of the lifeworld in relation to the process of modernization and to 'technologies of the social'; the politics of decolonization and partition, the latter leading to the formation of Pakistan; the differentiated effects of globalization for culture and for identity, and so on.

In this presentation, I am concerned not with the details, or with an explanation of the events, but with the demonstration of how the problem of locating the postcolonial already calls up ways of conceptualizing the colonial itself, and shows that postcolonial theory has already become part of the problematic to the extent that its intervention in the understanding of the colonial has already altered the picture of the processes involved and the stakes; it has, in short, redefined the agenda for analysis. The fact that Bhabha, Suleri, Viswanathan, Guha, Spivak, among those I have considered in my brief excursus on India, put to work an analytical apparatus drawn from cultural theory, literary criticism, poststructuralism, Marxism, critical anthropology, and subaltern history supports the argument that the problem is not about making disciplinary demarcations, or about hard and fast distinctions between indigenous versus cosmopolitan theory.

If we turn our attention to Vietnam and to Algeria, a number of other elements and dimensions will surface to add to the picture of the postcolonial as a problematization of the present that, while it has so far set its sight on (mainly) the ex-colonial world, can be shown to encompass concerns that make it very difficult to limit the postcolonial either at the level of territory or at the level of theory.

Now, in the case of both Vietnam and Algeria, we are looking at a later phase of colonization than the Americas or India and at the French model. Equally, we are looking at examples where decolonization involved the most intense warfare and forces operating across the globe. While the colonization of Algeria (itself a name of modern designation) and North Africa may be relatively recent, its analysis calls up centuries of the relationship between, on the one hand, Europe and Christianity and, on the other hand, Africa and Islam, which has been formative for both since antiquity. One must not forget that the Arab and Islamic presence in Europe lasted 700 years until 1492, a fateful date, and the effects of that presence remain and run deep indeed. The proximity of the two territories is important in a way in which far-flung colonies were not. The Arab world's iconic location in the European imaginary, reflected, for instance, in Napoleon's fascination with Egypt, refers to the fact that until the period of European imperialism Europe had knowingly benefited from Arabic North Africa's more advanced technology and knowledge and economy (Goonatilake, 1984; Harding, 1998; Yates, 1964). As a general rule, it is important to keep in view the fact that in speaking about the Arab world, we are talking about a vastly complex area, greatly simplified in today's political imagination, confusing territories, histories, periods, religions into a stereotype Islam. Many texts have appeared, for example, Hourani's (1991) history of the Arab peoples (note the plural), that have revived the reality of the different cultures and histories that have been singularized into the term Islam. The Christian version of the Crusades may have succeeded in producing in the popular European imagination an idea of an 'us' and a 'them' that is far from the reality at the time, the fact and longevity of the Moorish and Ottoman Empires may have been largely forgotten in Europe's retelling of the making of the modern world, the birth of Christianity may have been relocated within the perimeter of a (relatively recent) Western spatial imaginary that has Europeanized the cultures and figures involved, the post-Westphalian (1648) history of the emergence of modernity may have 'forgotten' North Africa's, Islam's and Arab's contribution to its possibility, the conventional history of European knowledges may have erased the debt to Arab and other knowledges before modernity, the social sciences may have repressed its debt to scholars like Ibn Kaldun. The fact remains nevertheless that the history of the relationship between Europe and the Arab world (refigured and reduced in the cold war period in terms of what the American geo-political spatial imagination calls the 'Middle East') and Africa has been constitutively intertwined for such a very long time that to speak of the postcolonial in relation to 'North Africa' immediately triggers deep discrepancies of time and cultural space that challenge the concept of postcoloniality in some fundamental ways.

To get back to Algeria, we note at the level of a straightforward narrative of events that modern colonialism in North Africa first begins with Napoleon's adventure in Egypt and is consolidated with Bugeaud's governorship from 1840. In the wider context, it is significant that the fact that the English had in the course of the nineteenth century wrested domination from the French in parts of North Africa, for example, offering 'protectorate' status to countries like Egypt, did not prevent French culture and language from gaining a strong foothold in Arab countries from the Lebanon to Morocco, especially among the bourgeoisie. Here the French colonial strategy of integration within the French state system through the apparatus of education, administration and policing signals an important difference from the English colonial administration. The French colonial system implemented a Jacobin strategy imposed from above aiming to reconstitute the population according to a rational model of order, generally, implanting French culture in all French colonies, in an attempt to eradicate ethnic differences and to pacify insurgent peoples through acculturation. Not surprisingly, the instrument of resistance took many specific cultural forms, as we find in many novels dealing with North Africa, say, in Khatibi (1971, 1990), or as demonstrated in the still admirable studies of Algeria by Fanon (1989). One must note the complicated stakes in the question of language, in the tropes of the veil (see also Chapter 3); the unifying function of a technology such as radio in the struggle (the Voice of Algeria, from 1954, for radio functioned as a constitutive technology in the imaginary institution of Algeria as a nation); the conscious appropriation of French language after 1956 for a counter-hegemonic strategy, in place of the official Arabic which many ethnic groups and tribes like the Berbers did not speak anyway. One interesting element is the international character of the decolonization movement, in solidarity with other liberation struggles throughout the 'Mahgreb Front' in the 1950s and with the wider international forces of the Left. The incredible violence involved in the struggle, including massacres (Setif as an iconic case), systematic tortures, the murder of potential leaders, a generalized form of warfare, has nevertheless left a legacy that is being played out in the repetition of crimes against humanity, now in the form of a postmodern Islamic fundamentalism against the legacy of colonial modernity and capitalist globalization (Venn, 1998).

Let us add the case of Vietnam before drawing out some conclusions, for it clarifies the wider global stakes involved. Again we find the regional peculiarities of colonialism side by side with its common elements, namely the project of a cosmopolitan cultural homogeneity that the French pursued, at home and in the colonies, forcing disparate ethnic groups and different histories to realign along the temporal trajectory of the French civilizing mission. The idea was that anyone could be 'French' and a citizen, provided one had been formed according to the educational and cultural apparatus set in place for that purpose throughout the French Empire. The Second World War disrupted this project in Indochina but the neo-colonialism which reappeared, refigured within the parameters of the cold war after the Potsdam redistribution of the world between the Americans, the Russians, the British and the French, gave new life, an after-life, to French colonialism in Indochina. Already decolonization from the 1920s had fixed the stakes; it inaugurated a movement of liberation from Europe that aspired to autonomy, to freedom of the individual, to the ideals of liberty, to the defence of human rights. Vietnam is not alone in this, for everywhere in the colonial world the same political demands were being articulated in the aftermath of the First World War, through, say, the Congress Party in India, established in 1922, the Chinese Communist Party (1924), the

Pan-African movement, launched in the 1920s, or revolutions in Latin America. These were very modern goals, one might say, yet sought in an old but still tenacious imperial world, albeit weakened after the First World War. The story of the liberation struggle in Vietnam after the defeat of the Japanese in the Second World War by mainly the Vietnamese themselves is well known. A few names will summarize the episodes: Dien Bien Phu (1954) and the defeat of the French, American military intervention from then on until it comes to grief with the Tet Offensive of 1968, the fall of Saigon and victory for the Vietcong. Since independence, in addition to the legacy of years of destruction through terror and the use of weapons of mass destruction by the Americans such as 'Agent Orange', Vietnam, like other ex-colonies, has gradually had to contend with the forces of corporate global capitalism, while it has felt more acutely the major geo-political events like the end of the USSR and shifts in Chinese economic and political strategy.

I have sketched these cases not only in order to point to the importance of local differences when it comes to theorizing the postcolonial, but also to put an emphasis on the often neglected historical dimension in approaching the question of the postcolonial, a neglect that Young (2001) has thankfully countered. This historical dimension in more recent times must take into account the fact of the cold war, followed by the demise of the USSR and the symbolic fall of the Berlin Wall, and currently the apparent triumph of liberal capitalism, increasingly in its neo-liberal form, that is fast becoming globalized as part of the attempt to constitute a 'new world order'. So, the problem of the postcolonial now has become inextricably bound with questions about the postmodern and the directions for change that may be open to those who seek alternative socialities. Inevitably, issues of identity and subjectivity reappear, rethought beyond a 'politics of difference' since the stakes have shifted to align such issues with the wider question of dissident politics and movements that are constituting a 'globalization from below'. We are left having to look afresh at the postcolonial world against a background of increasing crises and a permanent state of emergency. My arguments for a critical postcolonial approach relate to this situation; they bring to the fore issues of the relationship between analytical method and critique.

Outlining a critical postcoloniality

The approach that I have outlined above, I hope, gives a clear enough indication of the direction for postcolonial analysis that is offered in the book; it circumscribes the sense of what is meant by critique. For all the reasons already presented, it could be argued that the postcolonial is now everywhere, in the sense that if we are to understand the 'post' to refer to some condition yet to come, and if we take the idea of a global matrix seriously, then the 'to-come' involves radical transformations – even if not immediately or all at once – in all existing societies, altering in the process relations of power affecting the economy and gender relations, attitudes to the environment, forms of governance, ways of being in all cultures. A good deal of writing about the postcolonial supports this view that critical thought must target all forms of oppression and exploitation, opening its scope to rethinking the forms of societies to come after occidentalism.

Postcolonial critique therefore cannot but connect with a history of emancipatory struggles (Young 2001: 1), encompassing anti-colonial struggles as well as the struggles that contest economic, religious, ethnic, and gender forms of oppression, on the principle that it is possible and imperative to create more equal, convivial and just societies. It follows that the construction of an analytical apparatus that enables the necessary interdisciplinary work to be done is a central part of the task.[4]

To that extent, critique in this book includes the constitution of a specific gaze, that is, a standpoint and an orientation directed by its location in a postcolonial conceptual imaginary that self-reflexively positions the questioner inside/outside a postcolonial and postmodern reality that he or she seeks to transform. The point of view of political economy that I outline in Chapter 4 represents this sense of a politically engaged location. It takes the view that the everyday lives of people cannot be divorced from economic conditions, since the latter are part of the activity of constituting lifeworlds and of grounding a sense of place and belonging, even if that place for many is insecure and hazardous (see Chapter 3). The constitution of an archive[5] for analysis is an element of the construction of this postcolonial critical gaze. Such an archive cuts across the division between culture and the economy, so that postcolonial analysis can take on board the transcultural processes and forces at work in determining existing postcolonial glocal 'scapes'.

Furthermore, while the idea of gaze relates to the point about critical theory above, it extends beyond it because the gaze is additionally a constitutive element of subjectivity, as I show in Chapter 3 in the elaboration of the issue of the figuration and reconfiguration of identity and the diversity of politics relating to it. The problems of constituting postcolonial archives in relation to the space of belonging and the space of the reconfiguration of identity have been experimentally explored in the Documenta 11 series of exhibition and texts (Enwesor et al., 2002, 2003). This initiative recognizes the extent to which a postcolonial politicization of the aesthetic and the artwork is part of the goal of emancipatory adventures that contest subjugation. It emphasizes the fact that already other kinds of texts and cultural forms besides writing, such as film and music and other artistic forms, are becoming the focus of attention in working out the ways in which people in or from postcolonial situations express their identities, give form to their sense of belonging or marginalization, assert their difference, represent their world in its complexity, translate their hopes. Through the artwork, the gaze is pluralized and de-realized, but equally re-oriented. The aesthetic dimension allows affect to mediate the alignment of the expressive with political projects, a central task for the postcolonial critique of the present.

The range of issues above are explored in the next three chapters. In Chapter 2, 'Modernity, Modernization and the Postcolonial Present', the space for posing the question of what may come after modernity and what may open the way to the abolition of existing forms of exploitation is cleared by way of reconstituting the genealogy of modernity, charting its co-emergence in relation to colonialism and capitalism, and establishing the key features of the discourses that construct the modern frame of intelligibility. This is done through the reconstruction of the shifts that announce the break with pre-modern times in Europe, specifically the place of the logocentric subject, the key functioning of a positivist epistemology, the break with theology in the foundation of modernity as a secular and universal project of the historical development of 'humanity'. It examines how these features came to be inscribed in the conceptualization of the colonized other and in the technology of colonial and modern governance. The emergence of imperial governmentality as a hybrid form of biopolitics and a military model of sovereignty is detailed, and consequences for the postcolonial machinery of power are examined. The thrust of the chapter is to understand the material and socio-cultural effectivity of the legacy of colonialism and imperialism in the postcolonial present. It stresses continuities and discontinuities in the field of forces, for instance, capitalism and modernization, and the need to develop a historical or genealogical perspective that recognizes the mutations in these forces, the varieties of modernities they constituted, and the implications for theory and politics.

The third chapter, 'Questions of Identity and Agency', focuses on a problematization of the complicated problem of identity, using concrete examples as a basis for exploring the theoretical issues that arise from the standpoint of how subjectivities and identities may be transformed. This focus is prompted by the fact that identity, in the shape of a 'politics of difference' and an 'identity politics', has become a central issue for a complex set of reasons. These reasons have to do with the privilege of the Western, modern, masculine and Eurocentric norm of the subject and thus the need for those thus marginalized to valorize 'difference'; they refer also to racism and ethnocentrism – sadly not limited to white Euro-America, as seen in Rwanda and elsewhere – and the subtle and not so subtle mechanisms through which they operate; they concern also the process of resistance and the need to constitute or occupy cultural and psychic spaces that allow for alternative ways of being. They include problems of identity that relate to 'multiculturalism'; they highlight the focus on lifestyles and consumer culture that, at least in some quarters, has displaced politics towards an 'aesthetics of existence' and the commodification of the aesthetic. The aim in this chapter is not so much to engage with all these issues, but to introduce a theoretical apparatus for pursuing the questioning of the present that is one of the central themes of the book. The chapter begins with an extended account of Dangarembga's (1988) novel, *Nervous Conditions*, in order to disengage a number of theoretical problems, ranging from ideology to the formation and reconfiguration of subjects. These problems are then examined through an analysis of recent theorizations of subjectivity (Foucault, Althusser, Lacan, Butler) paying particular attention to the role of culture in the process, and to the functioning of the mechanism of recognition and of the gaze (Lacan, Fanon, Lichtenberg-Ettinger). The discussion is further developed through an elaboration of Ricoeur's view of the self as a narrated identity. This allows the analysis to propose ways in which identity and subjectivity can be understood in relation to the narratives and scripts existing in a culture from which one draws in locating oneself as a particular self, and as a member of a particular community or collectivity. The chapter moves towards the problematic of transformation in the light of emancipatory politics and expressive action.

The final chapter, 'Towards a Postcolonial Political Economy', addresses more directly these changes and goals, indicating the contours of a critical political economy that is seen as crucial for rethinking the present. I draw upon the analytical positions I have introduced in the methodology section to establish the theoretical bases for this postcolonial political economy, using Arundhati Roy's (1999, 2002) account of the Narmada valley big dam project as a starting point. The idea here is to show the inadequacy of the separation of culture, the economy and politics if one is to understand them in terms of their inter-related processual dynamics, and in terms of the embeddings and re-embeddings, de-territorializations and re-territorializations that accompany changes in productive activity and technology or in the spatiality of everyday existence. In the Narmada case, it becomes clear that the links between environment, economic development, and human rights are at once structural and existential, in that they are lived in the form of a way of life, that is, they are inscribed in the culture and in forms of subjectivity and identity. Furthermore, the emphasis on the active and inter-subjective constitution of community relocates the focus of analysis on agents' meaning-making activity and the inscription of norms, values and knowledges in such activity. The production of the means of existence is seen to be an important but not the sole determining part of modes of existence. The elaboration of political economy proceeds through a general critique of the neo-liberal apparatus of politico-economic governance. This critique is supported by a number of examples to illustrate the reality of globalization for the new stage of pauperization becoming horizontally and vertically widespread across states – through 'liberalization', 'structural adjustment' programmes, the commodification of knowledges and technologies, new forms of enclosures, the form of usury called debt, the use of 'terror as usual' (Taussig, 1993a). The analysis in the chapter shows that the problem of the postcolonial cannot be separated out from wider considerations regarding the postmodern, particularly the attempt to establish globally the rule of neo-liberal practices and patterns of behaviour and thought consistent with it. Issues of identity, of envisioning alternative futures on the basis of an heteronomous ethics, that is, of imagining transcolonial and transmodern futures, cannot but take account of this wider repositioning of the postcolonial. The view that the postcolonial is an idea to be realized means that the critique of the present must be oriented towards the institution of a world beyond the homogenization and privilege of a centre or an origin or a sovereignty that are at the heart of every form of colonialism and subjugation. Today this process is called neo-liberalism, a totalizing and autistic doctrine that threatens to institute an inhuman world; alongside other pathological forms of fundamentalism, it is the greatest danger.

Notes

1 The world has shrunk even further than with globalization in the wake of the generalized surveillance that has been put into place, combining technologies previously applying to different zones so that little is left of public and private space that is not open to the gaze of the new militarized governance. At the global level, the sign of danger has been generalized, and the state of emergency has become permanent. The fact that the USA has over 360 military installations located right across the whole globe is a stark reminder of the interconnections of capitalist business strategies and military strategy and of the big stick kept in readiness in case the locals should think of insurrection.

2 Concerning Introductory texts and Readers covering postcolonial studies, I have found the following useful for different kinds of reason.

Patrick Williams and Laura Chrisman (eds) (1993) *Colonial Discourse and Post-colonial Theory*. A first Reader, it helped to circumscribe the field, introducing among the many key papers both well-known positions and less familiar names; the thematic structure defined an early agenda for postcolonial analysis.

Peter Childs and Patrick Williams (1997) *An Introduction to Post-Colonial Theory*. The introductory chapter addresses the issues that have become central to postcolonial studies. These are developed in detail through the studies of Said, Bhabha and Spivak and an important last chapter on the intersections of postcolonial theory with other areas of critical theory.

Ato Quayson (2000) *Postcolonialism: Theory, Practice or Process?* This book focuses on the postcolonializing process, and on the intersections and affiliations of radical theory when one considers the stakes in discourses addressing problems of gender relations, the environment, 'imbalances' of power, inequalities throughout the world. So the approach is to ally the postcolonial with other forms and sites of struggle. The point is not to confine the postcolonial to specific territories and constituencies associated with the 'Third World' or the South, and so on. The specific studies examine feminism, writing, historiography, postmodernism.

Leela Gandhi (1998) *Postcolonial Theory: A Critical Introduction*. The book examines the aftermath of colonialism, ranging over issues of community, nationalism, feminism, and globalization, as they affect postcolonial analysis. A chapter on intellectual history introduces key concepts and developments, such as the Enlightenment. The book is a clear guide to the kinds of issues that postcolonial studies has engaged with or ought to.

Achille Mbembe (2001) *On the Postcolony*. This is a different take on the postcolonial question, written as a meditation on the state of power and violence in Africa in the shadow of colonialism. It addresses issues of sovereignty, of bare life, of alterity and the stranger, of basic existential questions that concern everyone, but examines them in the context of Africa, what meanings they have in the context of the havoc in the African postcolony. It is a challenge to the familiar categories and debates within postcolonial studies, whether about questions of identity, or the everyday, or forms of power and governance, going beyond generalizations such as Africanism, Afrocentrism, and so on, to look at the multiplicities of times, trajectories and rationalities that are inscribed in the African reality.

Bart Moore-Gilbert (1997) *Postcolonial Theory: Contexts, Practices, Politics*. For those looking for a text that examines the elaboration of theory by authors writing from a sense of belonging to the 'postcolonial', this book attempts to show the extent to which concepts and theories usually located in Western academe have been elaborated from the standpoint of (post)colonial experiences.

Robert Young (2001) *Postcolonialism: An Historical Introduction*. The intention here is to retrace and make visible the history of anti-colonial struggles, much of it forgotten or neglected now, and the thinking that accompanied them, showing the link between activism and intellectual work. Splendid archival work.

Ania Loomba (1998) *Colonialism/Postcolonialism*. Loomba's book clarifies key concepts in Marxist, poststructuralist, feminist and postmodern approaches to the postcolonial. It also deals with racial and 'subaltern' identities, pointing to the complex mechanisms at work in the colonial context. She uses literary texts to explore these and other issues. She argues that postcolonial studies must engage with the wider problems, arising from globalization, that now determine what is possible.

Iain Chambers and Lidia Curti (1996) *The Post-Colonial Question*. This collection is a wide-ranging engagement not so much with the postcolonial as with experiences and thinking – of diaspora, of marginalization, of displacement, of oppressions – that cut across disciplines and categories to indicate the emergence of new starting points for dealing with the often disjunct spaces and temporalities that inscribe postmodern, postcolonial realities. Stuart Hall's classic essay, 'When was "the postcolonial"? Thinking at the limit', critically surveys the issues as developed in the polemics, having in mind the political and theoretical stakes in thinking about the difference implicated in the post. It is a plea to create a disturbance in the field of theory so that the postcolonial critic may be able to break with the familiar terrains and ways of thinking that too often repeat positions that do not help one address the problems of global capitalism and relations of power or of identity as they are experienced in late modernity.

The essays collected in David Theo Goldberg and Ato Quayson (2002) *Relocating Post-colonialism* update the critical apparatus of postcolonial studies, providing instances of work that engages with the changing landscape of global culture, including information technology, the body, re-examinations of slavery and racism, and a wide-ranging conversation between Homi Bhabha and John Comaroff.

Additionally, I rely on the fact that several books, for example, Moore-Gilbert (1997), Ashcroft et al. (2000), Macey (2000), already provide adequate introductions to the range of concepts that would be useful for the analysis of the range of texts that postcolonial studies take within its purview.

3 The car is an interesting case to consider; it is itself the product of knowledges and techniques applied or derived from physics, chemistry, electronics, mechanics, ergonomics, economics, design, pragmatically put together or assembled to achieve specific performances and outcomes. It works by itself but requires to be inserted into other systems: of roads, traffic system, rules of good practice, spatial environments and so on. Interestingly, these have themselves developed in dynamic response to the car as a particular machine and what it makes possible; all these sub-networks mutually condition each other's development and operation. Assemblages over time generate structures and structural relations that are both enabling and limiting.

4 It is clear from the arguments and sources in the book that it consciously avoids the tired debate that divides postcolonial studies into two opposed, almost stereotyped, positions about the postcolonial. On the one hand, there is the view that the postcolonial is a discourse produced by intellectuals originally from the former colonies whose perception of the problems is directed by the Western theoretical apparatus they use and their locations in Western universities (Dirlik, 1994). They do not speak for or to the people in the former colonies. They operate in some kind of theoretical ghetto and have little of value to contribute in solving the real problems facing the postcolony. The other view is that the postcolonial is a decolonizing critical discourse which engages with the theoretical and analytical problems that have emerged since the formal ending of the older forms of imperialism; it intervenes productively in the understanding of the postcolonial world through the interrogation of the texts that have discursively produced colonial identities and spaces; its work attempts to gives voice to those whom colonialism had marginalized. There are, of course, many positions inbetween. But this book is not concerned with an engagement with these debates as such, whatever their merits.

5 It seeks the constitution of an archive that feeds into postcolonial studies as an inter-disciplinary terrain of critical discourses addressing the postcolony as a specific lifeworld, at once a material and discursive space, which has been historically constituted in the course of colonial modernity. This archive is concerned with the everyday reality of postcolonial local existence and with the broader, now global, field of forces which condition and limit that reality. A more

open-ended search beckons, drawing from the massive literature already established in post-colonial studies and cognate fields such as development studies, third world studies, diaspora studies, cultural studies, feminist studies and the important accumulation of historical material about the colonies: their histories, deeds, cultures, arts, knowledges and the constant mutations in them in the course of time. It would range through sources like the *New Internationalist*, reports by charitable bodies like Oxfam and Amnesty International, activist and pressure groups such as the World Social Forum, the Self-Employed Women's Association (SEWA) and Greenpeace, accounts of the activities of NGOs like the World Bank, the World Health Organization, international apparatuses of global governance like the World Trade Organization, in order to compile a dossier of information about wealth production, the state of health of people across the world, geopolitical activities, conflicts of various kinds: civil, ethnic, territorial, and wars of liberation, the grim data on debt or poverty or global wealth distribution, collusions between technosciences and capitalism as in the pharmaceutical and food industries, environmental problems and disasters (often to be found in the Business pages of newspapers). It also includes acts of resistance and the cultural and social machinery that sustains them, in short, the myriad forms in which the lived experience of postcoloniality has been expressed: in films, writings, music, the arts. The postcolonial here is not confined to the specialist literature about the 'Third World' but appears in relation to matters that affect all countries and that are dispersed in every aspect of the everyday world, for example, about whether the clothes one buys come from some sweatshop in South-East Asia. Of course, if one lives in a postcolonial country or situation, then it is impossible to avoid knowing about and living this reality and trying to make sense of it. The problem is to connect more clearly two distinct postcolonial worlds, the academic world and the experiential reality to which it is supposed to refer, and to show that our interpretations of the world is shaped by the way theory, implicitly or explicitly, cuts up the world in specific ways that make visible some particular underlying processes while throwing into invisibility other aspects. It is important to recognize that the terms and theories we have at our disposal for any analysis of our (life)world already belong to the history that directs the way we pose questions, or indeed how we recognize certain questions as legitimate and important or the right ones to ask. An important element of postcolonial critique, therefore, is a self-reflective awareness of the limitations that this implies.

2

Modernity, Modernization and the Postcolonial Present

Framing modernity

We are, it seems, living through a period of major transition, a period that announces the coming of postmodern and post-industrial times, or, indeed, the advent of 'a new world order' into which we are being pressed. Recent events have made it possible to speak once more in productive ways about capitalism; and after the massacre at the World Trade Center in New York in 2001 and the launch by the USA of the 'global war against terrorism', the analysis of imperialism in its various forms has moved up the theoretical agenda, evidenced in the massive success of Hardt and Negri's (2000) book, *Empire*, while its theses have been discussed in countless articles. However, the readiness with which older agendas – for example, the 'clash of civilizations', new wars of religion, imperialism as usual – have been revived should alert us to both continuities and discontinuities, for, it would be counter-productive to assume that nothing has changed. It is therefore an opportune time for postcolonial critique to think again about modernity and its relation to capitalism and colonialism. The central aim of this chapter is to understand modernity against both the long span of a history that began symbolically with the events of 1492 in the New World and in Europe, and in relation to the present. That historical scope should include the contribution of the Arabs to the emergence of the Renaissance in Europe, itself a condition of possibility for the birth of Western modernity. Additionally, this different **genealogy** would introduce a different dimension to the analysis of vernacular modernities and would add to the matter of 'provincializing Europe' (Chakrabarty, 1988). If it is true that one imagines the future according to how one locates oneself in a stream of history, then the particular way one narrates the past becomes vital, especially a narration that makes visible what has been 'forgotten' or disavowed, erased in the history of the victors, but equally that recovers the traces that 'marginalized' or 'minoritarian' narrations have kept as a memory.

It is impossible today to pose any question about the postcolonial without presupposing the history, the discourse and process of modernity and modernization. Yet much of this is taken for granted as background or unproblematic, routinized in existing apparatuses constituting the social and in institutional practices, for instance, in decisions concerning the strategies that would be appropriate with respect to the policies of the World Trade Organization or what institutions best deliver health care, or indeed in thinking about theoretical issues such as how one is to understand the situation of the postcolony in relation to the 'disorder of identity' (Derrida, 1998) and emergent forms of sovereignty and governance (Mbembe, 2001). This chapter is primarily concerned with constructing a different genealogy that disrupts this taken-for-granted character of modernity, appearing as doxa inscribed in the everyday lifeworld, its spatialities and its temporalities. The point is that, as I argued in the last chapter, the lives of most people in large parts of the world, particularly in urban areas, are circumscribed in one way or another by the transformations wrought in the name of modernization and by the limits determined by the conceptual horizon of modernity, for example, as expressed in the forms of governance and in cognitive-affective orientations of political philosophies such as liberalism and socialism. Indeed, the problem for postcoloniality is precisely how to contest and break out of prevailing parameters and limits, a problem which is central to thinking about the postcolonial as an idea and a project to be realized. Interestingly, the emergence of mega-cities, in Africa and other tri-continental countries has shown the degree to which such assumptions are no longer tenable anyway (see Bishop et al., 2003; Chung et al., 2002; Koolhaas, 2002; Simone, 2001; Venn, 2005; Yeo, 2003). The argument in this chapter is guided by the recognition that a critical engagement with the legacy of colonial modernization and the epistemic foundation of the Enlightenment cannot be avoided if one is to oppose 'globalization from above' and the spread of neo-liberalism as an ideology and a mindset operating through its colonization and integration of the public and the private spheres.

One major problem is that the concept of modernity has become one of the most frustrating concepts to address, complicated by the cacophony of views about the **postmodern**. It is thus crucial to be clear about what postcolonial critique understands by modernity, since ideas or assumptions about what it is continue to lie in the background of the most important debates and disputes today, from the would-be anti-modern thrust of religious fundamentalisms to the problematic notion of re-modernization, and the resilience of values and practices that, besides, prompt one to question whether we have ever been modern (Latour, 1993). One knows too that these assumptions about modernity are re-inscribed in the concept of 'development' and the goals thought appropriate to it, and the numerous questions that emerge in relation to the transformations gathered under the term globalization.

It is odd that most introductory books on postcolonialism do not directly examine modernity, through, in one way or another, the issues about the heterogeneous effects of modernization and modernism that they address constantly invoke it. This may well be because of the doxic character of the modern, so that the latter now dwells as a given in the mind as much as in the material culture of the everyday, or else because of a decision that the problem for postcolonial thought is to address its legacy, for example, in its signifying texts, rather than to rethink modernity itself. A few authors, for example, Gilroy (1993), and Nandy (1990) do explicitly interrogate this legacy in terms of a challenge to the presuppositions of modernity and the Enlightenment. One of Gilroy's goals has been to demonstrate the emergence of counter-modernities as part and parcel of the resistance to, and counter-appropriations of, the modern project of subjectification and subjection. Appadurai's (1996) analysis of modernities in the global cultural economy is another significant contribution to rethinking postcoloniality within that broader framework, drawing attention to the flows and scapes that characterize international and transnational economic, informational, technological, and cultural exchanges in the contemporary world. Canclini's (1995) work traces the history of the hybrid appropriations of modernity at the level of cultures, that is, at the level of the lived, making visible the dynamic character of transcultural interchanges between indigenous and Western cultures that create liveable spaces and preserve in a creolized form the temporal flux of indigenous communities. One conviction guiding this chapter is that an understanding of modernity in terms of its historical specificity has become both a condition for clarifying what is at stake in how one is to judge what is to be done in the moment of the 'post', and for assessing the policies that are currently altering, perhaps irreversibly, the postcolonial world.

In line with this reasoning, a central goal in this chapter is to establish the co-emergence of modernity, European **colonialism** and capitalism. Although this relationship is recognized in postcolonial theory, my objective here is to demonstrate that each of these broad processes historically and conceptually conditioned the others in determining their co-articulated development. The analysis will make visible the way in which a number of key concepts – the unitary autonomous subject, modern rationality, science, disciplinary power and knowledge – operated as relay concepts in that process of co-articulation, and constructed their discursive coherence, a coherence that abides. I will return to the idea of modernity as a project, organized according to the logic of a linear temporality, inscribed in the concepts of progress and development, and the specific functioning of modern notions of the subject and of knowledge in it. The thrust towards globalization, active from the beginning of European expansion and its universalizing and monotheist ambitions must be understood within such a conceptual framework or world-view.

My discussion necessarily focuses on the mechanisms that have been put in place to institute modernity globally from colonial times. In particular, the chapter will highlight three features of modernity and modernization: (1) the emergence of an imperial governmentality, which will be explored in terms of its specificity as a form of governance and in terms of its legacy; (2) the role of the Enlightenment in authorizing the European worlding of a world; and (3) the linear temporality of 'progress' and 'development'. The ambivalent effects of these developments for ideals of emancipation and becoming will be discussed. I will also propose the idea of neo-liberalism as a counter-Enlightenment idea, a line of analysis that suggests the convergence for critique of the problems of the postmodern and the postcolonial future.

The approach indicated in the first chapter means that the process of modernization can be examined from the point of view of vernacular appropriation or **creolization**. This approach, as I argued, relies on the proposition that creolization and transculturation are normal processes, associated with diasporic displacement and turbulence, occurring in the course of the encounter of cultures. They apply to the modern as well as to other periods throughout the world, and can be seen in countless examples of borrowings, adaptations, appropriations, exchanges, reconfigurations, graftings that take place in the history of the mutation of cultures. Cultures, as I pointed out in the first chapter following Edward Said, are intrinsically heterogeneous and polyglot. Their history from the standpoint of **diaspora** shows that the interpenetration and syncretic mixing of cultures have resulted in their being intertwined at the level of the everyday, although an interesting theoretical problem arises regarding the mechanisms whereby new cultural configurations acquire relative stability for a while, depending on the circumstances. Clearly, power relations inflect creolization and diasporic reconstitution as process, for such processes take place in conflictual or agonistic situations so that every aspect of the mutation in culture is marked by contestation. One can detect this process in the difference between the place and functioning of the study of English in India (see Viswanathan, 1989), or, with significant differences, in the transformation of the English language, well before its standardization, that followed Northern European migrations (of Saxons, Vikings, Celts, Normans) to the British Isles. This chapter extends this recognition to point to the different vernacular modernities that have developed in different parts of the world, inflected by different circumstances and dynamics.

In the retelling of modernity, I shall draw attention to the special place of the mediation of the aesthetic domain in relaying the cognitive and the ethical in the discourses underlying the idea of Enlightenment modernity. The canonical example is that of modernism as an artistic movement from the end of the nineteenth century, though Romanticism as a movement, most clearly in Early German Romanticism (Bowie, 1990), equally demonstrates this mediation. It is important that the postcolonial genealogy of modernity keeps in sight the transformative role of the 'arts of resistance' in emancipatory struggles against forms of oppression and exploitation (see Enwesor et al., 2002, 2003; Trinh, 1989, Venn, 2002a, 2002b).

Pluralizing modernity

Let me start with a number of concrete issues about modernity and modernization. Japan today is regarded as an exemplar of successful dynamic modernization. Yet, one might ask, does that mean that Japanese society is *ipso facto* Western? If one were to examine this question by reference to Japanese cultural values, to the place of the family in people's lives in Japan, to the still minor role of women in the public sphere, to ideas of loyalty and deference still determining of social relations in institutions, to prevalent belief systems and religious affiliations, to a multitude of mundane patterns of behaviour in the everyday, it is clear that, while Japan has appropriated key aspects of modernity and the 'West', it remains in some important senses Japanese. It is thus both modern yet different from Europe or North America; it is a vernacular modernity. A brief look at the history of modernization in Japan reveals the important fact that the Japanese government from the Meiji period (1868–1912) autonomously decided to modernize in order to counter the threat of Western domination, dramatically experienced through the invasion of Tokyo harbour in 1853 by an American fleet commanded by Matthew Perry, and subsequent demands for trade liberalization from Western powers. The event demonstrated the superiority of Western, modern military apparatus and the vulnerability of a non-modernized Japan to foreign domination, in spite of the draconian measures put in place in the Edo period to keep foreign influence at bay. It came at a time when an increasingly prosperous and ambitious middle class in Japan was already experiencing the Edo regime as a structural obstacle to its own advancement and the further development of Japan. A typical and very influential figure of that period is Yukichi Fukuzawa who travelled to Europe and returned to advocate the modernization of Japan, not in order to mimic Europe, but in order to adopt the spirit of the West as part of a strategy for Japan to break away from Asian culture – by which the Japanese meant China's historical cultural hold, thus revealing locally constituted blocs and stakes, for China and not Europe was Japan's other – and so become modern and strong. Fukuzawa ([1866] 1973) represented modernity as a liberating spirit favouring national independence against the fixity of the Asian spirit. He thought that for people to want the material and institutional rewards of modernization, such as a progressive economy and changes in government, one needed to first change the Japanese mind. Interestingly, this strategy was later (in the 1920s) reflected in the slogan 'good wife, wise mother' as part of the effort to transform the family so that it could spearhead the transformation of Japanese society (Tamari, 2002).[1] Furthermore, it is important to bear in mind the grafting of modernization with an imperial project, still in line with the European model, as Inoue Kaoru, the Japanese Foreign Minister put it in 1887: 'What we must do is to transform our empire and our people, make the empire like the countries of Europe and our people like the peoples of Europe ... we have to establish a new, European-style empire on the edge of Asia' (cited in Jansen, 1984: 64, in Myers and Peattie, 1984). The colonization of Korea, the expansion into China in the 1930s, and the extension of Japanese economic power through South-East Asia, and Japanese military objectives in the Second World War are fully consistent with this project. Yet, the goal of modernization for the Japanese remained the preservation of their independence and autonomy and the protection of Japanese culture against colonization, a Japanese culture that is itself reconstituted in the process, for instance, by reference to the construction of a national language (Sakai, 1997). This marking, and re-making, of a threshold are demarcated in real thresholds, particularly at the level of the familial, the domus, ritualized in, for example, the common practice of removing one's shoes in order to cross the threshold between the modern/outside and the Japanese inside or private sphere which additionally reconstitutes the spatiality of an imagined Japanese culture through a regime of familiarity instantiated in the disposition of furniture, artefacts of one kind or another, the food, the staging of the social relations within a physical and temporal space that is consistent with that **imaginary**. Modernization, then, was an instrumental and strategic form of appropriation, a creolization; the fact that it encountered modernity at a time when it was already moving towards modernization for reasons of its own is important from the point of view of the specificity of Japanese modernity.

Quite different factors and circumstances were at work in the case of the implantation of modernity in India (or in Latin America or Africa). In India, modernity came inseparably with the tactics of governance that were being invented as part of establishing colonial authority. It took the form of an acculturation, through pedagogy and the introduction of the English curriculum, as the detailed work undertaken by Viswanathan (1989) that I introduced in the previous chapter shows. The process was a complex one, involving ideas about the proper way to exercise authority, the choice of the right kind of texts to use, the place of a secular approach in the context of religious opposition, complicated by differences among the contesting missionary tendencies, disputes about the virtue of detaching English culture, as represented in the chosen texts of the colonizer, from the materiality of domination (ibid.: 20). Modernity and modernization do not appear as explicit goals in the early part of the nineteenth century when these apparatuses for establishing imperial hegemony were being invented. Rather, they were implicit in the notion of the West that had been emerging since the birth of the modern (see below), and as inscribed in the idea of the (at first fractured and ambivalent) superiority of Western sciences, learning and civilization, an idea emphatically expressed in Macaulay's 'Minutes on Education' of 1835 that explicitly denigrated indigenous Indian knowledge. In contrast to the case of Japan, modernity in India was implanted as part of Westernization (targeting an elite and an administrative cadre). Resistance to it took different forms, for instance, when we compare the appropriating strategies employed by the Japanese with those invented as part of subaltern resistance such as the form of mimicry that 'repeats differently' to disrupt colonial authority, as Bhabha (1994) has shown. Additionally, the bases for alternative ways of being that reasserted the validity and value of indigenous cultural and social norms of being were sought in practices of everyday life through the 'ruses of the weak' (de Certeau, 1984) that aim to secure spaces in which such norms could be performatively enacted, even if it meant inventing means of adapting to changing power relations, as the Subaltern

Studies Group has established (Guha and Spivak, 1988). The struggle for
liberation before 1947 abounds in stratagems of this kind. Foremost would
be Ghandi's subtle adaptations of elements of modernity such as the ideas
of democracy, autonomy and freedom in order to recast India's civilizational
project and valorize Indian culture. Similarly, Tagore (1922) reformulates
modernity in terms of a non-Western project, emphasizing the spiritual
aspect of Asian mentality that would infuse modernity in the East, against
what he saw as the mechanical, materialist, violent, urban, bureaucratic
character of modernity in the West. Asian modernity would free the human
spirit for a creative development at the individual and social levels, signalling
an alternative universal project that is nevertheless consistent with an idea
of the modern. In a sense we can talk about different, or alternative modernities
(Gilroy, 1993), perhaps co-existing or 'co-eval modernities' (Harootunian,
2000), developing in Japan and India, responding to counter-occidentalist
cultural and political imperatives and interests that have a purchase in the
local conditions.

Many issues surface in the contrast that I have introduced, for instance,
regarding the historical specificity of the processes and mechanisms involved,
the different time lags between Europe and the particular colony, the
retroactive accounts of what took place, the disjunctive times of belonging, the
forms of resistance, the problematization or amplification of processes often
conceptualized in terms of hegemony, the context-specific effects, the sense
of modernity that the colonized and non-Western peoples formed from
their experience. Given these different histories, it is not surprising that the
stakes in modernization today in India and Japan are different. Nevertheless
there are important similarities, especially by reference to ideas of the modern
and its institutions, such as the democratic state, its technosciences and their
universal implantation or reach, conceptualizations of the 'West' with-and-
against which these different cultures enter into relations of co-articulation,
and the reality of globalization in its various forms. These are some of the
issues that need to be clarified through establishing the specificity of modernity as a concept and as event.

The colonial birth of modernity

Most accounts of modernity from a Western point of view continue to mar-
ginalize or ignore the place of European colonialism in its institution (Venn,
2000). In a strange way this is the obverse of those accounts of colonialism
and the postcolonial that wish to see modernity and its forms, like nationalism, as only a 'derivative discourse' (Chatterjee, 1986), or else as an imped-
iment that may perhaps be cleansed out to recover an authentic national
culture, as fundamentalists everywhere are tempted to phantasize (see
Bhatt (2001) regarding Hindu fundamentalism). Yet there are sound arguments and historical evidence to indicate that colonialism altered in crucial
ways both the colonized and the colonizers – which is not to say that older

traditions and cultures have simply vanished; my analysis of identity in Chapter 3 shows their resilience and survival through a range of strategies such as creolization and hybridization. The story of the becoming modern of the world is very complex, since many momentous events and changes in Europe and throughout the world participate as conditions of possibility. I will summarize the main features, aspects of which I examined in detail in Venn (2000), beginning with a number of gestures that retroactively appear as inaugural in the genealogy that I am presenting.

The first act of the Spanish conquistadors upon landing at Guanahani in the Caribbean was to plant the royal standard of the King and Queen of Spain and claim the land in the name of Christianity and Spain (Columbus, [1492] 1988: 53). This gesture, profoundly inaugural, already binds sovereignty with conquest and a monotheist missionary project. In Columbus' account, we are meant to believe that first contact enabled the conquerors to immediately draw significant conclusions about the Caribs. He says:

> They should make good servants and very intelligent, for I have observed that they soon repeat anything that is said to them, and I believe that they would easily be made Christians, for they appeared to me to have no religion ... I will bring half a dozen of them back to their Majesties, so that they can learn to speak. (ibid.: 56)

This astonishing statement shows that from the beginning the people whose land and wealth they were appropriating and whose lives they were about to destroy were already categorized as 'primitive': without language or religion, fit only to be servants, a lesser breed. Equally it is clear that ownership, possession and conversion to Christianity went hand in hand. Loot was never very far from the minds of the colonizers. This gesture whereby knowledge, ownership, subjection, dispossession and subjectification are entwined was to be repeated in countless encounters in the history of European colonization, characterized by considerable violence. Todorov's account in *The Conquest of America* ([1982] 1992) argues that the discovery by Europeans of what they called the New World was fundamentally involved in the remaking of European identity: 'it is the conquest of America that establishes our present identity; [it marks] the beginning of the modern era' (ibid.: 5). The othering of **the other** as Other not only casts the other out of humanity and demonizes or objectifies him or her; at the same time it reconfigures the identity of Europeans as superior, with a divinely ordained right to take over non-Christian lands and goods. Columbus' gesture already marks European colonization as a process validated under cover of a mission, Christianizing at first, later 'civilizing'. More recently, a developmental or modernizing mission, increasingly directed by a postmodern monotheism, namely, neo-liberalism, has taken over the dispossessing and subjugating goals of the earlier phase.[2] Thus, 1492 already inaugurates a narrative of history whereby the rest of the world is positioned as always in the process of catching up with Europe/the West/the modern, always in process of casting off the obstacles of 'arrested development' that prevent them from being 'properly civilized'.

One may perhaps see this through the question that troubles Todorov, which is the following: 'not only did the Spaniards understand the Aztecs quite well, they admired them – and yet they annihilated them, why?' Among the explanations he proposed is that they did not regard the Native Americans as properly human, and so do not speak *to* them. Added to this is the obsession with riches – gold, silver, precious stones – convertible into money as the general signifier of value. In this respect, Todorov says: 'The homogenisation of values by money is a new phenomenon and it heralds the modern mentality, egalitarian and economic' (1992: 143). Todorov jumps the gun a bit here, for Spanish colonialism is structured by other more archaic forces, keeping a degree of continuity with medieval social structure and its structures of authority (Kamen, 2002). A properly mercantile ideology took some time to become established, ushered in by, among other mechanisms, the Protestant 'spirit of capitalism'. Nevertheless, it is true that from the earliest days, European colonialism was inflected by incipient capitalism and the crucial break with the Augustinian principle of the trinity of mind, knowledge and love that binds knowing with loving, as I examine below. Instead we witness at such an early stage the emergence of the epistemological and ontological bases for the co-articulation of knowledge with domination, later developed in mechanical philosophy and in instrumental rationality that acquires a totalizing force, as Habermas (1987) and Horkheimer and Adorno (1973) have argued about instrumental reason, although crucially, they fail to detect the conditions of possibility for this feature of occidentalism in the European form of colonialism and imperialism. These are crucial shifts because they explain much about the banishment of other forms of life that modernity initiates and legitimates by reference to its own discourse. I shall elaborate on them presently.

At this stage, I want to signal the broad direction of the analysis I am developing so that the stress I place on these shifts in the conceptual framework makes sense in terms of a narrative of modernity and postcoloniality. To begin with, the relay of knowledge with oppressive power and with ownership makes visible the deep affinities with capitalism, especially in its coupling with Protestantism (I am clearly extending the line of thought initiated in Weber) and its reduction of the human to abstract legal entities governed by (a specific form of) rationality and by contractual arrangements (when it is not reduced to the status of commodity as in slavery). Thus, when science came to be the signifier of the model for the instrumental control of nature and human beings, it made possible the gradual emergence of a disciplinary society – the term making visible the implication of a militarist mindset and techne that underlie the disciplinary systems in Foucault's sense of the term.

The dominance of instrumental reason in modernity, coupled with the institution of disciplinary society, both sanctioned by the epistemological privilege of Science, has **over-determined** the emergence of totalitarian and intolerant systems of thought encompassing every aspect of existence. Today it is inscribed in the technocratic rhetoric of neo-liberalism. It is worth signalling the political implications of the affinities of this technocratic reason with the postmodern reduction of the goals of social advancement to those of the self-referential notions of the system's efficiency, as understood in Lyotard's ([1976] 1984) critique of the postmodern. The result is the imprisonment of thought in the iron cage of this mindset and thus the elimination of the possibility of imagining alternative ways of life. We find the same mindset repeated in the appeal of new information technology, in its application in new military thinking, in the almost child-like wonder in the magic of dot.com, in the identification of superiority with technological sophistication that has become naturalized. They are all signs of the extent to which technique now operates as a transcendent realm (see Derrida and Stiegler, 2002), replacing the ethical foundations that grounded, albeit ambivalently, the project of modernity and concealing the metaphysical, occult and quasi-theological assumptions that sustain the neo-liberal postmodern ideology. Already, then, some of the parameters of modernity that I want to highlight begin to appear in the shifts that inaugurate the modern period.

The second inaugural gesture that I want to signal is that of *tabula rasa* that Descartes invokes in 1637 to explain the radical nature of his break with the previous system of making sense of the world and of validating knowledge. *Tabula rasa*, in one movement, brushes aside a whole epistemology; it symbolically discards centuries of learning, the vast accumulated store of the traditional scholastic knowledge, founded on sacred texts and their authorizing narratives of the world, that determined for educated Europeans at the time what could be said with confidence about the world. Instead, it installs the subject of logos – the 'I think', the logocentric subject – as centre and autonomous agent of the process of knowing. It thus positions the human subject at the origin of the process whereby the truths by which we are meant to live are established. The whole classical order that framed Renaissance and earlier European understanding of the world is at once subjected to the turmoil of a systematic doubt, with implications for the epistemological status of the foundational narratives that had held (relatively) firm until then. Descartes' gesture announces the emergence of a new form of knowing, independent of divine validation, founded on evidence and rational thought alone, a knowledge that grew to acquire the status of Science as the undisputed form of the truth in the nineteenth century. But this gesture does not appear out of nowhere. Epistemological shifts that begin to appear in the wake of Arab scholarship, and a series of developments from the fifteenth century, including, importantly, European encounters with other cultures and other ideas and their challenge to the medieval conceptual framework (Goonatilake, 1984; Ozment, 1971; Pagden, 1993; Sayyid, 2003), prepare the grounds for it. Space does not allow me to do any more than a brief summary of what I have established at length elsewhere (Venn, 2000).

I have chosen these two gestures precisely because analysis shows their intimate inter-relation. The first thing to note concerns the effects of the 'discovery' of the New World for knowledge, for the fact is that the sheer abundance of new objects and peoples encountered by the European conquerors radically challenged the whole edifice of knowledge put together since the Greeks. The picture of the world that had been taken for granted by European scholars, for instance, the classificatory systems for the objects of nature based in Aristotelian science, could not encompass the disruptive new-ness of the Americas. The conceptual framework of the old world was left in tatters by the challenge that was posed to its system of classification and its explanations of natural and cultural phenomena by what the conquerors found: the new species of plants and animals, the new geographical contours of the world, the new peoples, their cultures, languages, beliefs and ways of being. Pagden's (1993) study elaborates the implications, indicating that the net effect was to fundamentally disrupt the older world order and undermine the founding principles in which it was inscribed. After 1492, a new way of making sense of the world, for both colonized and colonizer, had to be found.

The effects of the new findings did not depend simply on the fact of their newness or the fact that the existing system of classification could not accommodate them. Several discoveries and new theories about the world at the time added to the disruption, such as the Copernican heliocentric model of the known cosmos that challenged the Ptolemaic model sub-scribed to by the Church, the invention of perspective (Brunellesci), new (Galenic) knowledges about the body, the cumulative effects of the trans-lations from Arabic that made available not only the old Greek store of knowledge but all the other knowledges that came along with it. Harding (1998) points to the fact that the Greek legacy had been created by many intervening cultures in Africa, Asia, Egypt and the Mediterranean. Goonatilake (1984) highlights the importance of the Arab critiques of the geocentric theory and their advances in optical theory, and that of the Chinese astronomical ideas founded on principles quite different from those of the Greeks, Arabs and Indians, as well as hermetic beliefs creolized from Egyptian and African thought (see also Yates, 1964). Additionally, given what I indicated in the first chapter about the technical conditions of possibility in the worlding of the world, I should point to the many borrowings – say, printing, the magnetic needle, the rudder, gunpowder, mathematical techniques like early calculus from China and India, Arabic alchemy and chemistry, knowledge of medicines, classification systems, plants, agricultural techniques from all parts of the world (Crombie, 1961; Diop, 1974; Harding, 1995; Sayyid, 2003) that together constituted the assem-blage of knowledge and techniques that fertilized the emergence of modern science and the new ways of thinking about the universe that usher in the time of Galileo and Newton and later the Enlightenment.

The shift from occult philosophy to natural magic and Baconian mechani-cal philosophy is a more complex and fascinating story than is usually told in Eurocentric accounts, illustrating once more the polyglot nature of cultures. From the point of view of hegemony, one must consider what was at stake, namely, not only the authority of the ancient texts, allied since Aquinas with Church doctrine, but also the fact that legitimate political authority and power in feudal Europe were founded on the principle of divine right, so that both the epistemological order and worldly power at the time depended on absolute faith in the truthfulness of the scriptural texts and their narration of the world as interpreted and authorized by the Church. It follows that any challenge to the received truths, either from the sciences or from within Christianity, undermined the established relations of spiritual and worldly power. Indeed, a challenge to the hegemony of the Church was categorized by the priesthood as heresy, and punished by an exemplarily cruel death.

At the end of this transformation, two major convictions came to provide the framework for the reorganization of knowledge. First, the idea that mathematics was the language in which the truths of the world could ideally be expressed; this principle gained a decisive hold on the imagination of the time, influencing the sciences, architecture, music, painting, and social hierarchy. Foucault (1970) has argued that a *mathesis universalis* became the principle replacing the older 'prose of the world' written on the basis of similitudes, resemblances, affinities, sympathies. Second, there is a vital shift from the notion of natural necessity to that of rational necessity, especially from the time of Galileo, so that it became possible to think of causality in terms not of naturally occurring relationships and affinities, determined within a natural order established with Divine 'creation', but in terms of necessary relationships that one could uncover through an appropriate rational experimental practice (for details, see Clavelin, 1974; see generally, Easlea, 1980; Foucault 1970; Koyré, 1971, 1978; Yates, 1983; and Crombie, 1961, discussed in Venn 1982, 2000). Such new thinking, as I have pointed out, finds another set of conditions of possibility with the translation from the Arabic of the corpus of knowledges that the Arabs had developed, building upon the Greek heritage they preserved, and new translations of the Scriptures that revealed mistakes and misconceptions. These developments found their most powerful expression in Cartesianism.

Before I turn to this key phase in the emergence of the discourse of modernity, I need to point to the radical challenges to the established hegemony that the break-up of the Holy Roman Empire and the loss of faith in Catholic theology represented. Dissident movements were fairly common at the time (associated with Huss, Wycliff, the Cathars, and so on), but it is Luther (1517), not so long after Columbus, who has come to be the figure standing for the new spirit. The main reason for picking out Luther is not only because he marked the beginning of the Reformation and thus the beginning of Protestantism and Puritanism, the importance of which from the point of view of capitalism Weber has long established. It is because Lutheranism introduced another hiatus between faith and reason (a complex issue for Christian theology, see Gilson, 1930; Ozment, 1971; Venn, 2000) in arguing that faith and reason could be separated, and that faith alone was necessary for salvation. Furthermore, he claimed that love of God was in a different category from the love of other creatures, rejecting the view (of Biel, for example) that associated the love of God with the love of his creatures, which included non-believers (Luther, [1517] 1971). Europe's conceptualization of the colonized as 'other', held in a state of 'arrested development', perhaps an ally of the devil, is consistent with that Lutheran thesis. Also, the detachment of reason from faith makes the task of Descartes easier; it allows science gradually to manage a distance from religion so that its claims are not seen to undermine faith; it helps capitalist thinking to remove from the responsibility of every Christian the duty of care for one's others, thus boosting individualism (foundational in Puritanism and, later, liberalism and neo-liberalism), and in an indirect way adding weight to the arguments countering the prohibition of usury, which is the basis of banking (though, interestingly, Islam retained the prohibition in principle). It also begins a different narrative of the principle of the Christian sense of salvation as a journey, rationalizing it in the concepts of work and discipline; it is an idea of a journey that could be universalized in the period of the Enlightenment in the thesis of the 'salvation' or emancipation of humanity as a project, expressed in the Kantian conviction of the 'sure march of progress', a reconfiguration that has become central for our understanding of modernity.

All this acquires added relevance when one thinks of the claims of fundamentalisms today, particularly the underlying connection between faith and reason which they make. In the post/hypermodern context, Christian fundamentalism is an interesting case. Several displacements mark its mutation to a doctrine that now explicitly aligns itself with capitalism. In a first phase, the Protestant and Puritan separation of the love of God from the love of God's creatures, and the emergence of the disciplinary practice of an asceticism and a calling, were aligned to the idea of salvation as predestination. More recently, Lutheran doctrine has been remodelled – modernized, perhaps? – to ensure the conversion of faith into a kind of insurance policy as in born-again Evangelical Christian doctrine, that uncouples faith from conscience and guarantees salvation in the form of a contract with God, cashed out in material prosperity. In the fundamentalist imaginary, the good Christian has become the good capitalist, a move mirrored in the parallel mutation in Islamic fundamentalism whereby the good Muslim has become identified with the good terrorist,[3] determined to erase all signs of the 'West' and Christianity.

My aim in sketching these shifts and displacements is directed at making better sense of the Cartesian gesture and what it means for the history of the subject of modernity and for the epistemology underpinning its 'grand' narratives. One immediate point is the rejection of any claim to knowledge resting purely on the authority and privilege of ancient or religious or sacred texts. *Tabula rasa*, though, introduces another element of modern epistemology that has had a distorting effect, namely the assumption that the knower acts alone, relying solely on the available evidence and on rational arguments. This position directly opposes the idea that knowledge is authorized not only on the basis of evidence alone but according to the judgement of a community of practitioners, as well as on the basis of factors that locate the intelligibility of arguments and theories within a wider cultural context (Foucault, 1972; Latour, 1993; Law and Hassard, 1999). The other side of this erasure is the move which installs the rational, unitary, solipsistic subject, the subject of the 'I think' or of the sovereign statement, in the position of the autonomous epistemic centre, the agent who owes nothing to anyone as far as the process of establishing rational thought and truth is concerned. This assumption is still central today, taken for granted in popular views of the scientist, and re-inscribed for instance in the model guiding the approach to the replication of the human mind in Artificial Intelligence, and in the attraction of genetic theory as the explanatory basis for human behaviour; it is present in debates about intellectual property and the ownership of knowledge. They extend the Cartesian epistemology that dictates that the subject be conceptualized as the autonomous self-present subject, inscribed in the point of view of the self-centred gaze, while the relation to the other is disavowed or 'forgotten' in the folding of the I upon itself to establish the 'I think', or cogito, as the 'first principle of the philosophy I was seeking' (Descartes, [1637] 1968: 54). Thus is denied the priority of the relation to the other in the formation of a self, and in the worlding of a world. In the foundation of the discourse of modernity, it was but a short step from this epistemology and ontology to the instrumentalization of the process of human enlightenment and emancipation. The separation of faith and reason relates to the Cartesian system in terms of another displacement, namely, it is the key move that evacuates God from the process of authorizing knowledge (though a 'non-deceiving' God remains the ultimate guarantor of the logocentric subject); this enabled a secular epistemology to emerge and become dominant, grounding the 'project of modernity' itself. The modern **episteme**, as Derrida (1982) has argued, nevertheless keeps hidden a metaphysics, precisely that which secures the modern subject as self-sufficient, as a self-present presence. Today, the conceptualization of transmodern, thus postcolonial, foundational discourses has to address such issues; the scope of this chapter allows me but to note it as a problem for the postcolonial imagination of the future.

My summary is meant to bring into the picture not only the conceptual proximity of these displacements and shifts at the level of the world-view that framed the intelligibility and self-understanding of modernity; they also point to the mutuality of their effects. Thus, the abstract economic subject of rational capitalism – cashed out in the model of the rational buyer or seller of a commodity operating within an abstract, impersonal system of exchange based on money as universal exchange value – echoes the epistemic and legal status of the subject-as-agent. Science, Capital, and Colony gradually came to constitute a fearful symmetry at the level of thought, capable of holding the same intensity of subjective investment as religions do. In Puritanism, the two levels – the ideological and the subjective – combined to great effect. It is interesting that historically, as in the anti-slavery movement, the only force that undermined it, or at least attenuated its inhuman consequences, remained the ethical imperative in Enlightenment humanism and vestiges of a humanitarian spirit in religion, particularly for those who heeded the principles that counselled respect and love for one's neighbour as fundamental to a Christian (and Islamic and Judaic) life. Of course, many Enlightenment intellectuals preferred to ground the same principles in secular philosophies. An examination of the Enlightenment will indicate the extent to which the dilemmas and **aporias** that nowadays continue to determine the terms of the debates about the 'postisms' (Derrida, 1994) find their beginnings in this key moment of modernity.

Science, reason, colony: the Eurocentric temporality of modernity

The relationship between modernity and the Enlightenment discourse is that the latter recast the former in terms of a project of emancipation and liberation of all of humanity: from inequalities, from lack of freedom and liberty, from the denial of fundamental human rights. Within the framework of that discourse, to enlighten meant to throw light upon the mechanisms of the natural and social world, thus banishing ignorance and, in the same movement, it meant showing in the clear light of rational knowledge what needed to be done in order to emancipate human beings from the systems of thought and practices that kept them in a state of bondage and oppression; in this way the goal of the Enlightenment project was to bring about a more just and free society. This promise of liberation and emancipation for all, and the elaboration of the means for achieving it, enunciated outside religious discourses, set a new target for human societies. The continuing hold of the Enlightenment resides in this promise, translated into political ideals represented by Marxism, socialism and liberalism. I have argued that since postcolonial critique is directed by a project of emancipation and liberation, it must examine the reasons for this history which is an important part of colonial liberation's own history.

A theoretical issue central for a re-evaluation of the Enlightenment and the project of the possible completion of knowledge correlated to the project of human advancement relates to what is at stake in the decision that only science – yet to be properly instituted in the course of the nineteenth century – can provide the foundation for rational action in the world. For the Enlightenment, this idea is grounded in two principles: first, the premise of a rational order in the world, and an order that a rational discourse can comprehend and explain. Second, the concept of the subject as the rational autonomous entity who is able to know that world and, thereby, disclose and take possession of it, and direct its history. Thus, the implication that knowledge confers possession, already inscribed in colonial modernity, as Todorov ([1982] 1992) has argued, is inflated with the normative claims of a rational project encompassing the whole world, concerned with its destiny as the progressive History of man, translated in the nineteenth century into the idea of a 'civilizing mission' to replace the Christianizing mission that functioned to legitimate conquest and dispossession in early modernity.[4]

The affiliation of knowledge with both power and with possession/ownership opens its analysis to the part it plays as relay in the intelligibility of the new order. One would need to add another important element, namely, the proposition in mechanical philosophy and modern science that the world is a purely material and inert entity, 'disenchanted', and thus available as property to be owned and to be placed under the sovereignty of 'Man' (Easlea, 1980). It is important to note that in the sciences supporters of a view of nature that later became inscribed in vitalism, although marginalized by the **hegemony** of Mechanism, pursued the idea that immaterial or liminal or irreducible forces – what Renaissance knowledge understood in terms of 'occult' forces – were at work at the heart of nature. Its genealogy runs from the Renaissance natural philosophy of people like Paracelsus and Agrippa to Goethe, Pasteur, Bergson and, more recently, Deleuze and Guattari. Equally crucial to the functioning of the positivist ideology of science were the correlations of rationality with masculinity, whiteness, Europe and the West, so that they became privileged as the markers of legitimate authority and agency.

Retrospectively, one can detect in Enlightenment thought two broad trajectories and visions that each rely on the privilege of the terrain of epistemology; they cross each other at crucial points, for instance in the ideas of freedom and liberty, to complicate the history of their genealogies and effects. On the one hand, we find the reconfiguration of Renaissance Humanism so that the rationality of social arrangements is judged by reference to an ideal of humanity in which justice and goodness prevail. On the other, a political philosophy and a project emerge that concern questions of order and peace, and thus questions of sovereignty, legality, legitimate violence, ownership, and reasons of state and capital. The dilemmas inherent in these discourses appear in the thought of figures of the Enlightenment like Rousseau who denounces inequality and supports republican liberty, yet is able to alienate individual liberty in the idea of a general will that acquires absolute authority with regard to singular wills (see also Hardt and Negri, 2000). They are repeated in different registers in the writings of other theoreticians, culminating in the project of Kant to reorganize the conceptual framework of modernity through the three Critiques, attempting to unite the epistemic, the ethical and the aesthetic instances under the troubled auspices of Reason and the rational subject. A brief summary of the initial project as described in Kant's 1784 essay on the Enlightenment will provide important elements from which to examine the geo-political stakes affecting the postcolony.

Kant defines the Enlightenment as the project of the becoming mature of humanity. He argues that 'man' is held in a self-incurred tutelage because of his 'inability to make use of his understanding without direction from another' (Kant, in Waugh, 1992: 90). Tutelage is the abandonment of autonomy in the use of one's reason through reliance on the authority of experts of one kind or another: doctors, priests, specialists. Yet, all that is needed to ensure gradual enlightenment is the courage to use one's rational faculties, though this possibility requires one basic condition, namely, that 'the public use of one's reason must always be free' (ibid.: 92). Tutelage, of course, acquired imperial connotations in its transformation into the project of a 'civilizing mission' of Europe, allied to the Enlightenment project, as Kant himself expressed it (see Derrida's 1997 critique of the Kantian view of the cosmopolitical). Freedom, then, is central to the project, but it is the freedom to criticize prevailing doctrines, beliefs, customs, and laws and thus to challenge the ideas and reasoning that legitimate existing authorities, something that contemporary tactics of power implicitly and sometimes explicitly repudiate (for instance, through anti-dissidence state terrorism). Kant argues that it is unacceptable for the prevailing state power to decree that the instruments of power cannot be challenged in rational debate, for that would halt human progress: 'a crime against human nature' (ibid.: 93). Freedom, for Kant, is central to critique; its importance for the advancement of humanity is instantiated in the progress of the sciences. A postcolonial narrative of the Enlightenment cannot ignore Hegel's version of the project expressed in terms of an historical logic and a teleology at work in determining the direction of change and the 'ends of man'. For, with Hegel, Kant's linear temporality is converted into History, with its laws of development and its dynamic, and with implications for the criteria that Hegelian-derived theoretical positions may use to judge the relative 'stage of development' of particular societies. I must emphasize the extent to which this notion of time is still central today, inscrypted, that is, inscribed and encrypted, thus buried, in ideas of development and modernization. After Kant, liberal humanism becomes aligned to the idea of progress, and the whole world is brought within the perimeter of the linear temporality characteristic of modernity as discourse, a characteristic of the occidentalist model of colonialism. In the nineteenth century, as we know, Hegelianism splits into left and right, radical/revolutionary and conservative/liberal. So, on the one hand, we have the liberal democratic option and its individualism and, on the other, Marxism and its structural forces, or processes without a subject, at work in the destiny of human history. Both, however, take for granted the possibility of a general science of 'man', central to the Enlightenment and its legacy, to guide the maturity of humanity and advance the cause of freedom; they retain a totalizing vision infected by totalitarian temptations whenever the ethical goals of the project become obscured. Both have profoundly affected the history of colonialism and colonial liberation, politically as well as in the discourse of 'development', from the liberal democratic model in India or post-Nasser Egypt to the socialist model of Cuba, but also the killing grounds of Cambodia.

In Foucault's (1984) reflections on Kant's essay on the Enlightenment, we find him shifting the concept of freedom away from the Kantian emphasis on its role in the elaboration of rational thought and science and its functioning in accomplishing 'History'. Instead it becomes a stake in a critical ontology, conditioning a critical attitude to the present that seeks the elaboration of an ethos that explicitly challenges oppressive forms of power. Foucault, however, avoids general theory and so his analysis is unable to direct political action except at the level of local struggles and in terms of underlying ethical commitments that reiterate the ethos in the Enlightenment project inscribed in the promotion of equality and human rights. Clearly, the analysis of freedom in Kant (and in Foucault) is very far from the notion of freedom as understood in neo-liberal discourse and rhetoric, where it seems to signify, on the one hand, the condition in which corporations are free to acquire as asset any resource, and, on the other, the status of consumers as autonomous individuals who are 'free' to choose, provided they can pay, in a world in which everything has been reduced to the status of commodity. Freedom here becomes either a condition for a postmodern recolonization, namely, the freedom to acquire the assets of the poor and of the collectivity – a counter-emancipatory project – or an attribute of a consumer culture, as the freedom to choose from a range of options that one cannot determine. The concept of rationality is reduced to the calculations agents make in exercising these freedoms; neo-liberalism is a self-enclosed system with no place for critique.

The Enlightenment: the context and condition of possibility

These differences in conceptualizations and stakes relate to the changed conditions from high modernity to the threshold of a postmodern social order. In the earlier phase, Europe was on the ascendant, energized by colonial expansion and the accumulation of new capital. I have in mind a broader picture in which to cast Kant's reflections of 1784. Let us remind ourselves that the greater part of the eighteenth century covers the beginning of industrialization, the growth of towns, the consolidation and expansion of trade, the emergence of banking and insurance, the setting up of quasi-governmental companies like the East India Company that take charge of colonization, the growth in the power of an emergent bourgeoisie whose bases of power extend throughout the colonies. Most of the major European countries participate in the colonial enterprise, except for Germany and Italy, precisely the countries without overseas empires tempted in the twentieth century to join the club and to construct the great nation–state through National Socialism, making race = nation = identity = destiny the principle on which to found the becoming of the people. The context of the Enlightenment saw the most extraordinary flowering of the arts, sciences and technology, alongside the transformation of nature which occurs with the extensive development of new modes of transport and communication, agricultural revolutions that altered the lands and landscape of the old and the New World; it also witnessed the great migrations and the forced displacement of peoples, as slaves and indentured labour, that transformed cultures right across the globe, producing modern diasporic or hybrid cultures, greatly neglected in the cultural analyses of this period. It was also the time of the consolidation of European expansion and the beginning of the establishment of a hegemony founded on Christian religion and colonial governance, backed by superior military and industrial technology (see, for example, papers in Schwarz, 1996).

So, an important element of the conditions of possibility of the Enlightenment project is the reality of what, by the mid-1750s had already been accomplished, the new knowledges produced – of peoples and cultures, of geography and plant and animal species, of new materials and products, of economy, government and the human subject – the new wealth created, the supremacy assured in the New World. Europe learnt to depict and to shape the world into the image of its phantasy of itself and to make it serve its own ends. It is an intrinsic element of the history of the becoming-West of Europe that I call occidentalism. It was, also, an age of revolution, as Hobsbawm (1962) has characterized it in his analysis of the century from the 1750s to just after 1848. The rumour of revolution came from the discontented masses or the 'dangerous classes', whose existence remained as wretched as ever, and from those intellectuals who regarded freedom and liberty to be inseparable from the exercise of a secular reason and who envisaged the ends of social progress to be consistent with an egalitarian justice. For instance, Rousseau, Diderot, Condorcet and Herder, for different reasons, condemn colonialism and slavery, as did many other intellectuals who belonged to the age of Enlightenment (Pagden, 1993).

In addition to the cultural conditions, I draw attention to the economy and technology to signal two other important dimensions.[5] The point of view of major scientific and technological breakthroughs from the time of Galileo and Newton has been amply explored. Most studies of the emergence of modernity have highlighted the advances made from the seventeenth century in the understanding of the physical world, including the body, and in chemistry, mathematics, medicine and the life sciences and their effects for military technology, navigation, geography, mining technology, metallurgy, architecture, manufacturing, and biopolitics. One would need to add to the list the new understanding of language and of political economy (Adam Smith in particular), and the emergence of the science of 'police' as part of a technology of social regulation (for example, the work of Beccaria in the eighteenth century and his influence on Bentham). I have already pointed out the extent to which colonial expansion, and the contributions of North African, Arabic and other non-European knowledges, had been crucial as a condition of possibility for this explosion in knowledge and invention. The point is not simply to argue for the acknowledgement of a debt, important as this is for postcolonial thought. It is to add a different dimension to account for the compelling need by the time of the Enlightenment for intellectuals in Europe to want to reorganize the accumulating and massive archive of knowledge and objects on the basis of a new post-Aristotelian general order, and to think of that order by reference to its universal scope. The fact that the Cartesian inauguration of a logocentric epistemology had freed the knowing subject from the limitations of foundations in theological master categories and in other relatively closed or restrictive classificatory **paradigms** is, of course, another crucial condition for the reorganization of society and knowledge, setting in process a different discourse of the relationship between the human and the natural.

It is clear from what I have just said that the consolidation of colonialism through further expropriations and appropriations is a constant backdrop in every scene of the Enlightenment. Its constitutive effects for modernity and for the emergence of the West as the hegemonic and sovereign centre of the world can be detected in a wide variety of discourses and practices. An indicative list includes Diderot's *Supplement to the Voyages of Bougainville* (1771); Herder's ([1800] 1997) thoughts about the incommensurability of cultures; the importance of the idea of cosmopolitanism in political and cultural debates; Humboldt's (1846) idea of the possibility of a unified knowing gaze encompassing the Cosmos; the functioning of Europe's others as 'supplement' – that is, as constitutive yet marginalized, and thus functioning as trace, an unacknowledged/'forgotten' presence (Derrida, 1982) – in the thought of Hegel and Kant, and in the 'invisible' presence of the colonies in the novel, as Said (1993) has demonstrated.

The constitutive aspect of colonialism should be extended to the formation of the material and social spaces in which a liberal culture could emerge and flourish, feeding into the growth of a civic culture in places like London and Amsterdam and Paris. The reality of such a culture was central for the emergence of modern political institutions. The liberal culture that was developing among an intellectual cadre in some European capitals, while providing fertile ground for the growth of a governing elite, incited revolutions in France and America with profound consequences for the history of modernity. The cosmopolitan character, the imperial scale, and the city spatiality of the transformations are exemplarily illustrated in Paris as the European centre of Enlightenment, functioning as a node in the great network of writers, artists, scientists, political activists (in spite of, or because of the politically illiberal conditions). The major figures associated with Enlightenment thought congregated there and exchanged views, constituting this network of radical thinkers. Among the better known, we can list Diderot, d'Alembert, Voltaire, Rousseau, Montesquieu, Condorcet, Buffon, and among the non-French: Paine, Wollstonecraft, Franklin, Goethe, Kant, Humboldt, and Hume. (The English, it must be said, are relatively thin on the ground, though not when it comes to the novel or painting.) The *Encyclopédie*, the first issue of which appeared in Paris in 1751, comes out of the attempt to gather together and re-order, according to new principles, all the great diversity of knowledges accumulated since 1492. It is guided by the conviction that properly validated and authorized knowledge can be the basis for the rational arrangement of human affairs, guided by an informed public that it would have helped to constitute. By and large, the axes that provide the coordinates for the elaboration of Enlightenment thought are a reconfiguration of the divide between the modern and the ancients, although it must be admitted that these are rather flexible classificatory categories, as the fate and vicissitudes of the French Revolution reveal.

When we think about the cultural component of the 'context' from the standpoint of constitution that I am developing, what is equally striking is the formation, among the elite, of a European sensitivity and aesthetic sense, so that, in spite of national differences, the idea of Europe and the West could be instantiated not only in the fact of European expansion across the continents, but also in works and in an experience of the arts and of thought shared across the different countries of Europe.[6] The biography of writers and artists, such as Voltaire, Goethe or Paine, Mozart and Beethoven, exemplify the European scale of their experience and communication network. In music, painting, sculpture, literature (including the beginning of the novel, see Watt, 1957), furniture, architecture, and so on, a cosmopolitan culture is formed and spreads across the world, beginning with the capitals of an expansionary Europe. It is in these circumstances that there emerges the figure Foucault calls the universal intellectual. An important aspect of this cultural revolution is the emergence of the idea of the aesthetic in the transformation of subjectivity and of society, that is, the idea that the development of a particular sensitivity, its exploration through artistic works and the existential challenge of the experience of a disruptive, unpresentable dimension, were part and parcel of the critique of existing social arrangements and the search for a better society (see Bowie, 1990, for a fascinating study). This functioning of the aesthetic in social transformation is repeated in the (post)colonial 'arts of resistance' from cinema to photography to fiction and music (see Enwesor et al., 2002, 2003; Gilroy, 1993; Morrison, 1992; Shohat and Stam, 1994; Trinh Minh-ha, 1989).

What stands out from this period is the extent of the disruptions to the old order, and the fashioning of a new order. Foucault, we recall, has characterized it in terms of the gradual replacement of the classical episteme by the modern episteme, marked by the importance of a science of order and calculation or *mathesis* and a system of signs or *taxinomia*. The work of Humboldt and Buffon exemplify this new standpoint or gaze that aims to make sense of the world in terms of a global system, thus in terms of a general science of order. The context of the Enlightenment reveals that crisis and the development of a new confidence are inseparable, for the logocentric subject comes of age in this situation, 'he' is construed as the rational, self-sufficient, male subject of knowledge and of history, the I of Reason, the Kantian agent destined to bring into being a new, modern world on the basis of the scientific elaboration of 'truth'. That same figure is of course shadowed by the secret anxieties and dreads bound up in the agon of freedom and the unfree – refigured in Hegel's reflection on the master–servant dichotomy whereby recognition among subjects is introduced as a central mechanism in the institution and positioning of subjectivities – that surfaced in the American novel, as Toni Morrison (1972) has shown with regard to slavery and the literary imagination. The same troubled soul appears throughout the European novel from *Robinson Crusoe* to *Heart of Darkness* and beyond, works in which the fact and presence of the colonized and the non-white provoke an existential crisis affecting the core of humanist thought.

Imperial governmentality

The second main theme that the analysis of postcoloniality needs to interrogate is the apparatus of administration, regulation and power put in place in the territories occupied by colonial Europe. This apparatus sees the institution of a new modern form of governance, a governmentality centred on the state, that, in Europe at least, aims to constitute the social through disciplinary techniques. The notion of governmentality enables one to do two related things: (1) to add a dimension to the analysis of the conditions of emergence of the modern period that the neglect of colonialism and of imperialism has obscured; and (2) to reconstruct the different apparatuses of subjection/subjectification instituted on colonial soil, such as through the missions, the introduction of European education and pedagogy, the shaping of the social through legal and administrative tactics, the elaboration of a 'savoir' in colonial discourse that supported and authorized the worlding of the colonial world that the postcolonial project has to deconstruct and dismantle. One of the points I would like to establish is that imperial governmentality itself functioned in the place of hegemony, that is to say, that a form of governance emerged with imperialism that combined elements of what Foucault calls pastoral power with the visible deployment of military force and with indigenous structures of power founded on different, traditional mechanisms of legitimation; it is in effect an assemblage, a pragmatic flexible combinatory that served the objectives of colonial occupation well. One could check this out in studies of different colonial regimes, for example, that in India as opposed to the regime in Nigeria or South Africa. There are important lessons to be drawn from this in accounting for conditions in the period after formal independence, for instance, concerning the continuing effectivity of these (social and material) technologies, and the often lethal break-up of former colonial territories, once colonial authority and power no longer hold together the territorial aggregates often arbitrarily lumped together to constitute colonial regimes of power, as has happened in India, Nigeria, Sudan, Rwanda and many other tragic cases. While geo-political and acquisitive interests shape these breakups and the ensuing violence, I should add that of course nothing whatsoever excuses the callous, hellish brutality of the killings.

Until around the end of the eighteenth century, power in many colonies was vested in firms like the East India Company, backed up by the force of arms.[7] This institutional integration of trade and warfare from the beginning is itself a revealing feature of the colonial process. As I will show, it is a feature that pervades the development of the imperial form of governmentality in the colonies, and may now be becoming generalized, in the period of neoliberal Empire, at the level of a mode of thought. The project of modernity had put on the agenda the possibility of a new economy of power, and new technologies of power allied to a new notion of the state. Its genealogy passes through the form of power that Foucault (1979) has described as pastoral power, that is, a power that targets every individual as well as the population as a whole in its attempt to constitute docile bodies and 'normal' subjects; it is a power that seeks both subjection and subjectification. Foucault tells us that the new technology of government, or 'governmentality', is characterized by the articulation of three elements: 'The pastoral, the new diplomatic and military techniques and, lastly, police: these are the three elements that formed the basis for the production of this phenomenon, fundamental in Western history, of the governmentalization of the state' (Foucault, 1979b: 21). I should point out that Foucault, in differentiating between the modern form of power and other forms, does not propose either a progression from one to the other or a system of mutually exclusive forms and interests. Struggles against forms of ethnic domination, against exploitation and against forms of subjection tend to co-exist. However, because of the emergence of pastoral power, he believes that the struggles against forms of subjection have become increasingly the mode in which in contemporary times we live the effects of the mechanisms of power, although he does make the point that, for this biopolitics, 'the mechanisms of subjection cannot be studied outside their relation to the mechanisms of exploitation and domination' (Foucault, in Dreyfus and Rabinow, 1982: 213).

Foucault's analysis of modern governance is vital for an understanding of modernity, yet his analysis hardly mentions the fact of colonization as a central feature of the conditions that enable this form of government to appear in Europe and to be grafted onto the apparatus of subjugation and regulation in the colonies to produce hybrid regimes of power. In contrast, in Edward Said's (1993) analysis of the relationship between culture and imperialism, we find him interrogating classics of Western literature like Jane Austen's *Mansfield Park* (1814) to establish how the values and ideologies operating 'outside' in the plantations of the English empire come to constitute the 'inside' of the English upper-class household in the form of a 'disposition'. He tells us that Austen:

> synchronizes domestic with international authority, making it plain that the values associated with such higher things as ordination, law, and propriety must be grounded firmly in actual rule over and possession of territory. She sees clearly that to hold and rule Mansfield Park is to hold and rule an imperial estate in close, not to say inevitable association. What assures the domestic tranquillity and attractive harmony of one is the productivity and regulated discipline of the other. (1993: 104)

In support of Said's view, one may recall that Adam Smith ([1776] 1812), writing at the time when the imperial countries were reconstituting the notion of nation – by reference to ideas of Englishness, and so on – in terms of an idea of empire, saw clearly that nation and colony were intimately correlated in the calculation of the wealth of the nation (*The Wealth of Nations*, Book 4, Chapter 7).

The neglect of the colonial dimension in Foucault, symptomatic of the 'forgetting' of the moment of colonialism in the institution of modernity as narrated by most Western scholars, is often reflected in a corresponding 'forgetting' in postcolonial writing, namely, that of the pervading effects of the implantation, through imperial governmentality, of the administrative, legal, pedagogical, medical, scientific, technical features of modernity in the colonies, a 'forgetting' that requires the work of historical reconstruction, as in Said (among many authors), and of 'hauntology' (Derrida, 1994) if the decolonization of mind is to undo the effects of cultural imperialism (Tomlinson, 1991) and open up new postcolonial socialities and subjectivities. The discussion below is meant to provide some tools for that work.

Foucault's analysis of power belongs to his broader interrogation of the specificity of modernity as a period. His genealogy of governmentality picks out the mutations in the discourse of the state from the Middle Ages, highlighting the shift from a concern with the proper conduct of the prince to the development, from the sixteenth to the end of the eighteenth century, of an 'art of government' when the concept of government becomes the focus of a problematization that ranges over questions to do with: 'How to govern oneself, how to be governed, how to govern others, how to accept him who is to govern us, how to become the best governor, etc.' (1979b: 5). For Foucault, the development of that new economy of power was bound up with the transformations relating to the dissolution of the feudal state, and to the processes concerned with the question of spiritual conduct and salvation. The new problematic of government was formed at the intersection of these questions; one text, Machiavelli's *The Prince* (fifteenth century) became central to these debates.[8]

Foucault's reconstitution of the emergence of modern governmentality sees him distinguishing two thresholds in the shift from an art of government based on moral principles and on the model of the family to a governmentality founded on rational principles intrinsic to the state, based on the model of political economy, that is, founded on contract, nature, general will. The first threshold is mercantilism, entailing the development of 'a savoir which pertains to the state and can be used as a tactic of government' (1982: 15). It does not yet mark a shift from the idea of sovereign power since it utilizes laws, decrees, regulations that are the traditional instruments of sovereignty.

Regarding this period, it is worth noting the relationship which Elias (1982) has tried to establish between the interest in disciplining one's passions and impulses, that is the interest in self-governance, and the process of the monopolization of the legitimate use of violence by the state. He shows that an apprenticeship into a form of civility is implicated in this 'civilizing process' whereby non-violent rules of encounter between adversarial parties emerge and the state becomes the ultimate juridical arbiter in disputes and conflict among citizens. Governance thus, and the role of law in it, could claim a moral force on the grounds of constituting community and good order. I point to this aspect in order to argue that the law thereby acquires a new authority in modern governance, gradually accruing to itself a moral premium (founded on religious or customary discourse in non-modern societies) to add to the force for compulsion that sovereign power already confers.

The next threshold in Foucault's analysis of power, coinciding with the demographic expansion of the eighteenth century, sees the emergence of a concept of population as the 'ultimate end of government' (1979b: 17). The population is brought within the sphere of the economy by means of the new instruments of statistics which establish its regularities and tabulate its characteristics, for instance, its rate of mortality, its birth rate, its geographical distribution, its habits of consumption, and so on. Gradually, the purpose of government is seen to be that of ensuring the welfare of the population by attending to the means for improving its productivity, its wealth and its health, and, more generally, its well-being and its security. The development of the notion of 'police' is a central element, addressing problems of poverty and pauperism, health and hygiene, public morality and public order, the security of the physical environment (see, for example, Procacci, 1978). The argument that Foucault proposes (in Dreyfus and Rabinow, 1982) is that from around the eighteenth century the principle of a Christian responsibility for salvation becomes inscribed in the form of a pastoral power, working at the level of a whole community as well as targeting individuals.[9] It operates through bodies and behaviour, developing through the psychological, medical and pedagogical sciences, ensuring the well-being of (in principle) every citizen. In its contemporary form, it is encapsulated in the promise that, in exchange for conformity to the norms of good order and for self-discipline, the state, in the form of the welfare state, will care for the citizen 'from the cradle to the grave', as W. Beveridge (1942) put it. Pastoral power helped to institute the state as nation-state, and later, as welfare and insurance-providing state, with implications for the colonies/occupied territories that I shall discuss presently.

I think it is important to point out another set of intersection left out by Foucault, notably, between an economy of the soul that has a basis in the Calvinist organization of the social as in Geneva from 1541, an economy of labour, on the model advocated by William Petty, co-founder, with Robert Boyle, of the Royal Society (1660), organized around a strict division of labour and the hierarchization of productive activity explicitly consistent with Baconian rules of rational and mechanical planning, and a political economy based on the principles of management pioneered by the same Petty in the course of his colonial survey of Ireland – the Down Survey – and which he systematized in his Population Arithmetic of 1682. One objective and incentive for the Down Survey was the redistribution of Irish land to English colonizers (Dickson, 1979). Thus, from around the middle of the seventeenth century, the new form of governance is articulated with the conceptual manifold or system formed from the correlations of colonialism, capitalism, and the new science that I established earlier by reference to the conceptual structure that framed the birth of modernity. The new economies which emerge occupy the terrain of a new order which a mathematization attempts to universalize and which characterizes the discourse of early modernity.

The problem that immediately arises concerning colonial and imperial power is the different genealogy that charts the passage from the

Machiavellian power exercised in the period of conquest and of rule by terror (see also Taussig, 1987), to the Enlightenment variation of pastoral power expressed in the ideology of a European 'civilizing mission' and of tutelage. The problem is also regarding the role of the colonial state in this, and how far the laws, institutions, knowledges, values, attitudes established as part of imperial governance continue to operate in post-independence times. From the nineteenth century onwards, imperial governmentality invents the new, modern technologies of the social, yet combines it with pre-existing strategies of power to constitute hybrid regimes that are locally specific. Colonized populations are reconstituted in terms of segments that function differently with regard to the exercise of power, for instance, either recruited as strategic allies in the case of amenable local elites, or categorized as adversaries to be eliminated or else chosen as potential source of labour to be domesticated. This has important consequences for the analysis of conditions in the postcolony.

One initial distinction that I would like to signal is that between colonialism and imperialism, both as a system of subjugation and in terms of periodization. I agree with Said's view that imperialism should be located not towards the end of the nineteenth century – for example, with the 'scramble for Africa' from the 1880s, coinciding with the 'second industrial revolution' – but with the emergence towards the end of the eighteenth century of the project which aimed at the 'complete subordination of colony to the metropolis' (Said, 1993: 108).[10]

Said's argument is worth repeating because it points to the correlations with several other developments that provide key parameters for understanding the specificity of modernity as a world historical and world-transforming project. He says:

> A closer look at the cultural actuality reveals a much earlier, more deeply and stubbornly held view about overseas European hegemony; we can locate a coherent, fully mobilized system of ideas near the end of the eighteenth century, and there follows the set of integral developments such as the first great systematic conquests under Napoleon, the rise of nationalism and the European nation-state, the advent of large-scale industrialization, and the consolidation of power in the bourgeoisie. This is also the period in which the novel form and the new historical narrative become pre-eminent, and in which the importance of subjectivity to historical time takes firm form. (ibid.: 68, 69)

Said's view adds specific elements to the correlation I am suggesting between subjugation on a global scale and the universal reach of the project of modernity and of Enlightenment; the latter is opened up for an interrogation in terms of the translation of its ideals into the paradoxical and opposite pulls of the liberal ideology of a 'civilizing mission' and the political philosophy of societal transformation – Marxist, socialist, liberatory. The paradox is repeated in the fact that the same process also produced resistance to it and a segment of Western and Westernized intellectuals – theoreticians, artists, writers – who have led the liberation movements throughout Europe and her empires, radical figures who belonged to hybrid or creole cultures, often living their split subjectivity in the form of a 'double-consciousness' (du Bois, [1903] 1989; Fanon, 1967; Gilroy, 1993).

Furthermore, we can explore how far the new 'government of the soul', and the ontology of being with which it is bound, becomes part of an imperial imaginary and is grafted in the colonized world. This is expressed, for instance, in the project of subjugation framed within what JanMohamed (1986) has called a 'Manichaean aesthetics', that is, 'a field of diverse yet interchangeable oppositions between white and black, good and evil, superiority and inferiority, civilization and savagery, intelligence and emotion, rationality and sensuality, self and Other, subject and object' (in Gates, 1986: 82). In the USA, in the nineteenth century, this imaginary found its model in the powerful idea of a 'manifest destiny', a divinely sanctioned progress that legitimated the push into the 'West' and the final dispossession of Native Americans who were herded into 'reservations'. It could be argued that the ideology of 'manifest destiny' is now being globalized, accompanied by new dispossessions.

It is important to emphasize at the outset that we are talking here about different durations, different conditions and different strategies, as, for example, between the Americas and India or Australia. In examining the apparatuses of colonial and imperial power, we should not forget that the aim of that power was to take possession, to accumulate land, to put the people and the resources to work for Europe, to establish the authority and rights of the new owners. It is a power over life, exemplarily exercised on the slave plantations, where the master exercised sovereignty over the slave's body and could decree death as an expression of his will. There is nothing pastoral in its conception.

The conditions that incited the modern form of governance include the fact of resistance and rebellion, in Europe and in the plantations and estates in the colonies, as well as the search for the mechanisms of the disciplining and rational administration of people. The new notion of the social that emerge, as a domain amenable to normalization and regulation through the exercise of power, is thus produced in a conflictual or agonistic field of forces. The absence of a pastoral form of power in the colonies, or its existence in the form of a tutelage, and the absence of a sense of a contractual obligation undertaken on behalf of the people – who are meant to be the represented in a democratic system and the source of legitimate power – mean that imperial governance is not primarily concerned with constituting the social, but with the partial constitution and management of a segment of the population for imperialism's own ends. Imperial power remains external to the social body. It targets different groups differently, depending on pragmatic and strategic calculations of political forces at work in the real world; thus, it often made an accommodation with existing elites, as in India in the nineteenth century or Nigeria this century, grafting imperial power onto existing mechanisms of power. Westernization is a tactic for forming an administrative and military cadre whose access to the machinery of power would be limited to a subaltern role. Other groups and communities are not drawn within this orbit, but are left to re-negotiate their position relative to the elite (see Chakrabarty, 1988). Imperial power undertakes the partial constitution of the social and the formation of colonial subjects, but it combines this form of governance with older, more visible forms of enforcing sovereignty, operating through laws, interdicts, military campaigns, terror, and through dividing practices that draw on a longer history of the tactics of subjugation. Thus, imperial governance in the occupied lands/colonies combined military forms of subjugation with a governmentality aimed at subjectification. In the process, it put into place a pragmatic apparatus of power combining repressive components directed against the people and apparatuses – educational institutions, the legal system, administrative mechanisms and bodies, new forms of taxation and property, religious institutions – that sought to form docile subjects, ideally subjects who would consent to Western domination and tutelage. This is why decolonization has often had to combine the decolonization of mind (Fanon, 1967; Ngugi Wa Thiong'o, 1981) with the violent overthrow of colonial power.

So, how does the disciplining process work for the colonized? The first thing is that the mechanisms target a subject categorized as other.[11] It is an other that the process of formation would transform into more or less the same as Western man: that is to say, make into 'white-but-not-quite', as H. Bhabha (1994) has put it in his analysis of mimicry. It is a process fraught with ambivalences and anxieties. Clearly, mechanisms for othering the 'other' were already in place, inscribed in colonial discourse and in systems of colonialist exclusion in existence well before the nineteenth century. In any case, subjectification requires that one must know, or presume to know, the other in order to transform or re-form 'him'. From the beginning, in 1492, as Todorov has shown, there is a massive production of discourse about the colonized and their world; it was part of the process of taking possession and destroying.

We should also remember the quote from Balfour's speech to the House of Commons in 1910 that begins Edward Said's (1978) interrogation of Orientalism, in which Balfour rebukes those who would speak simply in terms of superiority and inferiority when it comes to once 'great races' like that of Egypt; yet he goes on in the speech to support England's self-appointed role of absolute government over Egypt on the grounds that it would benefit both them and 'the whole of the civilized West' because 'We know the civilization of Egypt better than we know the civilization of any other country' (in Said, 1978: 32). The central Baconian theme of knowledge and power is clearly stated there, Said tells us. More specifically, the legitimation of domination on the grounds of superior knowledge draws attention to the standpoint of power/knowledge, a standpoint that returns us to the question of the discourses and the technologies in which modern forms of power are exercised and which participate in instituting the social. An examination of power/knowledge operating today in relation to theories of development and ideas of modernization and governance would reveal similar assumptions about superior knowledge and authorizing discourses.

The new apparatus of formation is at first, from the early nineteenth century, mainly that of pedagogy and law, aiming either for assimilation (the French strategy, systematic and universal in approach),[12] conversion (the missionary approach), or acculturation (the English aim)[13] centred on the introduction of the humanities curriculum in the empires. The work of, for instance, Bhabha, Viswanathan, JanMohamed, Mudimbe, Mbembe, Appiah, Spivak, and Trinh Minh-ha sufficiently detail the questions of ambivalence, of subalternity, of instability, of exclusion, and of the stratagems of resistance to this power/knowledge assemblage. It is also the case that the strategy of consolidating colonial subjugation by means of a process of constituting subjects did not penetrate as thoroughly into vernacular cultures as one might assume, a point that Appiah (1992) makes in relation to Nigeria.

In some parts of the former colonies, customs, old relations of power and privilege, notably about gender relations, changed little, except that often the former elites could end up deriving their authority from both traditional and colonial narratives and devices of legitimation, as I illustrate in the next chapter in the case of East Africa. The subaltern is a divided and fractured combination of traditional social groupings together with the new class of traders and petty state functionaries and a growing industrial working class. The state itself is often made up of contingently annexed territories, disregarding established cultural and ethnic differences, organized into opportunist administrative units. In the circumstances, the imaginary community of the nation-state is a very unstable artifice united only as a performative device for administrative and accounting practices; in the imaginary of the oppressed, it still often functions as a virtual community, or a legal fiction. While it is true that counter-imperial struggles helped forge a reality of community, the latter has in many post-independence states been split into conflicting factions because of the failures of the national bourgeoisie, a 'narcissistic, ignorant, cynical' class functioning as intermediary agents for capitalism, as Fanon (1967) once put it. A central problem for the postcolony is the remaking of communities of interest so that democratic and equitable forms of governance may operate, for instance, on the basis of an idea of a social contract, or of a just sociality.

I think that the explicit or implicit functioning of a notion of a social contract, or the idea of a 'deal' is vital in elaborating a more complete picture of state power in colonialism and imperialism. While contract and constitution underwrite the legitimacy of power in nineteenth-century England or France, they do not operate in the imperial situation. The notion of a civilizing mission does not involve the mutuality assumed in contract, for it is a decidedly one-sided and paternalistic aim. The absence of contract, and of a national community based on shared and agreed interest, has meant that post-independence states have had to invent constitutional arrangements that often rested on weak or thin nationalism, or, in some cases, have had to copy inappropriate Western models.

This relates to another important factor in analysing the mechanism for instituting the social, namely, the notion of community, and the concomitant relation of community to nation, and of the state to the community. In Enlightenment discourse, the ideal of community is posited in the notion of a *sensus communis* that Kant notably developed. For Foucault, it is implied in the boundedness of a population targeted by power, since such a population is constituted by all those whose action power recognizes, that being a condition for power to have an effect on their conduct (Foucault, 1982: 220). One must think of community in the sense also of an historically constituted unity of a people because, if, as Foucault explains (ibid.: 214), pastoral power is the mutated form of the ecclesiastical function of the Christian pastorate, then we need to take into account the fact that one of the essential aims of the pastorate was to build a Christian community in the form of a collectivity or flock. One main difference with imperial governmentality is the dominance of the relation of externality regulating the relation between the state and the people. One consequence of this relation is exemplified in the attitude of the military towards the people, for it was in its colonial form originally established outside the polity, directed against the community rather than for its protection. Today the military in many post-independence countries continues to see itself as above or outside the state, with the right to intervene and dictate and establish itself as the legitimate authority. It is a colonial mindset that suits well the militarist colonizing attitude and dimension of global corporate capitalism. Equally, the absence of a clear notion of contract between the state and the governed has added to the weakness of the bases for grounding the unity of the collectivity or 'nation'. This results in 'thin' or weak nationalism, in the service of what Fanon calls the local bourgeoisie and Kwame Appiah (1992) has renamed a kleptocracy. The weak or partial notion of contract and responsibility also leads to the break-up of the ex-colonized state into ethnic constituencies, especially in conditions of worsening inequalities and pauperization.

I would add to this analysis the fact that the unity of community has the character of narration, sedimented in a history of the community and in a memory. To the imagined aspect of the narration of a people must be added the materiality or worldliness of a constituted lifeworld in which embodied subjects enact the inter-subjective density of real communities. The lifeworld is a historically particularized entity. The past of the community, its achievements, the transformations it has wrought to its environment and landscape, the meaning it has constructed and reconstructed of its history, the sedimentation of deeds, events, biographies in the living memory of language, tradition, customs, sayings, stories, monuments, music, art and writings, the history that dwells in the material world that frames it and the capacities locked there, the institutions produced in the course of its self-formation, all these determine a community's 'coming into being' and its specificity as a collectivity. For example, it is this range of mechanisms and cultural objects, activated in the 'practices of everyday life' (de Certeau, 1984), that give a people its sense of locality and belongingness; it is the archive we must examine to figure out, and deconstruct, at any particular point, the Englishness of the English, the Frenchness of the French or the Indianness of the Indians. Individual lives are woven into the fabric of the community, which, in a process similar to narrative identity (see the next chapter), grows and changes yet retains a sense of identity at the level of the imaginary. The collective lifeworld is thus the ground that provides ontological security and the cultural space that sustains resistance and change.

In the period of modernity, the concept of nation operates in this field, gathering to itself in its swollen symbolism the 'social and textual affiliations' (Bhabha, 1990: 292) that weave the space and particularity of the imaginary to constitute a phantasized zone for cultural and subjective identifications. Retroactively, the time of the making of the community is projected into the archaic and timeless zone of myths (Faye, 1972) so that it appears as if the community has always been like this, equal to itself in an authentic moment of inauguration. Such an ahistorical notion of traditionality operates a closure in the space of the becoming of the community, feeding into conservative or regressive political tendencies (Bhatt, 2001).[14]

It is worth reflecting that, historically, the imperial nations of Europe have aligned the concept of nation with metonymies of race, purity, strength, and authenticity. Power legitimated itself on the basis of a promise of the prosperity, well-being and happiness of the nation, for which discipline and sacrifice were required. Good order and discipline were not themselves the ends of power but the means and conditions for the prosperity and happiness of the people or the citizen. For example, the notion of police in the eighteenth century was tied to the increase of 'public happiness' in the discourse of public administration (see Pasquino, 1978: 44 ff.). Nation, it can be seen, has functioned as a central ideological dimension of the modern form of power.

It would be interesting to examine the differences which separate and distinguish other, non-modern, empires – the Roman, Ottoman, Chinese, Japanese, Inca, and so on – particularly from the point of view of a project which defines the progress and advancement of the community and the well-being of the people according to secular, universal concepts and principles. Furthermore, with regard to the correlation of 'race', and nation and community, it could be argued that National Socialism in Germany, as a national project, was not projected outside the nation, it was not the possibility of measuring the greatness of the nation in the scale of empire and mastery over colonized others, as with France or Britain; instead it had to find the proof of its salvation and worth inside the (greater space of) the nation itself and its every member. The race-nation as coupled signifier of community became the intrinsic good, the foundation of the great future; therefore it became the entity that had to be purified or cleansed, so that it could stand for the authentic agent and bearer of its destiny. Similar temptations and dangers have been loosened today in the shape of ethnic and other fundamentalisms.

It is clear from the arguments above that the actual process of instituting new forms of constituting colonial subjects reveals a somewhat messier and undecidable state of affairs, for the colonial stage is the place where many dilemmas and ambivalences in the discourse of the West about itself and its 'others' are enacted. On the one hand, the discourse of modernity, in conceptualizing the other as other – as morally depraved and intellectually deficient, in need of improvement, yet also inscrutable, unpredictable and irrational – positions the other as the abject. On the other hand, the other is thought to be amenable to the same in the suppositions of the universality of the subject. From the point of view of the determination of imperial policy, the situation was resolved by emptying the other of historicity, devaluing cultural difference and conceptualizing the other as the dehistoricized empty slate, the non-agent to be inserted into modern civilization through the mechanisms of 'development'. The colonial scene is equally the place where the subjugated ward off the stratagems of the dominating power through counter-hegemonic tactics, that deflect the mimetic effect of colonial subjectification into the disruptive derealizations that Taussig (1993b) describes, or the (ambivalent) dissidence expressed in 'Negritude' and, of course as expressed in uprisings and the collective insurrections of decolonization. Colonialism provokes among the protagonists calculations of gains and losses, manoeuvres of escape and capture, plays of desire and loathing that cross each other to ensure that the state of emergency created by oppressive power is never lifted.

The end of modernity?

In the contemporary context, the standpoints of universalism and cosmopolitanism that had emerged with modernity have reappeared, still sundered by paradoxes and conflicts, differently located with respect to the global, with different politics at stake in their reformulation. Universality is now cast, on one side, against the claims for the valorization of difference, and, on the other, it is set against the pitfalls of relativism and the dangers inherent in the incommensurability implied in fundamentalisms. Discussions of **human rights**, for example, concerning sexual mutilation or the Sharia Laws in some Islamic countries or the treatment of refugees and workers in most affluent countries, bring out the need for an appeal to principles that have universal validity with regard to a notion of justice and to the relation to the other. However, a postmodern theory of ethics commanding widespread assent is yet to be properly founded. So, for the moment, one must still rely on formulations that first appeared with the Enlightenment – at least within secular philosophy – and, therefore, work through the memory of the violences inscribed in the history of Eurocentrism, as well as the violences that sustain forms of oppression in other cultures, for instance, regarding gender, ethnicity and the production of the means of existence.

Alongside the problematic of universalism we can locate different conceptualizations of cosmopolitanism, some still implicitly sharing the Enlightenment vision and temporality of a project of the maturation of 'humanity', as in the work of Habermas. One approach to the problem is the idea of a radical, non-Eurocentric and non-oppressive, diasporic culture to come, constituted out of the coalition of new social movements and forces seeking the transformation of all societies towards ideals of a just society in which systematic exploitation and oppression are absent or only provisionally tolerated. Meanwhile, a *de facto* cosmopolitan culture has surfaced in cities and among what Bourdieu (1984) calls the new middle classes, flourishing in the new global spaces and networks (Castells, 1996) or scapes (Appadurai, 1990, 1996). Another important development that comes on the agenda of new cosmopolitan cultures is the emergence of global diasporic cultures and identities, constituted in relation to cybertechnologies and teletechnologies, new spatialities, new networks of labour, producing new belongings and sense of citizenship (see Ahmed et al., 2003; Ong, 2003). This emergence of a postmodern, global, diasporic culture is one aspect of the process of globalization that now inflects every reassessment of the state of the world, though it could be argued that globalization in its contemporary form, while retaining core elements of occidentalism, differs in important aspects from the previous European enterprise of subjugation and the implantation of Western modernity globally.

Furthermore, following Lyotard ([1976] 1984), it could be argued that today the normative function of scientificity has been replaced by that of efficiency and performativity, criteria that are self-validated in terms of a discourse that has erased the externality of the ends pursued by the Enlightenment – liberty, freedom, equality, 'fraternity', universal rights – with the self- referential logic of the postmodern, erasing in the process the metaphysical suppositions that ultimately authorize it. The period of 'incredulity' with respect to the 'grand narratives' of modernity has triggered great uncertainty about the future, except for the supporters of the 'end of history', such as Fukuyama (1992), who wish to see in liberal capitalism the apogee of human development. New theologies, fundamentalist, autistic, homicidal, have emerged to fill the gap left by the failures of Enlightenment ethics. Furthermore, as I indicated earlier, a technocentric and technocratic reason bound to capitalism has become a *de facto* universalist reason. It has replaced Enlightenment ideals founded on a secular discourse of human emancipation with a postmodern dystopian corporate neo-liberal project in which ideas of democracy and freedom function as a cover for a totalitarian form of colonization. One may well ask if the future announces the coming of a new empire, organized around a new form of sovereignty, combining 'national and supranational organisms united under a single logic of rule', as Hardt and Negri have argued (2000: xii).

My discussion of the Enlightenment is meant to provide the backdrop for locating modern imperialism and postmodern 'Empire' and their forms of governance within projects for the constitution of a world order. Thus, the questions that now solicit our attention concern the lessons one may derive from the Enlightenment. They relate to a politics and to the basis for a reorganization of social scientific knowledges and the humanities, if it is no longer the idea of a science that should order their intelligibility and secure their legitimacy. Clearly, the critique of modernity and the interrogation of founding discourses put on the agenda the new legitimating discourses, perhaps in the form of a new non-Eurocentric 'enlightenment', that could direct political action in the postcolony and globally in the quest for just societies.

Notes

1 The Confucian slogan of 'good wife, wise mother' dictated a strict gender division of labour. Its reconfiguration as modern enabled Japanese women to enter the economy as working women before marriage, contributing to the economic development and participating in the new public sphere, then retreating to the private sphere after marriage to function as 'good wife, wise mother', but now educated in Western ways, able to consume modern commodities like electrical goods and Western clothes, and skilled in combining Western pedagogical skills with traditional ones in the home. Women's magazines, and the new department stores played a central role in this new disciplinary power (Tamari, 2002).

2 Monotheism, as in Christianity, it must be said, implicitly legitimates a sovereignty that declares a ban on other ways of being, other forms of existence (see also Agamben, 1998).

3 The term terrorism is, of course, open to all manner of ideological manipulation. Depending on which side of the conflict the speaker stands, the insurgent or member of the resistance becomes the terrorist and vice versa; thus Nazi Germany labelled French Resistance fighters terrorists. The term has become even more loaded today.

4 The support that colonial regimes provided for the Christianizing mission worked so well as ideological cover for genocide and dispossession, and in grounding the moral authority of the new masters that one cannot accept the argument that evangelization was the main motive for conquest. The arguments advanced by some Church authorities to legitimate war against a people who had presented no threat functioned admirably in demonizing the colonized and in precipitating their subordination, as the debate between Sepulveda and Las Casas at Valladolid in 1550 demonstrates. The universal claims of monotheism, that all are equally children of God, only succeeds in erasing the difference of the other by refiguring the other within the conceptual framework of the philosophy of identity, the other could only be 'saved' – though not freed – by becoming Christian, otherwise he or she remains a 'barbarian outcast' outside the family of man, or indeed, the vessel for the work of the devil.

5 The genealogy that I am reconstructing is guided by the proposition that our being-in-the-world is dynamically inter-woven with the materiality to which we are coupled, so that the very way we think about the world and its possibilities, the manner of our dwelling in it as one of the objects of the world, that is to say, our lived experience of its thickness and aliveness, are aspects of this being-in-the-world. One implication is that the historical specificity of that materiality and its technologies is correlated to the historical specificity of the ideas and discourses we are able to construct. By the eighteenth century, the colonized spaces of the world had become interwoven within that materiality, 'inscrypted', thus both visible/legible and invisible/unconscious – in the imaginary of Europe, with effects at the level of the 'real' as much as at the level of the symbolic.

6 It is important to recognize the existence of a European culture before modernity, for instance, during the Renaissance, through music, the arts, the diasporic reality of intellectuals, artists and craftsmen who operated right across Europe. The role of Latin as a common language among the elite, and, of course of Christianity, in spite of the sectarian conflicts, in establishing the reality of Europe are crucial. Perhaps today we have English languages (bearing in mind the variations) and neo-liberal ideology.

7 Interestingly, they operated very much like many transnational corporations do nowadays, through a mixture of alliances, theft, bribery, shady trade deals, non-governmental organizations for administration purposes, backed by military threat (see Chapter 4).

8 The disagreement dividing opponents centred on the relationship of externality that the Machiavellian prince is supposed to establish with respect to the governed, a relationship that seems to deny the relation of care that the (Christian) sovereign is meant to have for his subjects. The Church, as we know, underwrote the moral and political authority of the sovereign in the long-standing affiliation of Church and State in Europe; this guarantee was founded on the assumption of a Christian community whose well-being it was the duty of the sovereign to ensure, as earthly representative of God.

9 It is clear that the focus of Foucault in analyzing the modern technology of power derives from his assessment of the apparatuses that have started to appear since the Enlightenment which seek to institute the modern social order primarily by constituting particular subjectivities. The machinery of disciplining, regulation and normalization requires a knowledge of 'the inside of people's minds ... It implies a knowledge of their conscience and an ability to direct it' (Foucault, 1979a: 214). In that sense the new pastoral power is a 'government of the soul' (see Rose, 1989).

10 The 'second industrial revolution' saw the emergence of a range of new products, new materials and technologies that came to dominate industry for the next 100 years: oil and its by-products, new chemicals, the electrical industry including the telephone and telegraph, materials like aluminium and high specificity steel, the motor car. The major firms that operate in these industries are still largely those established from the beginning of that period. A commensurate shift in capitalism takes place, whereby closer structural links are established between technology, science, industry and the military, and a new globalizing vision emerges to match the interest in an expansion across the world to secure the new raw materials; the scramble for Africa, and the carve-up of the Middle East driven by oil interests are part of this process. The high stakes involved pushed the industrial powers towards confrontation and new alliances; one of the consequences was the First World War that itself started a new phase in the process of globalization.

11 This binarism of 'Europe and its others' was more clearly operative in the common-sense idiom of Europeans. A more complicated, and more unstable, narrative of the colonized emerges when we consider the radical discourse of modernity and the fiction that narrativizes the encounter between Europe and older civilizations like those of China, India and Egypt. For example, Europe looked to the East, say, China, for a long time until the nineteenth century. Suleri, analyzing English India, emphasizes how much colonial facts 'fail to cohere around the master-myth that proclaims static lines of demarcation between imperial power and disempowered culture' (1992: 3), but instead belong to an 'unsettling economy of complicity and guilt' (ibid.). This economy becomes clearer when we pay attention to the machinery of governance, and to the paradoxes and ambivalences in the Enlightenment discourse of rights, liberty, equality, freedom and justice.

12 The French reconstituted colonial lands as elements of the French Empire, in the form of overseas departments. The strategy of governance was directed at the assimilation of the colonies into French culture and nation-state. Even today, the French have difficulty, administratively, in acknowledging and dealing with cultural difference because of the erasing of difference in the notion of French citizenship and what it means for the relation of the individual to the state. For instance, because the recognition of cultural difference would imply the differentiation of the citizen into different legal categories, and thus fundamentally undermine the juridical status of each citizen and the whole constitution, there has developed no multicultural policy in France – though that is probably not a bad thing, given that most state multicultural policies seem set to manage difference by routinizing or normalizing it, that is, by incorporating difference within a tactic of governance.

13 The problem of imperial power in relation to the constitution of subjectivity, and thus in relation to the question of ideology, is illustrated in the role English literature was made to play in supporting British rule in India. Viswanathan's subtle and insightful study of the way in which the development of the Anglicist curriculum, driven by the 'motives of discipline and management ... served to confer power, as well as to fortify British rule' (1989: 167) shows that the (ideological) work performed by English literature was to cover the 'sordid history of colonialist expropriation, material exploitation, and class and race oppression' (ibid.: 20) under

the 'exalted image of the Englishman as producer of the knowledge that empowers him to conquer, appropriate, and manage in the first place' (ibid.: 20) To that extent, English literature performed rather different, though related, work in the colonial as against the metropolitan situation.

One of the earliest questions concerned the choice of the literary texts that would be appropriate for the task assigned to literature. This task consisted in the twin goals of moral and intellectual education that would dispose the native to look up to the colonizer with the respect and admiration due to a superior intellect and culture. Decisions about the literary canon were enmeshed in judgement of the literary as well as the moral worth of the texts. The moral interest complicates the history of the implantation of English in India, for the reason that the secularizing and humanizing orientation of the literature curriculum was often in conflict with the aims of the missionary movement and with the interest of commerce. As Viswanathan explains: 'The introduction of English represented an embattled response to historical and political pressures: to tensions between the East India Company and the English Parliament, between Parliament and missionaries, between the East India Company and the Indian elite' (ibid.: 10). The English model was therefore inadequate for transplant; new models had to be worked out, guided by the official discourse instituted in the 1813 Charter Act and in the 1835 English Education Act. Thomas Macauley's (1835) 'Minute on Education' expresses the bottom line of the policy: 'to form a body of well-instructed labourers, competent in their proficiency in English to act as Teachers, Translators and Compilers of useful works for the masses' (quoted in Bhabha, 1994: 106). Viswanathan's account details the conflicting pulls of religion and a secular pedagogy focusing on the development of a 'critical sense', highlighting the stakes in this conflict between a policy of alliance with the traditional ruling class and a concomitant respect for Oriental learning – Warren Hastings, Wellesley, Wilberforce (1989: 20) versus the more impersonal bureaucratized and judicial form of administration advocated by the Anglicists – Cornwallis, Macaulay – and, partially overlapping with the Christianizing policy of the Evangelists – Wilberforce, Grant, and others (ibid.: 36). The period up to 1835 marks the 'historical moment when political philosophy and cultural policy converged to work towards clearly discernible common ends ... [namely] ... questions of administrative structure and governance' (ibid.: 34). This convergence paves the way for the introduction of European knowledge into the curriculum, taught in English, with the aim of producing 'useful learning' (J.S. Mill). English literature functioned as a mediating device in providing the means for the secular, rational development of a critical sense that prepared the learner for the whole range of European knowledge and the acknowledgement of its authority without appearing to reject the value of education as a moralizing force, for literature could still be seen as 'a secular reinscription of ideas of truth, knowledge, and law derived from the sacred plane' (Viswanathan, 1989: 95). At stake in this was the emphasis on 'the legitimacy and value of British institution, laws, and government' (ibid.: 95) and, thus, the authority of British rule. By the time of Balfour's speech to Parliament in 1910, quoted by Said, authority, power and knowledge had become concepts that refer to each other within the conceptual grid of both imperialism and modern governmentality. But this authority, if it existed in the minds of policy- makers and in official discourse, was ever under siege. One of the mechanisms that fractures the authority of the colonizers' discourse refers to the process of ambivalence that Bhabha examines in 'Signs taken for wonders' (1985).

14 One consequence of the fact that the modern imperial Western nation was constituted in relation to empire, both discursively by reference to the subjugated, positioned as other, as well as in terms of a mastery exercised over other worlds and other peoples, has been that for many individual European citizens the validation of transcendent goals could subsume individual projects under the greater goal of national ideals. Thus, the building of empire added an extra dimension to the colonizers' individual sense of identity, by making their own subjective project contribute to the greater, collective objective. The affiliations of nation with race and with empire find anchorage in the colonial experience; they were inscribed in an imperial imaginary and are repeated in contemporary racisms, as in the resilience of an idea of empire or of the great race among racist organizations (see also, McClintock, 1995, Osborne and Sandford, 2002).

3

Questions of Identity and Agency

I noted in the first chapter the reasons for retaining the concept of identity in order to explore the range of questions that have surfaced in the debates about the lived experience of postcoloniality, and, more generally, in explorations of alternative ways of becoming for human beings, transcending present conditions. Among those reasons was the recognition that cultures are heterogeneous and polyglot, the result of appropriations, borrowings, graftings and reconfigurations that are processual and dynamic, responding to a field of force that includes diasporic displacement, material and symbolic exchanges of all kinds, power relations determining forms of exclusion and inclusion. I pointed to the fact that the constitution of social imaginaries are today inflected by tele-technologies and cyber-technologies that destabilize older **paradigms** for examining the formation of identities and socialities; I indicated that forms of worlding are grounded in a plurality of histories and experiences inscribed in temporalities and spatialities that now co-habit (Bishop et al., 2003) so that the analysis of the 'uprootings and regroundings' that shape contemporary identities must range from the 'micro-politics of embodied inhabitance and migration, to the macro-politics of transnationalism and global capital' (Ahmed, 2003: 2).

It must be emphasized that what is at stake is not simply the valorization of 'difference' in its various registers: gender, race, ethne, nation, class, sexuality, and so on. My arguments about the need for postcolonial thinking to break with the concept of the nation-state and that of logocentrism, and to transcend the conditions and assumptions that reproduce occidentalism in its various manifestations imply that it is important to move the debate beyond an agenda fixed by the limitations of the 'politics of identity'. This shift enables other fundamental questions about society and culture to become visible, here ethical and political issues underlying a counter-imperial '**globalization** from below' or problems relating to new cosmopolitical spaces and to alternative forms of sociality. Equally, it is important to bear in mind that the term difference and the 'politics of identity' have themselves emerged as political and theoretical issues for postcolonialism, as they have done for, say, feminism, to counter the assumptions and power relations buried in the model of the 'normal' or ideal-type subject as the 'developed', rational, autonomous, unitary, being who is ideally meant to be white, male, Western; a model that has been established and become normative or dominant in the course of **colonialism** and modernity. So, the politics of difference has only strategic but not absolute value. The essentializing of difference to which it is predisposed is politically debilitating and is in any case open to manipulation by the forces of exploitation.

Additionally, this politics has often been hostage to other instances of racism and ethnicism, outside the occidental arena of oppression, for the compulsion to fix the borders of identity within the boundaries of race and ethne knows no frontier. The emergence of identity as an object for theoretical reflection must therefore be located by reference to this contingent history, breaking with the narrow 'black and white' convention of the discourse (see papers in Brah and Coombes, 2000; Ahmed, 2000). In what follows it will become clear that the motivation for asserting a particular identity, or for resisting specific norms or for sustaining the investment of a large part of one's life in struggles for a cause or for a desired future, rely on visions of the good – the good society, an ethics of existence, ideas of living well – that find their basis in philosophical, ethical or theological arguments and concepts, even if these are often not recognized because they are implicit in the vocabulary of action. My approach, then, is guided by the recognition that in the background of the problem of identity one finds quite basic questions about the 'who' – of action, of agency, of lived experience, the one who answers the call to responsibility – and about belonging and ontological security, questions that are as old as the emergence of human self-consciousness. What is new, then, are the circumstances and the reasons for posing anew such questions, that is, for posing them in relation to a supposedly postcolonial, postmodernizing world, and in relation to material conditions and socio-cultural practices that are significantly different from what they were half a century ago.

Let us start with a couple of examples from which to elicit the kinds of problems this chapter will explore. First, the case of Muslim women choosing to wear the headscarf or *hijab*. It is immediately clear from the example that a conventional reading of the *hijab* as signifier of patriarchal authority or oppressive gender practice can be simplistic, though, obviously, such an interpretation is justified when applied to the policy of the Taliban in Afghanistan before 2002. Even then a woman artist like Samira Makhmalbaf in her films, for example, *At Five in the Afternoon* (2003), explores the difficult and complex political and affective economies in which the headscarf and the *burka* as signifiers are inscribed. We recall too that Turkey has banned women MPs from wearing the headscarf in parliament, a decision that one would not want to attribute to the (surprising) conversion of the (male-dominated) Turkish parliament to feminism, since we know the ban is primarily tied to the policy of modernization which Turkey has pursued for decades going back to Kemal Attatürk's project of the creation of a secular state, and the different interests involved in that project. The mutations and variations in meaning of cultural objects such as the headscarf oblige one to attend to the circumstances and to the historical and cultural context that locate their specificity as sign. The givenness or facticity of the visual and the visible, here the article of clothing itself, can hinder analysis, preventing one from properly recognizing that signs have meanings in relation to acts of communication, and thus, in relation to the inter-subjective framing of social action that may reiterate but could equally alter previous meanings. This multi-accentuality of the sign and these shifts in meaning participate in stratagems of signification tied to the mobility of social and power relations, and are integral to what is at stake in the politics of identity. Wider issues, both theoretical and political, are implicated in this, challenging dogmatic simplifications (see *Interventions*, special issue on the veil, vol. 1, 1999).

To explore this further, it is necessary to consider the point of view of the mechanisms that constitute and reconstitute identity and subjectivity, and turn to the accounts of participants and to the stakes in communicative action, and thus to the embedded knowledges and meanings and the social relations which provide the wider frame of reference. I will begin by clarifying an important distinction between these two terms, as I use them in this book, for they are complex concepts, trailing other terms like the self, that are often the source of confusion. I use the concept of subject to refer to its theorization in the philosophical and psychological discourses that posit an epistemic and ontic entity who is the agency of statements and acts. The 'philosophy of the subject' in particular stands for a position that dissimulates the who of experience and responsibility into the 'I think' of logocentric epistemology. The concept has come to be associated with the discourse of modernity, notably by reference to the Cartesian subject and to the abstract legal subject (which, incidentally, need not be a human being, but can be a corporate entity). The references to the 'death of the subject' relate to critiques of that concept of the subject.

The term subjectivity refers to the entity constituted as a position with regard to real processes and mechanisms of constitution of subjects generally. In current theorizations, it is located by reference to general norms of behaviour and disposition specified in discourses and technologies of the social (Henriques et al., 1984, 1998), although one must point to the other sites of sociality, outside direct state interventions, in which subjectivities emerge (see Arendt, 1959). It could be argued that this is one reason why the substantive acting, thinking and feeling being often does not conform to these norms or to all of them; it is a self, the product of an interiorization of attitudes, values, expectations, memories, dispositions, instantiated in inter-subjective relations and activities that, through historically specific self-reflective practices of recognition, constitute a particular named person, a singularity (see also Taylor, 1989). The 'who' is the agent who takes responsibility for his or her action, including communicative action, and recognizes him or herself as the person who is answerable by reference to an ethical imperative or a demand from an other.

Identity, on the other hand, refers to the relational aspects that qualify subjects in terms of categories such as race, gender, class, nation, sexuality, work and occupation, and thus in terms of acknowledged social relations and affiliations to groups – teachers, miners, parents, and so on. These categories are correlated to particular performative practices and routines of action, for instance, regarding parenting or masculinity, in which identities are instantiated. Identity as a concept thus always directs attention to the relational aspect of subjectivity (see also Hall and du Gay, 1996). Subjectivity and identity are necessarily inter-related when it is a matter of analyzing conduct or beliefs, obliging one to take account of the following mechanisms and their co-articulated operation: those revealed from the perspective of ideology in accounting for the normative content of specific identities, those that inscribe power effects relating to systematic differences such as gender, and mechanisms relating to the historical and cultural specificity of the processes. Together they institute subjects as specific selves; their analysis directs attention to the linguistic, discursive, technical, temporal, spatial and psychological reality of the processes and to the locatedness of identity and subjectivity by reference to their imbrication or embeddedness within the technico-material space of culture in which they are staged.

Fanon's (1989) analysis of the policy about wearing the veil or *haik* in Algeria during the period of French occupation will illustrate the point about the relationship. In 1954, in an effort to subvert the indigenous Algerian way of life and undermine the basis of national consciousness and resistance, the French colonial regime launched a cultural offensive against what was seen as a centrepiece of Algerian Arab culture, namely, the wearing of the veil. The policy calculated that the veil was the symbol and sign of the subordination of the Algerian woman in traditional Arab culture, and thus a key signifier of the difference between modern Western culture and the 'backward' indigenous culture; it was assumed that the Algerian woman could be won over by a show of solidarity from the French administration. Campaigns were launched to encourage the Algerian woman to liberate herself from the yoke of the men, and to transform herself into the progressive force for a modern Algeria. The men were left in the double bind of either opposing the policy and thus fitted the stereotype of the cruel, masculinist or patriarchal Arab resisting modernization and determined to maintain the inferior status of 'his' women, or accept the French policy and thereby acknowledge the 'superiority' of the colonizer's culture and values. The unveiled woman's face, as Fanon expressed it, became a symbol of French 'civilizational' mission and a measure of the success of the policy of assimilation: the formula, repeated in Fanon was: 'Let's win over the women and the rest will follow' (ibid.: 37). Insinuations about sexuality were of course part of the underlying stratagems of power. But one must also think about the intervention in the domain of the private in terms of the desire of the colonizer to cross the threshold of the public and penetrate the intimate domain of personal relations, the place where the colonized could still salvage and keep intact some core elements of the threatened indigenous identity. The stakes in the matter of wearing or not wearing the headscarf reached beyond personal problems of identity, and occupied a central place in the battle for hearts and minds, that is, for the colonization and the decolonization of minds.

A scene from the film, *The Battle of Algiers* (dir. Gillo Pontecorvo, 1965), makes visible other dimensions in the analysis of the disjunctures and ambivalences that cross the question of identity in the colonial and postcolonial contexts. The underlying reality, especially in the city, of the co-habitation of different temporalities and spatialities – modern, traditional, colonial, postcolonial (Venn, 2005) – is a feature that the film implicitly deploys. The film, photographed in grainy black and white dramatizes the uprising in Algeria led by the Front National de Libération against the French regime. The background is the extreme violence, including massacres (Sétif, as an exemplary case) and systematic torture, with which the French colonizers dealt with the demand for independence in Algeria. The defeat of the French in Vietnam in the 1950s and the cold war situation in which many colonial liberation struggles were caught up, added to colonial 'terror as usual' (Taussig, 1993a), explain the viciousness of the French response. The film covers the period from 1954–57, one focus being the bombing campaign that targeted cafés and other places frequented by the French. The scene depicts young Algerian women insurgents as they go through their preparations for planting bombs. The camera follows them in *cinéma verité* style from the time they begin the careful transformation of their identity into Westernized subjects, focusing on the women's activities as they put on make-up and Western clothes and adopt the posture and conduct of urban cosmopolitan women in order to be allowed untroubled through check-points and into cafés. The scene shows them behaving in the appropriate manner, their appearance and body language playing out the deadly mimicry of the colonizer's culture as they set about their mission with bombs in their baskets and bags, ready to explode. The sequence in the film shows that the decision to wear or not to wear particular articles of clothing such as the veil or a skirt cannot be read off from a check-list of stereotypes, but must be considered in terms of situated action. The distantiating effect produced by the particular filmic techniques separates the gaze from processes of identification so that a critical space opens up, beyond mimetic identification (see below), to encourage the relocation of the event within the arena of colonial struggle. One question that arises concerns the effects of power on the social relations, and the mobility of these effects according to circumstances, illustrating the performativity of power for subject positions. Identity, it can be seen, is not simply a matter of personal choice from a range of already-labelled options, nor is it independent of the political field and the variable stakes in it.

We could pick out a number of questions about identity and subjectivity from the example of the veil. For instance, who is the agent in the case I have presented? How are dissident subjectivities and identities constituted? What grounds dissident subjectivities? What continuities and discontinuities can one trace in the actions? Are the actions the result of autonomous individual decisions, or do they arise out of cooperative, collaborative mechanisms embedded in the inter-subjectivity of socialities? What structures of power determine or condition the subjective positions of participants? Would concepts like hybridity, **creolization**, transculturation, doubleness, subalternization,[1] ambivalence, and so on, deployed in the work of Bhabha (1994), Gilroy (1993a, 1993b), Hall (1996), Spivak (1988), and Canclini (1995), enable one to get hold of the underlying mechanisms and processes? What other concepts and theories could we bring into the analysis? These are the kinds of issues that are thrown up when one considers identity and its disorders to be an issue within socially grounded action. At the level of theory and politics, more general issues appear, regarding the process of the constitution and transformation of subjectivity and identity in all cultures.

Nervous Conditions: troubles of identity in the postcolony

I will begin to examine this range of problems through the elaboration of an example from a postcolonial situation, namely, the narrative in Tsitsi Dangarembga's 1988 novel, *Nervous Conditions* (NC). In order to provide the equivalent of an ethnographic 'thick description' that will enable me to give concrete density to the analytical apparatus I am deploying, I will give a detailed account of the diegetic elements of the plot. It could be argued that since NC is a work of fiction and the material is textual rather than ethnographic, the extrapolation one could make with regard to the analysis of real situations is rather limited. However, the narrative in this case describes a veridical world that allows all the basic problems of subjectivity and identity in postcolonial situations to be played out, and thus it adds the thickness and density of the quotidian and the experiential to the datum available for analysis. The appropriateness of fiction or other forms of expression, such as film, depends on whether they are exemplarily able to reconstitute within their imaginary space the characteristics of the real material and affective world; such works are part of the 'arts of resistance' and make present liminal and unpresentable features of human becoming that 'objective' discourses cannot. Clearly, not all expressive works qualify.

   In the novel, the mutations in postcolonial identity incite a fundamental interrogation of belonging and unbelonging, of tradition and change, in the course of which are disclosed the fragility of the worlds that have been instituted in colonial and 'postcolonial' times. Indigenous or vernacular culture in NC is enacted in the everyday routines and allocated subjective positions inscribed in the spatial and material reality of village life, its '*lieux de mémoire*' (Nora, 1984–93), while the West and modernity are at first depicted as an outside entity or force, occasionally intruding into the world of the settled community. But, as the story unfolds, we find that this picture of the local and the global, the indigenous and the cosmopolitan conceals a more complicated and mobile reality, so that we discover that mutations and cultural translations across the vernacular and the Western have been in process for a long time already, triggered within living memory by the imperial project of Europe, affecting identity and self-identity. It is a familiar story that will enable analysis to disclose both the ordinariness of the everyday world and the disorders of postcolonial identity inscribed in it.

The narrative begins with the narrator, Tambu, remembering her life as a village girl in Zimbabwe in the 1960s, it then moves on to the beginning of her initiation into Western culture through schooling – a familiar pattern in many postcolonial countries – and her formation as, in her own words, an 'emancipated' young woman in the household of her 'middle-class' Westernized uncle (Babamukuru). We are presented with a picture of her early life enclosed within the horizon of the 'traditional', 'age-old' tasks, routinized into a fixed pattern of life, concerned with the homestead and constrained within the already determined limits dictated by her destiny as female. The description of the activities of the characters shows that the household and the economy interpenetrate at all points in village life, the women bearing the brunt of the labour, while the men regulate and direct, and complain. The pattern varies little. It constitutes an apprenticeship into the skills, conduct and values that are deemed suitable for a girl, acquired through helping the womenfolk with the tasks of cooking, cleaning, fetching water, gathering firewood, working in the field to grow the crops and tend the herd on which the family survives. The description of village life allows the reader to imaginatively apprehend its instantiation through the interaction of objects, tools, bodies, crops, animals, the built spaces that form the elements of the assemblage that the communicative action set into motion. The narration of this apparently settled way of life with its seemingly undisturbed temporality includes accounts of happy recollections of long unhurried walks to the river, picking wild fruit in the woods, resting in the shade of trees, stories told of the life of the community so that the material reality of village life, its habitus – the intimate, taken-for-granted and interiorized inter-relationships of words and objects, world and deeds which modulate inter-subjective encounters and shape what is possible – is infused with a sense of belonging and ontological security as well as moments of disruption and quiet freedom. Her identity as a member of the village community is locked into the everyday tasks, the ways of speaking, conversations and quarrels about the endless little problems, the mundane actions that enact the network of relationships between the characters, the objects and living things, the landscape that actively create the village as a particular spatio-temporal reality which is materially and culturally framed. She attends school occasionally, for it is not a priority for girls, their duties and formation as future wives, mothers and agricultural workers taking precedence over education. The family is ruled by her affable but custom-bound father, Jeremiah, who has done his best to keep his daughter confined within the parameters of the 'traditional' village. Her brother (Nhamo), on the other hand, is given the task and opportunity of 'lifting our branch of the family out of squalor' (NC: 4) through education, a familiar strategy in (post)colonial countries. He finds ways of avoiding any work in the house or the field, clearly thinking that it is the women's lot to toil and fetch and carry. Equally, we find him already distancing himself from the traditional way of life, schooling taking him away from the village anyway; in his mind, becoming 'Westernized' and becoming 'superior' slide into each other.

The narrator had imagined that life had always been like this for the community, though she remembers her grandmother, who had a vague recollection of different times, telling her that once her ancestors had lived well on the land until 'white wizards' arrived, avaricious and grasping, 'well versed in treachery and black magic' (NC: 18); they had gradually appropriated everything, forcing the indigenous folk off their farms into poor quality land. Many had to leave to find a living toiling in the mines in the south. For the grandmother, this tale of English occupation had a lesson, not about colonialism, except implicitly, but about how suffering can be overcome if one 'endured and obeyed', as her son Babamukuru, Jeremiah's brother, had done. He had been sent to the mission school, had won scholarships and succeeded beyond all expectations, studying to postgraduate level in England. His return had been crowned by being appointed head of the mission school, so that he now enjoyed the combined power and authority of the head of the village and the head of an important state institution. This situation whereby indigenous and occidentalist relations of power have amplified each other's effects in sustaining systems of oppression is an important, if often neglected, element of (post)colonial culture, for example, concerning class and gender relations; it is a central theme in the novel. Nhamo, the male heir, was meant to follow in his father's footsteps and maintain the new postcolonial social hierarchy.

Tambu dreams of an education and a lifestyle like that enjoyed by Nhamo, who had every privilege at home because of his studies and because he is male. He would often humiliate her when she complained about the drudgery of her duties while trying to get him to help; he would settle the matter by reminding her about her status as a girl and her inferior position. Her chance comes when Nhamo dies of an unspecified illness and her father reluctantly agrees to Babamukuru's wish to let her pick up the opportunity to take on 'this job of raising this family from hunger and need' (NC: 56). Thus began a journey to a different identity, and a different future. It is marked by a radical shift in the horizon of experience and the horizon of expectation, and poses for us questions about the ambivalences of time and identity, and the specific narratives, for instance, of indigenous belonging versus Westernization, and the possibility of a 'third space' (Bhabha, 1994) beyond that polarity that may help the reconfiguration of subjectivity. It is clear though that the space of belonging in the postcolony is already pluralized, already inscribing fractured social imaginaries.

The change in Tambu's life is signalled through the narrator's decisive and dramatic displacement away from home to live in her uncle's house and attend school there, 'the place of death' as Tambu's mother had called it because Nhamo had died there (NC: 56). The narration presents the car journey as an experience of translation from Africa to the 'West', a rerouting from tradition to modernity; in Tambu's description it marks the passage from what she sees as 'peasant identity' and the fixity of women's place in the village community towards the discovery of 'another self, a clean, well-groomed, genteel self ... [concerned with] the creation of consciousness ... an emancipation' (NC: 58, 59). Village life appears in these description as the place of abjection, at least for a young girl dreaming of emancipation. We learn through the story that these lifeworlds turn out to be more unsettling and complex than that, for they interpenetrate in subtle ways that have shaped the overt action and understanding of the characters as well as the collective unconscious – the inscripted memory of place and time – invisibly animating their way of being. A kind of creolization has already reconfigured these worlds, not least through Christian religion, and its association with being 'educated' and modern, as the narration in NC gradually reveals.

For Tambu, the encounter with Westernized life is one of defamiliarization and de-territorialization, experienced in the different materiality and spatial distribution of the new world, the car to start with – a key trope, laden with connotations of wealth, modernization, technological sophistication, freedom, displacement – then the size of her uncle's house, experienced as immense compared to the houses in the village, and its disorienting layout, for the house is differentiated according to a Westernized spatialization of everyday activities. It is a world of dining room, sitting room, bedrooms, fireplace, bookcase, cutlery and china: 'proper' spaces and 'proper' objects for the initiation into modernity and the time of progress, quite at variance with the spatial disposition and feel of the parental house in the village in which labour, leisure and everyday living seep into each other without clear borders. A crucial element in the re-formation of identity is language, for English replaces Shona at school and for conversation between the 'educated'. This experience of speaking in a language which is not one's own is exemplified in Nhamo's behaviour who lived this troubled identity in the way he would address his father and Tambu in a careful English when visiting home during school breaks, though his fluency in Shona would 'mysteriously return' (NC: 53) when aroused.

What, then, is the postcolonial world in NC and more generally? Regarding identity, we could turn to theories of identity that conceptualize it in terms of its inscription in narrative, that is, its dispersion in the stories that one constructs to tell others about one's action and about who one is and the stories that others tell about us, as the characters in the novel do. Such stories generally refer to or are grounded in the material conditions and in the history of relationships with specific others, and with a world of objects, so that the self can be conceptualized as also a fold in the fabric of the world. The postcolonial form of sociality that NC brings to life is a messy, disjointed yet familiar cultural space, allowing for slippages and drifts in identity that play out the tensions provoked by transculturation and creolization. I shall develop this further later on in the course of my analysis of the text. Interestingly, the description of the incidents at Tambu's uncle's house and the school indicates in a striking way the performative character (Butler, 1993) of the process of formation and change of Tambu's identity. This is because terms like modern and so on do not appear in the narration; instead, in Babamukuru's household, it is a matter of requests from her aunt and uncle to act in a certain way, to read particular books, to use particular objects, to conduct herself according to particular rules, without any kind of guide or explanation, so that the only way for Tambu to find out, for example, which cutlery to use, when to speak, and so on, is learnt through watching and repeating: do this, eat like this, read these books, conduct yourself in this way, behave as we do and you will be modern. She is rewarded with unspoken signs of approval whenever she shows that she has cracked the code. The iterative and performative aspects of the process of formation have a lot to do with the fact that the cultural mimicry of Westernization which shapes the practice of everyday life in the Babamukuru household remains that of surface appearance, without a clear commitment to the underlying values and without its embeddedness in a network of inter-subjective action that extends beyond the household into a community of shared values and understandings.[2]

The absence of what Ricoeur calls 'traditionality' (see below) underlies the communicative action in the household, so that the reader increasingly imagines it to be a nowhere place, out of place and out of time, neither African nor English or even hybrid, although for Tambu it eventually functions as a transitional space (Patterson, 2002; Turner, 1986). Does Babamukuru's regimented place, scrubbed clean everywhere, and arranged for comfort according to 'British interior-décor magazines' (NC: 70), differentiating it from the discomforts and dirt of the family home in the village, succeed in warding off the vestiges of 'tradition'? First of all we find that nothing is quite what it is supposed to be; the 'antiseptic sterility' of the house turns out to be an insecure front breached by constant little invasions from outside. A point immediately follows: it concerns the absence of explicit 'empowering' narratives in the culture that could mediate the process of reconfiguration of the self and provide anchorage for forms of empowerment and resistance that do not simply re-inscribe already established forms of sociality and belonging. These come from elsewhere, as I shall examine in the theoretical discussion in the rest of the chapter.

Now, a central figure in the novel in terms of its diegetic development, is that of Tambu's cousin, Nyasha, who accompanied her parents to England when she was little and who now knows herself to be, in her own terms, 'hybrid', her head 'full of loose connections that are always sparking', as her mother had put it (NC: 74). She is the 'too Anglicized' little African girl who has 'forgotten', as she claims, how to speak Shona, and so does not participate in the communicative exchanges that bind together the members of her enlarged family. The loss or abandonment of the indigenous language is a symbolically vital cultural and ontological dispossession; it will leave her mute and bereft when searching for a language, and so for a community of discourse, in which to ground ontological security. This experience of unbelonging finds expression in a sense of rootlessness that triggers a series of disagreements with her parents about the rules of proper behaviour and conduct, a situation which the latter find disturbing because they cannot imagine the stories and exemplars with which to counter Nyasha's arguments. Babamukuru simply resorts to the invocation of parental authority and ineffective threats, and when everything else fails, punishments. The underlying current of violence that courses through the relations of authority and power in the 'hybrid' habitus of the postcolony is striking in these examples, though they do not have the stark intensity of the cases of the warfare states discussed by Mbembe (2001). (See also, Brah and Coombes, 2000.) Nyasha already shows a rebellious independence of mind, evidenced in the arguments with her parents, and acts of transgression such as her secret habit of smoking and her choice of material to read, including disapproved of novels like *Lady Chatterley's Lover*, but also historical works about South Africa, Palestine, the Nazis, and so on. She discovers through each dispute the contradictions between the values of autonomy and emancipation which she learns in the books she reads and the authoritarian patriarchy behind the veneer of liberal civility that masks her father's power. A bond of solidarity develops between the two girls as Tambu is gradually drawn into this new world, seduced by its secret pleasures, its promise of discoveries and liberation from patriarchal authority, and her dream of becoming like her cousin.

The conflicts of 'double consciousness' (Gilroy, 1993a) come to a crisis when Babamukuru decides that Tambu's parents had not been properly married, since their marriage was based only on a tribal ceremony, and he decides they must now have a church wedding to redress this situation. This rejection of the validity of the norms recognized by the local community and the delegitimation of the relations of obligation, and so on, instantiated in the inter-subjective network of action and communication in the community, show how the authorizing narratives from the colonizer's world can still disrupt the values and attitudes of people in postcolonial times. Many of the villagers do not accept the superiority of modern Western values as intimated in Babamukuru's arguments, and consider them incommensurate with their form of sociality – in other words, when it comes to a way of life, the two sets of values are lived in the form of a 'differend'. The lack of a possibility of compromise brings into visibility the effect of power in constituting incommensurate worlds; here it reveals the power of colonial discourse and the multiple points of its exercise, a power that had appeared absent from village life. Through Babamukuru, described as 'a bloody good kaffir' by his daughter (NC: 200), the authority of Western values and its denigration of indigenous values continue to reshape the community. The narration of the events surrounding the dispute shows Westernization to have become a force operating inside the postcolonial community, and thus not lived as a force imposed from outside the community (such as a colonial authority). Westernization is seen to be at work at both visible and invisible levels, that is to say, it operates through the apparatuses of subject formation, like schools, and so on, but also, and in more intractable ways, through the subjectivity of the agents and actors. The effects are therefore more difficult to resist and work through because the conflicts and ambivalences have become invisibly folded inside the psyche of subjects, and routinized in the everyday reality of the experiential world, as I shall explain below.

It comes as no surprise that the rest of the extended family is browbeaten into submission to Babamukuru's wish. Nyasha's and Tambu's ambivalences about the wedding, together with the disrupting effects of psychic torments provoked by several incidents, precipitate a crisis of identity for the girls. For Tambu, this is experienced as an out-of-body experience of doubleness, at once uncanny and liberating, for at the end she is set on a principled resistance. The narration of the events enables one to reconstruct several sources that nourish her resistance: the distantiating experience of Westernization, the countless little cuts inflicted by patriarchal oppression, and something that resides in the 'essential parts of you [that] stayed behind no matter how violently you tried to dislodge them in order to take them with you' (NC: 173). This violence of dislocation has a name that her mother, secure in her African identity, calls 'Englishness', that she describes as a kind of 'disease' that Tambu comes to recognize. It is a violence that takes one away from oneself, a dispossession that, as she puts it, makes you 'forget who were, what you were and why you were that' (NC: 178).

So, in the novel, the discourses and tropes gathered in the signifiers Englishness and Africanness are made to configure the spatiality and temporality of colonial modernity in terms of incommensurable worlds and incommensurable identities. This is why the Babamukuru household becomes a nowhere place, and a place of mimicry, as camouflage in the case of Tambu, and as the repetition that repeats differently in the case of Nyasha, thus subversive to power, as Bhabha (1994) has argued. Nyasha, unable to come to terms with the fact that she knows herself to be neither 'one of them' not 'one of you' (NC: 201), and lacking the narratives – for instance, the discourse of diaspora or feminism – to give voice to her experience of unbelonging, suffers a schizophrenic breakdown.

Tambu survives her 'hyphenated' existence to tell the story, or, better, she survives by telling the story, a cathartic telling since it is also a re-transcription, drawing strength from the experience and resilience of the women in her life and from her own sense of rootedness. Her narrative is a reconfiguration, or rerouting, implicating a transfiguration of her identity. In attempting to mend the disjunctures of temporality in 'postcolonial' modernity, she overcomes the kind of abjection that her cousin experiences (see Kristeva, 1980). Postcolonial modernity, as depicted in NC, seems to indicate an inbetween world, cobbled together through mistranslations, and split between custom and the modern, past and present, agency and subalternity that the havoc of colonialism had thrown together. It awaits its alternative becoming in an imagined future that the narrator apprehends and allows to grow, nurtured by an emergent postcolonial critique and feminism (NC: 204). In making visible the experience of colonial alienation relating to the effects of the colonizer's language and culture, the narration allows several problems to surface concerning diaspora and creolization (Glissant, 1999; Khatibi, 1971, 1990) that refer to the strategies of appropriation and subversion and issues of translation that relate to the problem of dwelling in a culture or speaking a language which is not one's own (Derrida, 1998).

Identity in these circumstances is lived as being on loan and thus in suspense and under siege, as it is for several characters in NC. The narration, importantly, indicates that the process of anamnesis is required if one is to deal with the trauma that often accompanies such experiences. Anamnesis brings to the surface not only problems to do with affective economy, as Fanon discussed in his work, but also the polyglot, heterogeneous character of cultures and languages. It could be argued that artistic works such as NC, more than theory, make available the space and the scripts that enable these complex aspects of identity to be expressed and worked through.

When we begin to examine the theoretical problems that emerge, we are faced with such a range of issues that we need to widen the scope of identity into the problematic of subjectivity generally. This means that the specific character of the problem of postcolonial identity, to do with the historical, economic, social and cultural conditions that determine that specificity, needs to be grounded in a more general theoretical understanding. Pursuing this line of reasoning, one can specify some key theoretical questions such as: How are subjectivities and identities, colonial and otherwise, constituted in the first place? What is the part played by culture in the process of constitution? How do subjects as particular selves come to recognize themselves according to norms of being or types of action or descriptions or by reference to specific group belonging and so on? How do identities change? What circumstances or discourses inform resistance?

At the more general level, one encounters a further range of problems that refer to the modalities of the self–other relation and its variation according to culture. Equally, one comes across the ontological assumptions that motivate subjects to seek or anticipate forms of life that respect the dignity of the human being, or provide for existences worth living. What 'grand narratives' establish the values that should determine 'worthwhile' existences?

Let us try and group them into three sets. On the one hand, there are general theoretical issues about the mechanisms whereby subjects appear, or come to occupy specific positions, and recognize themselves as specific subjects, and, on the other hand, a range of concrete issues about effects and content relating to identity and self-identity in specific postcolonial circumstances. Beyond these issues reflections of a philosophical or religious nature surface to remind one of the underlying questions concerning values and beliefs that answer to the fundamental existential problems of being.

The first set of issues turn on theorizations of subjectivity generally. I shall consider, to begin with, the standpoint of the subject as constituted, that is, the view that the subject is the effect of processes of constitution whereby an 'outside' comes to be interiorized as an 'inside'. The social sciences understand this process in terms of socialization, but since that term simply offers a redescription of what takes place without problematizing the inside/outside distinction (Adlam et al., 1977), it lacks explanatory power; I shall not discuss this approach. One must bear in mind also the associated issues concerning the theorization of the self, relating to the idea of the who of action and of agency. It is important to clarify these general theoretical positions if one aims to avoid any collapse into unhelpful dichotomies, such as between tradition and modernity, which are part of the discourse of a constitutive subject central to modernity (see Chapter 2), or the reduction of the issues of identity and difference to species of essentialism, for example, in fundamentalisms of one kind or another, including racisms, genderisms.

I will assume that we only need to examine theories that leave behind Cartesianism in its various forms, that is to say – summarizing arguments developed in the previous chapter – theories that break away from the privilege of the 'I think'/the cogito/mind, and from the idea of a self-sufficient, rationalist, autonomous, unitary subject who would be the agent of History. Instead one can focus on those theories that propose that identity is an entity that emerges in relation to an other or others; it is a plural self who is constituted by socio-cultural, corporeal and technico-material mechanisms of formation that can be described.

I will examine the following approaches or, more accurately, problematics of subjectivity. First, the idea of the subject as an ideological subject. This is mainly because problems about decolonizing the mind, or about why people in the 'Third World'/former colonies still buy into occidentalist values and world-views, or problems about the language of resistance are often analyzed in terms of the complicated and problematic concept of ideology; the latter thus continues to have a purchase for thinking through the mechanisms of subjectivity. I will do this beginning with Althusser's theory of ideology because his approach emphasizes not only the functioning of state apparatuses but also draws attention to the psychic economy, thus the subjective dimension involved in this process. Second, I will cover Foucault's notions of discipline and normalization, and the point of view of the embodiment of subjectivity, attending to the implications for governance in postcolonial times. Third, I will introduce Ricoeur's idea of narrative identity, because this concept grounds identity in the ontological dimension of intersubjective action and signifying practices, and extends the discussion of subjectivity to encompass questions of the ethical and affective bases of desirable forms of sociality and becoming. Finally, I will develop the idea of the gaze, deploying a range of psychoanalytic concepts in order to draw together a number of themes that open up the issue of identity and subjectivity to a cross-disciplinary frame of analysis. The problem of the reconfiguration and transfiguration of subjectivity and identity will provide the basis for clarifying the mechanisms, such as the work of mimesis, using the conceptual combinatory established in the course of the different sections.

The point of view of ideology: interpellation

The starting point for the classical theory of ideology is that people act in accordance with a set of values and beliefs about the world and about themselves that have a normative and legitimating force for them. Familiar examples would be the belief that men should be rational and strong or that the market is the fairest and most efficient mechanism for determining the deployment and distribution of resources. Usually such beliefs and values are locked into each other through relay concepts or nodes to constitute coherent enclosed systems of thought, for example, as in patriarchal or masculinist, or white supremacist ideologies. Often such beliefs are held in spite of the evidence, although standpoints outside the specific ideology can detect inconsistencies and contradictions. A basic claim about ideology is that particular sets of ideas and values and representations in a culture acquire an authoritative force because they relay the interests of the dominant group or class and because the intellectuals who produce the authoritative knowledges and narratives of becoming either share these interests or are the functionaries of the ruling elites, that is, a clerisy. Of course when subordinated or subaltern classes and groups accept the authority and worldview inscribed in the dominant discourses and representations, they are predisposed to see the world from the point of view framed by the ruling ideology, which means that they would then regard the established social order as legitimate, and thus consent to the existing distribution of power and goods, status, opportunities and subjective positions. When ideology works, the result is a docile population, because the consolidation of **hegemony**, in Gramsci's sense, guarantees consent and the absence of challenge to the founding premise of the ruling social system. Religions are the ideal exemplars, combining one's willing subjection to the Law with the promise of salvation, provided one conducts oneself according to the norms of the established order. The important aspect to highlight at this point is the idea that ideology constructs a grid of intelligibility and thus makes sense of the world in a particular way; this grid is ultimately founded on 'grand narrative', such as in a religious doctrine or a political philosophy like liberalism. Often this grid of intelligibility presents itself as custom or tradition or common sense. It is only when it is challenged that the underlying value assumptions and foundational or master narratives are made visible. In *Nervous Conditions*, for example, it could be argued that Babamukuru, through his formation, and because of his own interests in the existing social order, was ready to accept some determining values we could describe as colonialist: here the attitude of the 'good kaffir'. My account of the novel has tried to show that the grid of intelligibility is more complex and fractal than the classic theory of ideology allows.

The problem with the orthodox concept of ideology is that it assumes it is possible for people to change through a rational process of recognizing that their way of making sense of the world has been the result of indoctrination or a particular formation, even to the extent of acting against their better interest, a situation that the concept of 'false consciousness' is meant to theorize. The analysis, in its positivist version, presupposes a domain of objective reality and rational unitary subjects who can objectively weigh up the arguments. All that is required would be a process of re-education that would demonstrate the conflict of interest between their own 'objective' position and the values they support, and indicate the means whereby they have become ensnared. The critique of the logocentric and Cartesian subject and the epistemology affiliated with it implies the rejection of this positivist concept of ideology, for it shifts emphasis onto the idea of a subject-in-process and the constitutive character of the relation to the other, thus opening towards cognitive as well as affective and ethical considerations in ideology critique and for the changing of subjects. An associated problem is the assumption that there is something like the 'truth' that can be revealed through something assumed to be a non-ideological discourse, for instance, a 'science'. To think these issues through we could go back to the case of wearing or not wearing the veil in the UK; it is clear that the decision does not depend in any simple way on how being or not being modern is valued. The wearing of the veil is not necessarily intended to signal attachment to so-called 'traditional' values, although clearly it does for many Muslims and for those whose opposition to it assumes it is an effect of patriarchal power. We know that many of the young Muslim women who choose to wear traditional clothing nevertheless support key values that would be seen as modern, or regard themselves to be modern by reference to what they aspire to be and in defying a number of specific values associated with 'tradition'. It is a matter of strategic choices that are located in a wider political context, perhaps invoking Gramsci's (1971) notion of 'war of position' here.

However, the action has to do equally with problems of identity in relation to roots and the assertion of difference when faced with negative stereotypes of the Muslim woman or the Muslim community; that is to say, they are part of a politics of difference and the ruses of resistance that put into play affective as much as political considerations. Similarly, Nyasha's ambivalence about Western as against African/Shona values and identity are not reducible to rational calculations of interests. Relations to parents and to the whole community and forms of life are at stake, and the way these relations and forms are lived in the psyche. Hence her breakdown, itself symptomatic of her inability to resolve the conflicts at the affective and intellectual level.

The limitations in the orthodox theory of ideology have been the spur for Althusser's ([1971] 1991) own recasting of the theory. A starting point for his theorization is the rejection of a self-centred Cartesian subject, that is, the notion of the subject as autonomously constitutive, and everything that is implied in that epistemological position. For my purposes, I would highlight in particular the failure to recognize, in classical epistemology, the inter-subjective character of the production of knowledge and the inscription of the subject through language in the culture, so that autonomy must be qualified with respect to heteronomy. The central propositions that Althusser wants to demonstrate deal with the mechanisms whereby subjects, although constituted, end up thinking of themselves as constitutive. His theory proposes the mechanisms whereby this misrecognition is produced as effect, a misrecognition which is absolutely central for his account of the functioning of ideology. For example, it is clear in NC that Babamukuru is convinced he has rationally and autonomously decided to be the way he is, a way of being he considers progressive and proper, the right thing to do, in contrast to what he perceives as the 'tradition-bound' retrogressive beliefs and lifestyle of his brother and sister-in-law. Yet the rational arguments of Nyasha have no effect on his position and values. A clear case of ideological resistance one could say. But then, Nyasha herself supports values that, it could be argued, are not in her best interest given her privileged 'elite' position in the village. Yet, from a postcolonial and feminist point of view, the values of autonomy and independence, of anti-patriarchal and anti-colonialist struggles for which she suffers are in her better interest. So, theories of ideology that privilege the cognitive dimension fail to theorize the other dimensions involved in the transformation of identity.

The point of introducing Althusser's theory into the argument is precisely because it does introduce for the first time an account of the manner in which ideology does its work at both the psychic and the cognitive levels, a theory that enables one to address the question of the resilience of the constituted subject when faced with contradictions in interest. In his account of the functioning of ideology in constituting subjects for it, he distinguishes between ideological and repressive state apparatuses. The latter at least at first glance appear to be fairly straightforward in their operation, for instance the police. But closer inspection reveals that for an institution of 'repression' like the police to work, it requires that subjects acknowledge their authority and the rightfulness or legitimacy of the way they function. The example that Althusser himself uses – that of a policeman shouting 'Hey you!', and people automatically turning to look and to position themselves as if they were the person hailed – indicates that something else happens elsewhere prior to this moment of hailing or interpellation that over-determines the response or action. That something else is the prior constitution of the subject as an ideological subject through the working of the ideological apparatuses of subject formation. There is too the hint of a 'guilty conscience' that predisposes the subject to respond to the call of the Law and submit to its injunction, as Butler has argued (1997: 112). Ideological apparatuses are institutions like schools and the family that function mainly through interpellating particular individuals as specific subjects. In practice, both sets of apparatuses work through a mixture of repressive power and interpellation. For instance, schooling involves norms and goals and practices set up and regulated by the state, enacted by agents like teachers, together with the action of (suitably already constituted) parents who reinforce (or not) these norms of the good student and good parenting and the relations of authority inscribed in them. One can see this taking place in the Babamukuru household in the pattern of dos and don'ts, the system of reward and punishments, the judgement of conduct that inscribes particular values and legitimates particular courses of action. However, as we saw in the case of Nyasha and Tambu, an ambivalence lies deep in the cognitive and affective economy at work, for as Butler has remarked: 'Submission and mastery take place simultaneously, and this paradoxical simultaneity constitutes the ambivalence of subjection' (1997: 116).

Althusser's theory introduces one element that has proved productive for exploring this **aporia**, not least because it highlights the processual character of the mechanisms involved. He draws on Lacan's psychoanalytic theory, especially his account of the mirror stage, concerning the relationship of Subject and subject, and the imaginary character of that relationship both in the psyche and in the domain of the symbolic, to show that ideological interpellation works in a similar manner. Intrinsic to the process is the effect that Lacan calls misrecognition. Lacan uses the analogy of a person who looks at herself in the mirror to explain the positioning of the subject in relation to the Subject, and the effect this has for the conceptualization of oneself as a particular (self-)image. In the process of subject formation the mirror is symbolic and imagined: the infant imagines itself according to the image which it projects of itself as if in the eyes of **the Other**, as I explain in greater detail below. Everything happens in the 'imagination' of the infant/subject: the Other exists at the level of phantasy and projection: it is a (specular) play of mirrors in the mind. The domain where such practices of signification occurs is the **imaginary**, which is constituted in that process. Althusser gives the example of the constitution of the Christian, arguing that actions like kneeling and praying in the Church, intrinsically ask of the subject that she recognizes herself in the position of the faithful Christian. This means acknowledging the authority of the Church, and recognizing oneself in the image of the Christian subject, that is, a subject who submits to the will of God who is positioned as Subject. To recognize oneself as Christian entails acting according to a set of norms and rules that performatively establish one's identity as Christian. At the same time, according to the theory, the Christian subject, in principle, does not consider her action to be in any way forced, but willingly undertaken: I do these things because I am, and wish to be, a good Christian, that is, I am someone who consents to the norms of the good Christian as defined in the authoritative texts and teachings of the Church. Besides, the implication in the example is that the performative activity itself – praying, kneeling, and so on – has a constitutive effect for subjectivity. But we know too that most religions, for example Christianity, also promise punishments.

Similarly, it could be argued that to be modern one must abandon wearing the veil; yet my example shows that this is not such a transparent act. Something else is evident in my example: had orthodox Muslim families and/or ideological state apparatuses like schools been completely successful in their work of interpellation, the act of wearing the veil as an act of resistance to Eurocentrism/ethnicism, or as an assertion of difference, would not have happened. So, one must acknowledge that some people are not so successfully interpellated, and that the mechanisms operating are more complex and processual working in the manner of assemblages, allowing for degrees of indeterminacy. Furthermore, one must be able to imagine a space of resistance already existing within a culture, uncolonized or discrepant, inscribing different values and forms of life, different socialities, a space-in-process for a subject-in-process. For instance, on what basis do Nyasha and Tambu resist in their different ways? What mechanisms operate there? What informs it and what identities are at stake? Or, in a different context, what makes Fanon turn to the writings of Negritude and to a critique of the Western project of emancipation?

It must be said that the Althusserian model allows the economic to remain as determining factor, even if 'in the last instance'. However, it makes visible the point of view of consent as well as misrecognition, so that the problematic of the constitution of subjects calls up that of hegemony, thereby keeping visible too the relationship between the economy and the process of legitimation which is central to a discussion of power. In the divided and dividing spaces in NC, hegemony is at best fragile, since consent is seen to be the volatile and provisional product of fractured socioeconomic and cultural processes.

The point of view of normalization

A similar list of questions appear when one considers the Foucauldian problematic of subjectivity. I introduce this approach because it highlights some of the elements one needs to consider, especially at the level of the discourses that speak about the subject in terms of the norms of 'normal' behaviour and in terms of the normative dimension in the functioning of the institutions and mechanisms of constitution of subjectivity, operating through the assemblage made up of schools, hospitals, the family, the barracks, and so on. Foucault's theory must be relocated in the context of the conceptualization of modernity as a form of sociality and as 'a form of power which makes individuals subject ... a form of power which subjugates and makes subject to' (1982: 212). Now, the idea that the subject could be the object of a systematic technology of formation is born with modernity and the modern state, specifically, as part of the emergence of the 'sciences of the social' from the Enlightenment period, sciences that take the social and the subject to be the target of their theorizations and their concern. Indeed, modernity itself can only have a virtual existence without these apparatuses and the subjectivities that give it an existential reality as a distinct historical period. But the discursive formations and technologies that appeared had to constitute an idea of a 'normal' subject in the first place, and they had to suppose the possibility of an objective and objectivizing domain of statements about the subject and the social. The philosophical discourse of modernity, as I have shown in the previous chapter, already provides the foundational principles for such possibilities, specifically in the 'philosophy of the subject' and its dividing practices – for example, regarding madness in Foucault's work – that establishes the concept of a logocentric epistemic subject as an entity able to constitute discourses that have the status of a science. To these early developments in the

95

history of the modern form of subjectivity, one needs to add as condition of possibility the regimes of power/knowledge developed in the context of colonialism, as I argued concerning imperial governmentality. Furthermore, the inscription of power in knowledges about the social and the subject (say, in psychology and sociology) grants them a normative authority in the determination of what they themselves define as normal. In a sense, because of its role in establishing normative rules, power/knowledge, as a concept, takes the place of ideology. For this reason, the Foucauldian analytical method does not have a place for the concept of ideology, relying instead on power/knowledge and 'regimes of truth' (Foucault, 1979) and mechanisms of normalization and disciplining.

In the following paragraphs, I shall summarize a number of lines of departure and general propositions that Foucault has established in the many and varied concrete studies in which he has elaborated his analytical apparatus for the theorization of subjectivity. His focus is the new form of power he calls pastoral power, discussed in the previous chapter, an individualizing power that targets individuals and the whole community, thus bodies and populations that they constitute through their own practices, mobilizing in the process new institutions like the hospital and old institutions like the family (1979: 213–15). For instance, pedagogy constitutes populations of junior school students, students with special needs, mathematics students, and so on through the correlated application of, on the one hand, discourses like psychology that provide the theoretical basis for what is supposed to constitute 'normality' by reference to capabilities and cognitive development, and, on the other, classroom technologies of teaching and learning, including textbooks, teaching aids, programmes of activity and techniques that are themselves framed by the discourses. They seek to achieve specific objectives measured in terms of norms of the 'normal' regarding activity and ability that the expert discourses and the technologies have themselves determined. In this way, in principle at least, each subject is moulded according to specified capabilities and values, ready to act in accordance with them.

These assemblages of subjection–subjectification have their own specific genealogies, quite apart from the conditions that I have pointed out earlier concerning the emergence of modernity as a discursive formation, and the central functioning of the ideas of science and of the logocentric subject in the modern form of sociality. The genealogies reconstruct the formation of the discourses in terms of a history of stratagems for dealing with theoretical and technical problems relating to subjectivity that have arisen in response to the specific interests of governance. A classic case is the emergence and introduction of intelligence tests (IQ) in schools in response to the perceived inadequate level of numeracy, literacy and general education of the workforce given the requirements of new industrial and military technologies (Rose, 1979). Thus, when we consider sociology, we have both the wider framework of modernity, especially Enlightenment discourses about the social and about governance as a general concept, and the specific history of reflections about culture and about the mechanisms for forming and changing the subject – importantly, to do with colonialism, but also with class – that refer to the interests of administration and to the formation of the nation-state as a new kind of entity for administrative and political ends.[3] These genealogies show the intricate correlation of knowledge and power, so that at the level of epistemology, what is fruitful for the analysis of subjectivity and of the social is not so much the objectivity of the claims, but the effects of power/knowledge for constituting subjects and for constituting particular populations.

The effectivity of power/knowledge in the process of normalization and disciplining is grounded in the apparatuses set up on the basis of the knowledges that make a claim to truth. These apparatuses establish technologies of the social, that is, practices that constitute particular subjects and regulate specific populations in accordance with the norms they specify. For example, the analysis by Viswanathan of the role of literary study in India reconstructs the dynamic interactions involving a complex network of institutions and interests and knowledges, namely, British colonial rule, the initiation of a properly imperial governmentality (see Chapter 2), the goals of evangelization, the sensitivities of the Indian elite, the requirements of the Indian colonial administration, including military personnel, and ethnographic and pedagogical knowledges. It is clear from the study that the **genealogy** of the discourse of pedagogy, and the role of literary study in it, passed through the practices instituted by the British colonial administration in pursuing their interest, namely, the recruitment of particular categories of subjects through their prior formation in a system of education. The concept of interpellation by itself does not encompass this range of mechanisms and their different and co-articulated functioning.

One of the innovations of Foucault was to direct attention to the body in the process of formation of subjects. The interest of power in developing specific capabilities and the focus of its exercise on populations suggests a 'biopolitics' (Foucault, 1976) that takes life itself to be the object for power. Biopolitics is not confined to sexuality alone but encompasses the regulation of general physical and mental health, the development of productive skills, issues of birth, death, longevity, demographic policy, child development, in short, the whole range of practices that concern the formation, disciplining and regulation of individuals and populations. Increasingly, governance operates as a biopolitics, for example, with regard to policy about how to deal with the unemployed. It is interesting to note that in this case the problem is being reconfigured as a problem arising from the psychological or mental health of particular individuals, or a problem of appropriate skills and attitude, rather than an economic or social one. An additional advantage for neo-liberalism is the privatization of disadvantage and suffering through the conversion of social and economic problems into purely subjective ones, thus transferring responsibility to the 'dysfunctional client'; the message is: own your own problems and your own solutions.

Another element concerning the embodied character of subjectivity is the sense that capabilities are not simply inscribed in bodies but are instantiated through action. Such a perspective has developed into the idea of performativity, as in Butler's work. In my example, Nyasha and Tambu could show their modernity not simply through declarations, but by acting in particular ways in everyday practice: their modernity had to be performed. However, a problem here, and a problem with the idea of performativity – more specifically with the way the concept is often used – is that the concept either assumes a self-centred agent or neglects the inter-subjective co-production of meaning in relation to action. In the case of the girls, when Tambu is all set to become modern and 'educated', she relies on signs of approval from the adults rather than her own intentions in working out the meaning expressed or performed through her action or speech. There is thus a relation of authority and power, as well as a relation of recognition, at work in the performative action that directs analysis to the inter-subjective ground of action. My point counsels against analyses that re-inscribe the ego-centric, autonomous subject. Furthermore, the claim from Nyasha that in reading the classics of English literature, such as D.H. Lawrence, she is only reading what's 'good to read' and is not really showing 'Anglicized' disrespect or rebelliousness, presents for analysis the recognition that the site where meaning is performatively constructed in terms of inter-subjective exchanges is a space of plural codings and overcodings of the normative and the desirable, and a space where the play of power shapes outcomes. This will need further exploration.

Foucault's problematic of subjectivity shows that other factors and mechanisms are at work that oblige one to revise the standpoint of ideological interpellation and misrecognition. In Foucault's perspective, subjects act according to a formation, that is, they act as subjects endowed with specific skills, dispositions, values, orientations (e.g. numeracy, 'masculine' characteristics, modern, etc.) that they have acquired as a result of their construction and normalization as specific subjects positioned in relation to specific practices, and who position themselves as subjects of power, that is, subject to it and exercising it to varying degrees. Does Babamukuru, for instance, misrecognize himself as a free and autonomous African agent or is he the 'good kaffir' that his daughter describes, the result of his specific formation, yet at the same time recognizing his interests as tribal head and head of a state apparatus and performatively enacting that position? Is he, in other words, answering the call of his own desire? While the psychic dimension of the question of subjectivity makes the problem more complex, by introducing an economy of desire into the equation, one must equally take account of the cultural location of ways of being and the formation of imaginaries. It is possible to examine this complexity through a theorization of a relation between identity and subjectivity, which I shall introduce below through the concept of narrative identity.

The analysis of the relation of power and discourse points to the constitution of 'regimes of truth'. These refer to both the system of the legitimation and authorization of action, as well as to practices that instantiate the regimes, that is, to an assemblage. Ideology, conceptualized in terms of true and false consciousness or, more usefully, in terms of the economy of recognition and misrecognition as in Althusser, although it directs attention to the processual aspect of the constitution of subjects, does not exhaust the picture. For example, for Babamukuru, the regime of truth is a hybrid of 'Western' colonial discourse and narratives and memories of indigenous ways of being and ethos that pluralize the regimes, introducing disjunctures at the level of subjectivity. For Nyasha and Tambu, we saw that the problem became that of either being imprisoned in the space of unbelonging – with traumatic consequences – or inventing new narratives, and new spaces (third space? Transitional space?) that have a transfigurative effect. The time has come to sketch the point of view of narrative identity. First, I must introduce the analysis of the process of identification and disidentification, so that the turn to Ricoeur will appear as a logical next step.

The point of view of identification and disidentification

It is important at this juncture to clarify some rather complex problems concerning the mechanisms of identification. I shall need to elaborate the problematic of Lacan with respect to what's going on at the level of the psychic apparatus, briefly introduced in the discussion of interpellation, and extend the analysis by indicating how the social enters into and has effects on that process. I shall do this through a discussion of the gaze. Apart from allowing me to bring into the picture the psychoanalytic, indeed a post-psychoanalytic, problematic of subjectivity, the gaze, just as importantly, acts as relay and threshold between body and mind, the corporeal and consciousness, so that the break with the dualism of body and mind can be seen to be a necessary aspect of fully addressing the question of subaltern, subjugated and postcolonial identity. My example here is once more taken from Fanon (1970) in his essay on the 'lived experience' of being a black man (mistranslated as 'The fact of blackness'). Fanon's narrative, briefly, is constructed from a key episode in his encounter with metropolitan France. He recounts the incident in which a white child points him out to his mother and shouts: 'Look, Mother, a Negro' and again: 'Mother, look at the Negro, I'm frightened' (ibid.: 79). He at first tries to take the gaze of the child in his stride and to remain unperturbed, but the addition of fear in the white child's language triggers for Fanon a journey of self-interrogation and transformation, described in a brilliantly insightful and honest account. The reference to fear trawls a chain of signifiers of an alien otherness attributed to the black person, inscribed in colonial discourse. That discourse has become an accursed inheritance for Fanon, reminding him of the stereotypes of savagery, intellectual inferiority, cannibalism, tribalism, and so on that insert the black person into white racist representation of black identity. He felt split into three different or disjunct states or spaces of being, namely, as a body, as a race, and in relation to ancestry. No reconciliation seemed possible. The language he uses to describe his feelings is rich in allusions, informed by psychoanalysis and philosophy, particularly existentialism. Thus, he puts to work terms like 'corporeal schema', 'epidermal schema', presence, recognition, objectification, historicity, and **over-determination** to try and make sense of his situation. It must be pointed out too that the narrator, the 'Fanon' of the incident could have responded in many other ways: he could have dismissed the incident as below contempt, smiled in irony, made a suitably cutting remark, scolded the mother/child for racism and ignorance, and so on. Fanon's response in the text is at first to live out the humiliation arising from the other's mis-recognition by embodying the negative stereotype, to fling it in the face of those in whose eyes he was nothing but a fearsome savage, those who could not recognize him as simply another human being. His exploration of identity then shifts to a discussion of the texts of Sartre on another racist discourse, that targeting the Jew. His account brings to the surface the fixity of identity which racism operates, and to the feeling of a 'determination from outside' that even the play of camouflage and invisibility does not change: his attempts at performing a non-stereotypical subjectivity or tactic of 'striving for anonymity' (ibid.: 82) do not work. There is no way out for Fanon but to confront what it means to be black in a white culture, that is, in a culture in which the humanity of the black person has been erased along with her/his own history – I emphasize once again that agency and history mutually condition each other in the discourse of modernity – and in which there is no position in language except as an **abject** or subaltern subject. Fanon's interrogation directs him to the writings where an alternative, dissident discourse of blackness has been enunciated, namely, Negritude, particularly, the works of Senghor, Césaire, Diop, in which he discovers a discourse that rescues and validates the history and culture of black people, constructing a new identity and self-esteem out of the poetic imagination of an other way of being. Yet, this too is a straitjacket for identity, for it is a memorialization that brings psychic and emotional comfort but does not provide an opening for a de-territorializing transcendence, that is, for operating a displacement and for supporting the anticipation of a future that could escape both terrains – that of racism as much as that of subaltern re-inscription of Afrocentrism. He works through the aporias of identity he has revealed by developing a critique of social scientific conceptualizations of the black person, thus joining the epistemological level of addressing the problem of subjective transformation with the affective level, the level of the 'lived'. This transformative process requires a rupture with the past and an inaugural gesture, intricately linked, as Verges has argued: 'Fanon removing chains contains, in its projective representation, decolonization, emancipation, freedom from the chains of madness and freedom from the chains of colonization, all powerfully linked' (1996: 48). This approach has been followed by many other postcolonial writers, for example, in Trinh Minh-ha's (1989) excavation of representations of the native 'other' in ethnographic work and the need to counter the subjectivizing gaze of the Eurocentric knower/epistemic subject inscribed in them. The direction of Fanon's analysis points towards the possibility of a world that would have overcome the limitations of the present dualisms and racist oppositions through a transcendence achieved in the course of a politics of transfiguration.

The gaze

I want to re-examine this episode, and the implications for theorizing the transformation in subjectivity that Fanon advocates, using the concept of the gaze to tease out the mechanisms that operate at the level of the psyche and of the social. In line with his text, I will extend the concept to take account of the cognitive level of the process of making sense of the world and acting in it.

The gaze from the point of view of subject formation has been first developed within psychoanalytic theory. Freud – and later Mulvey (1975) – notably pointed to the pleasure in the gaze, scopophilia, which I would like to dislodge from his understanding tied too tightly to sexuality, and relocate it away from the Oedipal model. Additionally, I want to emphasize instead the pleasure in the relation to the other – say, as happens in the process of recognition through the gaze of the other at the earliest stage of the infant's encounter with the other and the Other (a process harbouring existential traces of the 'face relation' in the Levinasian sense). This means recognizing the pleasure derived by the infant in its encounter with the world and with significant others (the mother, principally): the intimate body language between mother and child, the exchange of gazes, the touch, the feel of bodies, the play of voices, the little recognitions, the intricate you–me choreography whereby an infant enacts its entry into a social world. The co-activity and exchanges that describe the mother–infant dyad are marked by hospitality, generosity, pleasure, attachment, as well as conflict. Necessity plays a part here too, for the survival of the infant depends on this adjustment to a world, the world into which it is thrown by the act of birth. An element of seduction enters into this process too, not yet sexual but erotic: precursors of affective bonds (see also Laplanche, 1989). It is clear that from the earliest, a human being encounters a world of others and objects which it has to make its own and interiorize through active engagement in an inter-subjective process of constitution. It is an apprenticeship through a choreography that not only inaugurates subjectivity through the mechanisms of identification, but also constructs correlated affective, cognitive and ethical worlds that are instantiated at the level of the experiential. Choreography mingles the 'time of the body' with the 'time of the soul' (Ricoeur, see below). Clearly, and sadly, some of these encounters are painful or traumatic, the result of wrong choices or mistaken anticipations, but equally sometimes occasioned by uncaring or misguided or thoughtless others, including parents. It is a fraught process, and the outcome is uncertain.[4]

101

However, one of the key senses (at least for sighted people) active in the process of becoming a subject concerns the visual, although one should bear in mind here Lacan's (1966) own distinction between the visual and visibility, enabling him to say that the gaze 'is prior to the eye'. From the earliest, then, the visual and the visible are associated with knowledge and with pleasure – an enigmatic pleasure – as much as with anxieties about the strangeness of that world. I would add to this the importance of other senses: touch, sound, smell, so that in the encounter with the world the visible is overlaid with these other registers of being-in-the-world; in this way visibility extends beyond the visual: one sees more than what meets the eye. The salient aspect of the choreography I am proposing suggests that the gaze enters into a relation, and a play, of recognition and misrecognition (Venn, 2004). One reads the other's gaze for signs of understanding, signs of desired responses, of engagement with a common world, mediated through objects. The gaze inaugurates a journey from the initial solitude of thrownness towards entry into a familiar and (hopefully) secure common world.[5]

A more comprehensive problematic of identification emerges from these lines; it proceeds from the recognition that even before the infant has separated from the mother/Other and has not reached the stage of language proper (although vocalization takes place), the body retains an affective and signifying bond with the mother's body that prolongs intra-uterine experience. Kaja Silverman, in her exploration of the female voice has suggested that the maternal voice is experienced by the foetus as a 'blanket of sound', a 'sonorous envelope'; one could think about it as an acoustic space that would be the 'originary psychic space' (1988: 72). Female vocality invokes for the infant a 'primordial experience of corporeal harmony' (ibid.: 88); it is saturated with affect binding the infant's embodied experience of being-with and being-in-the-world with a maternal musical sound. Similarly, Bracha Lichtenberg Ettinger proposes the existence of a 'layer', 'the matrixial stratum of subjectivization', a 'beyond-the-phallus feminine field, related to plural, partial and shared unconscious desire (for both men and women), which has an imaginary and symbolic impact, and not only a real ex-istence' (1995: 22). She links it with the standpoint of the 'co-emerging I and non-I, prior to I versus others', thus a non-Cartesian standpoint.

What is clear is that it is not enough to claim that the 'self' or the 'I' emerges in relation to or in opposition to an other – for instance, in Lacan's metaphor of the mirror stage, implicating separation from the Other in the formation of the ego and recognition of the difference of the other as an other (or in the Hegelian problematic of the I–other agonistic relation, and even more clearly in socio-biology's assumption of a self-serving competitive instinct). While this separation does happen, the co-emergence of the I and not-I points to the dynamic and reciprocal co-production of subjectivity. This understanding cashes out the idea of the I–other relation as one of compossibility (Merleau-Ponty, 1968), emphasizing the idea of being as being-with and as being-in-the-world.

I should juxtapose in this context Merleau-Ponty's analysis of the body – which lies in the background to a good deal of the rethinking of embodiment and being-in-the-world – that starts with the proposition that an invisible connection binds the being who feels with what is felt:

> A human body comes into existence when, in-between the being who sees and the visible, between touching and what is touched, between one eye and the other, between one hand and the other, a kind of folding over takes place, when the spark of the sensing-sensed being is set alight. (1964: 20)

This radically anti-Cartesian view argues that the body is the mind's body and the mind is the body's mind; it proposes a dynamic inter-relation between psychic and bodily phenomena founded in a diachronic relationship between body and mind. The implication is that the body is altered in the course of its encounters with the phenomenal world of objects and people. Furthermore, Merleau-Ponty says: 'The experience of my own body and the experience of the other are two sides of the same Being ... the other is the horizon or other side of this experience' (1968: 225). He argues that there is an articulation of the other's body with mine which 'does not empty me ... but on the contrary redoubles me with an alter ego' (ibid.: 233). The idea, then, is of an intertwining of the world and the human, of interiority and exteriority, of the I and the other; it evokes, analogically, the relation of a curve to its hollow. For him the relationship of world and body is understood in terms of the chiasm binding the outside and the inside such that the one cannot be reduced to the other; it is a folding that preserves both since the visible exterior 'has a prolongation, in the enclosure of my body, which is part of its being' (Merleau-Ponty, 1968: 271). (See the 'Tenth Study' in Ricoeur, 1992; Lakoff and Johnson, 1999; and Grosz, 1994; Venn, 2000, 2004; Silverman, 2000) One can therefore imagine a compossibility, that is, a dynamic and constitutive interaction between the world and every being, between embodied experience and consciousness that fundamentally breaks with the body–mind dualism and with mechanical philosophy. Such a standpoint doubles the visibility of the world with an interior visibility but in such a modality that one comes to know the world according to perceptions and sensations that encompass all the senses, yet exceeds the givenness of the world, to refer equally to the un(re)presentable trace of the world that one experiences as dwelling.

One can now unpack the matter of the gaze in Lacan with a critical eye. In theorizing subjectivity, he brings into the forefront the mechanism of recognition, and the gaze, through the trope of the mirror phase or stage. This phase describes the process whereby an infant, not yet able to speak – though clearly able to communicate – the not-yet-subject or subject-in-process – first recognizes itself as if in a mirror. A specular mechanism is at work here. It all happens in the imagination. The mirror stands in for the place from which the other appears to look at the infant as an other, so that by reflection the infant can imagine itself as another subject. The mirror is the metaphoric site of the moment of constitution, through the gaze, of the subject as 'whole', that is, as an 'I' (but not necessarily as an 'I think'); the process, however, involves a splitting and separation from the Other, so that the process of identification, from the beginning, is fractured and ambivalent from the point of view of the economy of desire. It is important to remember that the whole process of interaction, the choreography of co-action, including communicative action – which involves a good deal more than vocalizations and utterances alone: the world is more than discourse – leads to this point of recognition in the mirror. Desire and loss and pleasures are played out in this choreography. It includes apprenticeship into language, which thus in the course of its development, provides for the infant the anchorages in a shared communicative medium for what the infant imaginatively constructs as its world, and which it comes to recognize as a shared symbolic and material world. The use of the personal pronoun, of proper names, attached to action in the world, is an important element in the process whereby the symbolic domain is brought into the formation of subjectivity. Communicative action thus links the economy of desire with the economy of significance. (See the essential Silverman, 2000; *jouissance*, Thing, Law, in the Glossary; and Venn 2002, 2004.) For the discussion here, I will limit the sketch to the point about the centrality of the gaze for identity, as the key mechanism in psychoanalytic theory (as I am refiguring it), alongside language, in the co-articulation of the psychic and the social. From the point of view of recognition, at this early formative stage, as well as in later life, the gaze – or whatever substitutes for it – remains central. Through it the economy of desire continues to be inscribed or inscrypted in the process of communicative action. Through it, therefore, analysis can keep visible the level of affect – of ambivalences, of loss, of secret or veiled yearnings, of mourning and melancholia, of displacements and repressions, of the life of the body and the yearnings of the spirit – that structures one's responses in real situations, and informs, at another level, the process of resistance and the transfiguration of subjectivity.

Fanon's text is analytically fruitful for the position I am developing because that level of affect is explicitly addressed in his accounts of oppression, and it is addressed at the level of the 'lived'. For instance, returning to the question of the gaze, his interrogation of black identity starts with precisely the disruptive and alienating effects for his identity of the gaze of the white other, a gaze that refuses him recognition as another human being and fixes him in an otherness – the black/savage – that he cannot accept without abjection, yet must confront and come to terms with. If one follows his account, the picture that he had of himself, or presented of himself, was that of a cosmopolitan and educated doctor, a French citizen, as worthy of respect as any other being. But concepts of oneself are validated, and acquire reality, only to the extent that they are cashed out in terms to how others perceive us and interact with us. Outside of this inter-subjective grounding of selves, one is but a potential self, a virtual being. The narrative that Fanon reconstructs in his essay is of course a discursive device, enabling him to explore with the reader the issues of racism and identity. The insertion of the gaze into the question of identity relocates it, as a theoretical and political issue, in terms of its relation to identification. In this respect, two discourses fix Fanon the black man as an identity: that of the humanist discourse of the general subject (which Fanon attributes to himself as a human being), and that of a white racist and colonialist discourse that denies his humanity and positions him as a brutish, uncivilized thing, unworthy of any respect or dignity, outside the law/Law and history, indeed, outside 'proper' language: 'Sho' good eating' (Fanon, 1970: 79). The mechanisms of identification involved here, apart from those that occur within the familial scene, are those of the educational apparatus that formed him, and practices of the everyday in the disjointed geographies called Martinique and France. The facticity of being black is an effect inscribed in the relay between the two, it marks a relation; the gaze is a crucial nodal point in the process, as I explain below.

The refusal of recognition, as I have indicated, precipitates all kinds of dread for Fanon. These are interestingly lived in the body, and through bodily responses such as aggression, anger, wild laughter. This bodily level of the responses is consistent with both the perspective I developed earlier about the relationship of compossibility between being-in-the-world and the insertion of oneself as self and body in that at once social and material world. The racist gaze reduces Fanon (and the black person) to bare body, to skin, a violence provoking the counter-violence of his response. His account brings to light precisely the connection between the psychic and the social levels of the constitution of subjectivity, levels that are, in any case, inextricably connected for every subject. It is clear that he desires recognition as a human being, and that this desire is expressed both at the level of ontology: securing or confirming his status and value as a human being, and at the level of the social: recognition as a particular subject: a French man, a professional, educated man. In a racist culture, since the black person – and, more generally, the other racialized, that is, categorized as racial other – is positioned as naturally inferior, unable to be properly civilized or cultured because of a presumed intrinsic inferiority as a being, she is forever the 'not-quite' subject (Bhabha, 1994). As Fanon puts it:

[E]very ontology is made unattainable in a colonized and civilized society ... In the *Weltanschauung* of a colonized people there is an impurity, a flaw that outlaws any ontological explanation ... For not only must the black man be black; he must be black in relation to the white man. (1970: 77)

So, it is in the eye/gaze of the white man that the black person lacks in being. But this is so only if the black person sees him or herself as if with the eyes of the white subject. This is brought out clearly in Fanon, whose narrative is calculated to make visible the mechanisms whereby the black person sees her/himself with the eyes of the colonizing or dominant other; this tactic is a condition for exploring the effects of such mechanisms and the ways of countering them. The interrogation is part of making clearer the process of disidentification.

In my account of how the gaze is a determining mechanism at the level of the psychic apparatus of identification, I have stressed the importance of the relation to the other for identification, pointing to the way the other is constitutive of subjectivity, and comes to be inscribed, or folded as an inside when one considers the domain of the unconscious and the economy of desire. The gaze is equally constitutive at the social level, something that will become clearer when I introduce Ricoeur's idea of narrative identity below. At this point, I will draw attention to the way that in learning a language one occupies, from the beginning, specific and specified subjective positions, already existing in a culture, for instance, regarding gender. Such positionings, though over-determined, are not unitary, so that spaces exist for dissidence – witness feminist politics. In particular, when more than one language, thus more than one culture, is involved, as in many colonial and postcolonial situations, translations across heterolingual and culturally heterogeneous and polyglot borders allow for the feints, the camouflages, the displacements, ambivalences, mimicries, the appropriations, that is to say, the complex stratagems of disidentification that leave the subaltern and the subjugated with the space for resistance. A difficulty, however, is that the spaces allowed the subjugated are already colonized, or partly colonized, by the dominant power in that the latter has effects on the discourses that authorize or legitimate the norms of the normal. This means that in entering a culture, one buys into a world-view – note Fanon's reference to *Weltanschauung* – with its system of classification, its values, its way of making sense of the world, its structure of feelings.

In other words, one enters into its cognitive as well as its affective framing of the world. Racist stereotypes, as described in the Fanon account, are examples of such colonized spaces, so that in occupying them – here as a black man – one locates oneself in the already assigned place of the 'inferior savage', and one sees oneself as the other sees one. The gaze, thus, operates as a point of identification as well as the point from which a grid of intelligibility depicts the world in a particular way. The gaze is the mind's eye for the imaginary, though the latter in turn orients the gaze. The process explains how the gaze can participate in subjugation, relaying and doubling the economy of desire in the mechanism of identification with a cognitive economy. However, the effects of subjugative and subjectivizing mechanisms may be countered, provided narratives and spaces exist that undermine the authority of hegemonic disciplinary and normalizing discourses. It is this matter of the ground which sustains, or not, resistance/dissidence that leads me to Ricoeur's work on the self and the agent of action.

On the narrative character of identity

My line of analysis will start with the argument that while every subject is grounded in mechanisms such as the ones discussed above, there is still a problem left over about the 'who' and the agent of action; this view follows from the recognition that this is the important element left unaccounted for in the explanations about the formation and positioning of subjects as elaborated in Althusser and Foucault and in subject-centred accounts. We know that people speak of themselves as particular, named persons, who remain the same self in spite of changes over time concerning personal circumstances and self-understanding. This sense of a self is tied to everyday practices in which people locate themselves by reference to a routine of ways of acting in the world and interaction with others that inscribe expectations about themselves and others that remain relatively stable in particular social situations. I should note here that there nevertheless remains an undecidable element in action in that it is always open to the initiation of newness, as Arendt (1959) has argued. Furthermore, it is the assumption that, although conditions change, responsibility can still be ascribed to a named agent that enables one to speak of the 'who of action'. The term iterability, drawn from Derrida and Butler, is often used to point to what is significant about subjectivity in relation to acts, that is, the fact that patterns of action, indicative of relatively stable material conditions and inter-subjective relations, are repeatable over time in a specific habitus or lifeworld. Such performative action, in its reiteration, instantiates a particular subjectivity, and locks it into the web of relationships established by reference to patterns of behaviour recognized by significant others. Variation, or difference-in-repetition, occurs that points to a play of stability/instability in the fixing of a self. A self exists as a knot in a network of intersubjective action and understanding. It follows that change implicates transformation in that whole world. So, the problem is: how is one to account for the fact that people by and large in everyday interaction – in the family, at work, in relation to obligations and responsibilities – recognize themselves as particular selves who remain constant over time? And how is one to account for, or even bring about, change in these positionings, since the idea of post-coloniality as a to-come implies new subjectivities?

The concept of narrative identity is today readily associated with the work of Paul Ricoeur. At different points in his analysis, he has pointed to the idea of a self as a storied self, as an entity made up of stories told, indeed, entangled in the stories that a person tells, or that are told about him or her. Yet, this very mundane aspect of human beings is also a profoundly enigmatic element. We could say that human beings are characterized precisely by this fact that they invented stories, or rather narrative, as the form in which the events of a life and of a community can be figured and communicated and, importantly, kept as a memory and so transmitted across generations. Indeed, I would claim that the emergence of narrative and symbolic forms of communication are co-extensive with the emergence of consciousness and of language, specifically with the elaboration of the complex signifying systems structured in terms of the communication of temporality that today we take for granted.

To clarify this view, I will introduce the (ontological) arguments that consider temporality to be the defining characteristic of human beings. In a very fundamental way, time determines the horizon for any understanding of being. As soon as one thinks of oneselves as conscious beings, one thinks time, indeed time as lived temporality, and one cannot think time without bringing up the question of consciousness, specifically, the consciousness that one exists as a being in time, dispersed between a remembered past, an evanescent present and the anticipation of a future without precedent.[6] We know ourselves to be fateful and fatal beings, we judge our sense of being-in-time by reference to the spacing and trace of time. I am here rephrasing key elements of Heidegger, read by way of Derrida, to contextualize the arguments which explain why Ricoeur considers the having-been, the making-present and the coming-towards to be the three moments, indeed, the co-articulated moments, of the temporality of being: they mark the temporal space or horizon within which being questions itself as to its way of being. This questioning, which is the defining and distinguishing characteristic of all human beings, is thus inseparable from the consciousness of the tempo-rality of being.

Now, a basic aporia of time is its inscrutability, in that it cannot be rep-resented directly. This may well be because we are encompassed by time, so that it is impossible to stand outside it. The avenue that Ricoeur follows is to explore the possibility that narrative is the form in which the unrep-resentability of time can be overcome (when one thinks of it in the singu-lar), and the device by which one expresses the lived, or phenomenal, aspect of the temporality of being. The underlying idea is that the act of telling a story 'can transmute natural time into a specifically human time' (1984: 17). In Ricoeur's approach, the term narrative identity seems to join up two problematics, one which is about subjective identity, and a second problematic concerning the relation of history and fiction in the process of the figuration of temporality. It does so by establishing that time, and the way it is lived, provide the common ground for their co-articulation. In the elaboration of his position, Ricoeur draws a distinction between identity as sameness (*idem*) and identity as selfhood (*ipse*), that is to say, on the one hand, identity as something that remains identical to itself over time and, on the other, an entity that considers itself to remain the same in spite of changes over time, for example, in a person's biographical history. Identity is not the sameness of a permanent, continuous, immutable, fixed entity; it is instead the mode of relating to being that can be characterized as self-hood. Self is not a fact or an event, it is not reducible to the facticity of things-in-themselves. The identity of a person, or a group or a people, takes the form of stories told.

Now, although '[L]ife is woven of stories told' (Ricoeur, 1988: 246), these stories are not purely imaginary or fictional, for they make reference to a domain of reality that can be verified. On the one hand, the stories we tell about ourselves are segments of other people's stories about themselves and us, so that a self 'happens' at the point of intersection of many real lives, confirming the polysemy of otherness and selfhood. On the other hand, some of these narratives tell of events involving – indeed, constituting – a whole community or period of time, that is, they inscribe a history and a memory, so that every self occurs 'at a point of intersection between fictive and historical narratives' (Ricoeur, 1991: 186). The process whereby biographical accounts include narratives of the nation or the ethne would be a case in point – recall Tambu's grandmother's account of what happened with the advent of colonialism and her decision to overcome the limitations it imposed through hard work and acceptance. They invest concepts like the nation with an experiential thickness that unites self-identity and national identity in the imaginary.

Narrative, Ricoeur tells us, 'constructs the durable properties of a character' (1991: 195). It does so by emplotting the events of a life according to the rules of story-telling, relying upon models and styles of emplotment already existing in a culture. Furthermore, the sense of narrative identity that Ricoeur develops stresses the view that every self is 'mingled with that of others in such a way as to engender second order stories which are themselves intersections between numerous stories … We are literally "entangled in stories"' (Ricoeur, 1996: 6). But, one may ask, how do we choose them, how do we know which scripts apply to us? Is self-recognition simply the retroactive effect of a process of constitution, recalling in part the Althusserian concept of interpellation, and in part the process of (self-) disciplining and normalization that Foucault has described? Or is it more than that? Is narrative identity but a supplement to these other ways of accounting for the emergence of particular subjectivities?

Narrative identity, however, should not be understood simply as another name for biography or limited to the description of the process whereby the storied events of a life are interiorized to constitute personal identity. Indeed, Ricoeur's analysis is not primarily located on the terrain of a psychology but on that of the theory of being or ontology. Narrative identity appears in his discourse of being as the concept that enables one to think of the mediation between the phenomenological and the cosmological apprehension of time, that is to say, the mediation between time as lived, inscribed in activities in the world, pluralized in its dispersion among events and places, and time in the singular, the intuition of a dimension that cannot be derived from the experiential but encompasses and transcends it. As Ricoeur (1992) put it, narrative is the way of joining up the 'time of the soul' with the 'time of the world'. In a sense, the 'self' as a meaningful and meaning-making entity appears at the point of intersection of two kinds of reflection on our being-ness or existence. On the one hand, one finds the stories and memories that express the time of being-in-the-world and of being-with, the duration of events and experiences in the everyday: the time we reckon as we watch our children grow into adults, the time of birthdays, commemorations, the scansion of the temporal flow in each life that we keep and memorialize because they involve our 'care'. On the other hand, bound up with phenomenal time, are the questions which surface about time in the singular, thus about finitude and death, and about what gives meaning to life at the general, cosmological level. It is a matter of evaluation, guided by a history of reflection about what is liminally present in the significant events of our existence, yet that transcends biography, for it concerns the apprehension of a sublime dimension to human existence, an experience, besides, that links up with the ecstasy and epiphany of being, that is, with the apprehension of a spiritual or liminal dimension to human existence.

Although what I am saying refers to universal aspects of the experience of time, I should note that the cultural specificity of the experience of phenomenal temporality is a matter that is too often neglected in Eurocentric (and logocentric) theorizations of time, as ethnographic studies have demonstrated for some time (Fabian, 1983). Thus, in Dangarembga's novel, the interpretation of childhood in terms of readiness to embark upon household work and school differs significantly between the official early age of entry in school, stipulated by the state, and the way the villagers experience abilities and development, grounding the latter in the everyday activities of material reproduction and play rather than in abstract pedagogical concepts that assume a linear temporal process of development and privilege cognitive measures in charting its progress, as Babamukuru does. It can be argued that the alienation of Nhamo from his family has partly to do with the different perception and experiential reality of time that schooling into Western culture produces. The modern form of colonialism colonizes time as well as other dimensions of being.

So, at one level, temporality encompasses the historical and cultural space of the emergence of the who of action and meaning, and at another level, it opens onto a critical hermeneutics and to a reflection which points to the apprehension that a self 'does not belong to the category of events and facts' (Ricoeur, 1991: 193). The implications for the formation of subjectivities and issues of reconfiguration and transfiguration link up with Ricoeur's approach in a way that avoids a conceptual collapse into species of psychologism, determinism and essentialism.

On disidentification

If we try and apply the analytical apparatus suggested in the problematic of the self in Ricoeur to the lives in *Nervous Conditions*, we can see how the main characters locate themselves in their social world and understand themselves as particular selves by narrating events in their lives that link their past to the present and to the anticipation of a future. Significantly, Nyasha who claims to have 'forgotten' the past and her mother tongue, Shona, is the one person who does not have a clear idea of what or who she wants to be in the future; she appears to live in the present, the future is indeterminate. The language, English, in which she speaks this loss, this disorder of identity, is not her own but that of the other; she is unable to dwell or be at-home in it; it is the monolingualism of colonial dispossession (see Derrida, 1998). The claimed loss of the indigenous language, Shona, the language of her past, is symptomatic of this forgetting. For her, then, displacement and the loss of the mother tongue are an amputation that closes off the space for her questioning of herself as to her way of being, disembedding and de-historicizing her existence with respect to the lifeworld, so that she is thrown back upon the disjointed spatiality of her household. Tambu, by contrast, is able to reconfigure her experiences by, among other things, drawing upon her past and imagining an alternative and emancipatory future; she is able to find the tools for change.

In order to understand the mechanisms at work in subjective change, I will start with the three mimetic functions of narrative as described by Ricoeur for they provide indications for thinking through the problem of becoming otherwise. Mimesis 1 refers to the prenarrative, prefigurative features that express basic human desire; it describes a 'semantics of desire' (1988: 248). From the point of view of a particular subject's configuration of experience, one can understand the prefigurative to refer to the corpus of the already-known and the already-said, the stock of narrative understandings of the world and of subjects, inscripted in the lifeworld. It would also relate to the chiasm in the relation of body, psyche and world that was indicated earlier, so that the 'semantics of desire' can be grounded in an affective economy. In some way the prefigurative forms a cultural unconscious in which elements of a culture are mingled with elements from the psychic field.

This brings me to Mimesis 2 which for Ricoeur arises from the creative process of the (re)configuration of experience, the implication being that emplotment is not automatic or routine but involves the imagination in the selection and ordering of elements, linking the imaginative dimension of the story to a domain of reality, so that the narrative refers to real events that can be verified through testimony. This mimetic function is constantly subject to repeated rectifications that occur in the course of the subject's examination of her life. For Ricoeur, narrative identity is the result of these rectifications proceeding by way of a third mimetic function that fixes these new figurations of identity. Thus, the third mimetic relation relates back to the first by way of the transformative praxis occurring in the second mimetic function (1988: 248). In this way, every narrative identity is a reconfigured identity involving the action of a *poiesis* that accomplishes the weaving of the phenomenological and cosmological dimensions of being, working the fictional and imaginative into the historical narrative to constitute a 'third time' (1988: 245).

The models for the emplotment of experience already exist in the culture, inscribed in the practices of the everyday, dispersed in tales, novels, films, parables, stereotypes, and so on. That is to say, the models or plots or scripts that one uses to make sense of one's experiences exist as a given in the culture; we do not invent them from scratch or choose them as 'free' autonomous agents, though clearly new models and emplotments are constantly generated, especially in modernity. They include narratives that construct the horizon of expectation, instructing the subject about what he or she is meant to anticipate and desire, for instance, in the discourse of modernity about the autonomy of the subject as a desired goal. Culture, therefore, delimits the space of experience and the horizon of expectation; reconfiguration takes place within these parameters. The plots or scripts in discourses of 'identity' provide the elements for the figuration and the reconfiguration of experience, so that every named subject is not only a figured self, but one who is constantly reconfigured in the light of the narratives that all human beings apply to themselves in the process of self-questioning by reference to acts and deeds, (Ricoeur, 1988: 247), for instance, what one does and says in everyday life relating to what it means to be a man, or a mother, or a friend, or a black person, and so on.[7] The process of reconfiguration and mimesis, one can see, rectifies previous identities as a result of a self instructed by the norms and values that are constructed in discourses of identity, although the who, as singularity, remains the same, as the named person, the one who is called to responsibility (see also Taussig, 1993b). Thus, the self-reflective activity of the examined life performs a hermeneutic and critical function. Tambu's account has the characteristics of such a hermeneutic activity.

The constant reconfiguration of identity, or its possibility, raise the question of the kind of narrative, and hermeneutic practice, promoting such a process, so that narrative would allude to the 'name of a problem' (Ricoeur, 1988: 249). Theorizing this problem involves the recognition of several co-articulated elements. I would note to begin with the fact that at any point newness may ensue from action, so that the routinized habitus is constantly open to initiatives that problematize the already-said and the already-figured. Furthermore, in modernity and diasporic conditions, a disruptive newness in the form of discrepant scripts of existence or violent disruptions of the customary way of life becomes endemic. Novels, for example, at least in principle, as in NC, can provide narratives that set out to problematize the ordinariness of life. Similarly, film and other artistic forms can disrupt the givenness of the world through alternative ways of telling that affect the mimetic function of reconfiguration, leading one to question oneself in relation to the events they depict or the experiences one has (see also Shohat and Stam, 1994). Modernism in the arts was meant to introduce the disruptions of perception, and of the taken-for-granted character of the routinized world as part of its contribution to the critique of the present and thus in support of radical change. Increasingly today, the media, and specific sources of narratives such as news are shaping how people refigure their identities (Matar, 2004). It is important to point out too that the privatization of culture by media corporations and conglomerates (Canclini, 1998) has perverting effects in not only narrowing the range of the models of emplotment that are available or have authority in the process of reconfiguration – for instance, in relation to the cult of the celebrity – but in eliminating counter-hegemonic narratives. The fact that an economy of desire is an integral part of the process of transformation in subjectivity and identity means that one needs to interrogate the narratives produced and available from the point of view of the power relations they inscribe and the world-view they support through their ideological functioning.

The concept of the gaze that I introduced attempts to theorize the systematic connection between the process of identification and the process of signification by way of the functioning of the economy of desire, and what Ricoeur indicates by a semantics of desire. It is meant to keep visible the psychic level of the process of figuration and reconfiguration, thus, the level of affect, a level that is not so clear in Ricoeur. In the example about 'blackness' from Fanon, and in the case of Nyasha's return to the village after having lived in England, the positioning of the subject is brought to a crisis or problematized because the place of the gaze is disordered, interrupted. But crisis in itself is not sufficient, as Nyasha's story reveals, or in the case of forced displacement, say, with refugees, so that a problem remains about the motivation for change if one sets out to search for explanations that propose mechanisms not specified or elaborated in either the theory of ideology or in Foucault's problematic, that is, if one wants to add more specific mechanisms to the transformative role of collective agency as instituted through class or gender struggles, or broaden the view of the immanence of resistance in bodies and desires. The exploration of the diachronic dimension in the process of subjective change, already present in these other accounts, will provide further clues.

This dimension is taken up in Ricoeur when he refers to the inscription of a notion of 'traditionality' located in the conceptual space bounded by the three-fold relation of mimesis. The concept of traditionality, irreducible to tradition, is used to try and account for the effectivity of history upon narrative identity, the way in which the past affects one independently of one's will and the way one responds to the effect of history through an articulation of the past and the present. In that sense, traditionality can be understood as the term referring to the interweaving of two 'temporalizations of history' (Ricoeur, 1988: 219) that intersect, constituting particular narrative identities at the points of intersection. A 'self' happens at that point of intersection or relay where the history of a culture, sedimented and transmitted as part of its stock of knowledge – its memories and memorials, its sayings, parables, songs, myths, and so on, that is, the narratives and 'texts' in a broad sense that constitute and inscribe a 'structure of feeling' – is intertwined with the history of a named subject, constituting a particular consciousness. This is the mechanism by which we are, so to speak, sutured in history. But this suturing, which is more of a folding, requires the participation of others: as interlocutors, imagined or not, as models or ideal egos, as those in the gaze of whom recognition is bestowed or refused; they are the social elements of the lifeworld that validate particular selves. Equally, the process of suturing knots the ties that bind, as Fanon realized when his blackness became a defining trope in fixing his identity.

Ricoeur's understanding of traditionality, besides, precludes the forgetting of the past, whether it is an active forgetting (as advocated by Nietzsche), or the forgetting that result(s) from repression or disavowal (as with the occidentalist history of colonialism, or the reality of state terrorism in nationalist discourse in many postcolonial countries), or whether it is achieved by means of the obliteration of the past through a brutal break with its reality in the present, for example, in ethnic cleansing and in some forms of fundamentalism, or, more mundanely, the repressive 'forgetting' associated with disturbing and traumatic experiences. The narrative of the present must remain open to the recognition of a heritage, or roots, with which one must come to terms. There are no 'roots' without 'routes' (Gilroy, 1993a), so that roots or a sense of belonging and of place refer to the manner in which one locates oneself (or a community) in a stream of history, the attunement to a memory, an apprenticeship to a 'structure of feeling'. The problem concerns the way in which this dialogue with the past can be both dialogical and dynamic, that is, the conditions in which the reconfigurations of the past and the present can condition and mediate each other while relating to the future as possibility and as difference, implying the effects of different 'routes' (ibid.). Gilroy's work, and postcolonial history, show that the past itself, or 'tradition', must remain open to a process of rectification, and not be closed off in the assertion of a phantasized 'authentic community'.

It follows from my arguments that issues of debt and of responsibility are implicated in the notion of a judgement of history, and, by the same token, the point of view of an ethics in the temporalization of history.[8] In other words, the way history is narrated – whether as difference, repetition, as logical necessity and so on – carries with it normative and prescriptive values since, in constructing the world in a particular way, every narration attempts to persuade or direct the reader or listener to act in a certain way. For example, an account of someone's action that relies on explanations in terms of genetic determination or essential tendencies – such claims still cripple the debate about gender or ethnic difference – removes action from the possibility of a transformative practice, and thus from the possibility of change on the basis of ethical considerations such as an idea of justice (Levinas, 2001; Venn, 2000).

In this regard, one should add to the analysis of the reconfiguration of particular selves the standpoint of 'working through', by analogy to what takes place in psychoanalytic practice, and by reference to the work accomplished in the process of rememoration (see Morrison, 1987) when the biographical content of narrative identity encounters the historical rectifications performed by historians. This is demonstrated in the way that feminist and 'Black' histories have participated in the reconstruction of identity by giving to people a reconstituted past, say, in feminist history, and a different temporal framework for anticipating possible subjective projects.

In everyday practice, it is important to recognize that the most common narratives and narrations that function as models or scripts for 'identities' are now to be found in tele-technologies and novels, rather than in traditional tales, parables and so on, in which lives are emplotted and secrets of 'living well' are revealed or communicated in the form of lessons or exemplars. Furthermore, the practice of everyday life is suffused with knowledges of all kinds, including ideas drawn from or authorized by theoretical accounts, for example, about the function of sexuality in the formation of the psyche as described by psychoanalytic theory, which has become diffused as part of the stock of knowledge that people apply to themselves. In that sense, the three mimetic functions as described by Ricoeur should be read as shorthand for a very complex process irreducible to a simple linguistic event or to a cognitive process alone. The reconfiguration of identity depends on the conjunction of particular phenomena, involving action with others, and the retelling or re-emplotment of the biographical elements of a previous identity: it is a labour. It depends, too, on the quality and provenance of the narration, that is, their density, richness, depth, insight, emotional weight, voice, point of view, or more generally, everything that makes it an inexhaustible, creative source for the hermeneutic task of the 'examined life', a poietic resource that operates to disrupt normalizing closure and create newness. It is clear from my discussion that I regard *Nervous Conditions* and *Battle of Algiers* to be suitable for such a critical hermeneutics. It is clear too that theory is intrinsic to the task of reconfiguration, for neither the text nor experience by themselves tells us what to think.

A further dimension is indicated when the concept of embodiment that I sketched earlier is added to the analysis of gender, racial and other differences in the constitution of identity. To recall, Merleau-Ponty's radically anti-Cartesian view asserts, against dualism, a dynamic inter-relation between psychic and bodily phenomena, expressed in the idea of an intertwining of the world and the human, of interiority and exteriority, of the I and the other. The relation of a curve to its hollow that I have used to express it is not representable as such. It can only be apprehended in the mode of the sublime, if – developing some indications in Lyotard (1994) – one understands the sublime to be the experience through which the invisible part of the visible is disclosed to being. The sublime makes present the absent-presence which inhabits it, the elements beyond representation that thicken and endow what appears with a transcendent yet ontic or phenomenal dimension.[9] The embodied and performative character of the human relation amplifies the idea of the subject as an heteronomous, rather than an autonomous, 'I'. The world of other bodies and the world of objects constitute the 'dwelling' for subjectivity (see also Grosz, 1994). Embodiment then, according to my analysis, inscribes a relation to the other, a relation to mind and psyche, and a relation to the objectal world. A different conceptualization of subjectivity begins to emerge with this approach, consistent with a critical phenomenology, far from the modernist (or the religious) projection of Being into the endlessly deferred moment of a plenitude to come, and its inherently totalizing temptations.[10]

At the level of description, then – as opposed to the level of the economies involved – the process of subjectivity involves three dimensions – the inter-subjective or social, that of consciousness, and the material – that are analytically distinct but experientially triune. The question of affect is relevant to the analysis of the details. For now we can distinguish the three modes of temporality involved in subjectivity according to, first, historical time or inter-subjective time, which is also the time of the community or collectivity (and its metonymies, like nation, race, and the implications for how concepts like nation and race can gather to themselves the iconic force of the authentic community, erasing differences). Second, the temporal dimension of subjectivity refers to memory time and biographical time, it being understood that memory is the form in which subjective as well as inter-subjective experiences and narrativizations of events and action are folded into the interiority of particular selves. Finally, my arguments so far indicate that the body and its spatiality also function as archive and monument, the living and material repository of the time of one's life enfolding that of the collectivity. One could say that the body remembers everything, but in codes and folds and capacities. For example, there is a sense in which the hand that has learned to play a musical instrument is no longer the same hand. An associated point is that it is in an alteration occurring in the entanglement of body and the objectal world that newness is grounded.

The three modes are co-articulated in the process of constitution of every particular subjectivity. The relays and mediations linking the different dimensions of being-in-the-world are established through tropes, chains of signifiers, displacements, embodied memories, activities, and so on, each with their affective charge, that construct the symbolic and semiotic universe of signifying practices. I have tried to show that the transformation of subjectivity involves two inter-related activities: on the one hand, an anamnesis that relays the cognitive, the affective and the embodied dimensions of subjectivity in a complex, mobile and indeterminate process in which neither element is privileged,[11] and, on the other, an emancipatory politics. One implication is that for the transformation of subjectivity the domain of the aesthetic must be brought into play to provide the material and the experience through which the various dimensions and their complex flows and interactions can be worked through and reflected upon according to a critical hermeneutics. Emancipatory politics and critical hermeneutics are in solidarity for changing the subject and the world.

Agency and the politics of transfiguration

The problem of agency is central to the problematic of politics. But, since this chapter is not located on the terrain of political theory, I will not rehearse the arguments about class, or gender and other collective categories that, in some theorizations, provide the basis for thinking about the relations of force that structure political action. I will instead draw out from my discussion of the problem of identity a number of remarks that, while keeping the focus on issues relating to the (re)constitution of subjectivity, open towards other discourses, including the political. As far as the latter is concerned, it is sufficient, I think, to start with the pragmatic recognition that acts of resistance at the individual and collective level have been a permanent aspect of the history of (post)colonialism, as the long history of struggles demonstrates. All the examples that I have put to work so far in developing my analysis of 'identity' and subjectivity illustrate acts of resistance, expressed at both the individual and collective levels, often linked as in the case of Fanon and fighters of the Algerian war of liberation, and in all the other wars of liberation that continue in one form or another. Yet in each case, resistance comes to have a meaning in relation to a wider context that relays individual acts to collective goals and interest and to a political frame of reference. For example, Fanon moves from talking about his own feelings to the development of a number of lessons for the 'black man' generally and the elaboration of a theoretical position concerning identity, and an emancipatory discourse for the colonized.

If one starts from the premise that people resist, and recognize that the reasons for the 'individual' decisions and responsibility are not so obvious, one is left with the problem of a more thorough understanding of the mechanisms involved. For instance, many people in real life, faced with the kind of options available to various characters in NC, arrive at similar decisions, such as to acquiesce (Tambu's father), or 'keep a low profile' (Nyasha's mother), or indeed, to join the 'winning' side (Babamukuru). The point is that class or gender belonging, or even the recognition of injustice, though they are motivating factors, do not automatically incite resistance or dissidence. While consideration of interest, relating to a pragmatics of action, often accounts for the choice, the problem of change deals with the less visible processes relating to the judgement of the present and to politicization. My discussion of the concept of narrative identity and of the process of the reconfiguration of subjectivity triggers the question of the kinds of narrative and the kinds of critical practice that inform the process of self-reflection. All the cases I have introduced have the following in common. They appeal to narratives that invoke a common experience, for example about colonial oppression and humiliations, or gender differences that privilege males. In doing so they bring into play second order narratives. Such narratives, for example, 'grand narratives' or a narrative of the 'race', the 'nation', or narratives that Ricoeur has demarcated using the term 'traditionality', are those that constitute categories like class or the people or humanity as reference group and as agency. They involve action with others, or identity projects that assumes the participation or the gaze of others rather than an autonomous self-centred project. The affective as well as the ethical dimension are bound up with the standpoint of heteronomy or a plural subjectivity indicated in my analysis. In referring to a collectivity – 'women', 'humanity', the 'postcolonial/the colonized' – they involve appeal to categories that transcend the personal world as well as the recognition of a wrong or injustice done to the group, that is, they appeal to categories that have become politicized in the course of struggles. With regard to effects for subjectivity and identity, one must locate politicization in the context of ongoing struggles and the political culture they generate and rely upon, so that narratives can be seen to play strategic roles through insertion into such dynamics; their effects become mobile, conditioned by strategies such as counter-appropriations, creolization, transculturation, and so on, all of which are at work in the cases I have described.

They keep in view the important fact that second-order narratives inscribe a historical or temporal dimension; they keep alive a memory of resistance and oppression and direct the (reflective) gaze to a different future that can be brought about by the action of agents. Social theory (for instance, Marxism), political philosophy (say, socialism), theologies like Christianity or Islam, operate as second-order narratives; they make a claim to epistemological as well as to ethical value. Subjects are caught up in such narratives from the beginning of their formation, whether implicitly or explicitly. From the point of view of changing the subject then, one of the functions of second order narratives is to give coherence to and assign their place to the scripts that a subject draws from in reconfiguring his or her subjectivity. That is to say, they have an ideological function, if we understand the term to refer to both cognitive and affective mechanisms. Fanon's use of concepts such as blackness or (a different) humanity is an example of the way in which second-order categories and narratives, that is to say, theory, are embedded in an agonistic territory; certain narratives therefore have a tactical purchase for politics. The existence of politicized accounts of history, that is, accounts that can act as counter-discourse or in counter-hegemonic moves, means that consideration of the content of political culture becomes relevant. An impoverished or colonized political culture would minimize the possibility of discontent developing into a will to change society.

They implicitly or explicitly engage with an aesthetic dimension. For instance, a slogan such as 'black is beautiful' reorganizes the gaze in relation to the desirable. I would emphasize the central importance of the expressive arts – music, film, painting, photography, writing, dance, and so on – as the imaginative space that is able to keep as a trace the memory of other ways of being, or transmit a history of resistance, or give voice to those not allowed to speak in the public sphere. There are too many examples to cite here, a rich world of subversions, alternative visions, laughter, aesthetic pleasures, simple humanity without which one loses sight of what is really important: the dignity and fragility of human life, and so loses heart.

They implicate an emancipatory imagination, in the sense of the imagination of a future in which a current injustice would have been eliminated. A judgement of the present in terms of concepts like justice, goodness, and so on is involved here, that is, an ethical dimension is implicated.

So, the following standpoints become visible when one unpacks the mechanisms involved in agency: the political, the ethical, the aesthetic and the affective. The point is that the process of change indicates that they are co-related in practice, with the implication that the transformation of 'identity' and subjectivity must operate simultaneously at all these levels. I have tended to use Fanon as a canonical case[12] to demonstrate this co-relation because his reflections on 'blackness' and his subsequent analysis of the condition of the colonized 'other' brings all these dimensions into play: in the assertion of a different, counter-occidentalist humanism and universalism, in the recourse to a psychoanalytic standpoint about the body and identity, in the indications for a politics of resistance to colonialism and its legacy, in the search for new ideals of beauty and an aesthetic-expressive register in which to re-inscribe what it means to be black or African or postcolonial.

There are no obvious answers to the many problems implicated in my remarks above. What my discussion puts on the agenda is the importance of this whole range of problematizations, and their inter-connectedness in the search for socialities that reduce suffering and injustice. The point of critique is to make the mechanisms and processes visible. In this regard, it has been one of my aims to show the centrality of general theory in working one's way to the point of recognizing what the fruitful questions are. I have tried at the same time to show that it is the process of thinking through the issues by reference to concrete instances, rather than primarily by reference to existing theoretical debates, that enables one to problematize both theory and an existing reality. The recognition that narratives of subjectivity and identity are embedded in politicized and historicized cultural territories leads on to the kinds of issues and questions that are the subject matter of the next chapter.

Notes

1 The subaltern invokes a relation of subordination. Within the wider theoretical context of the concept of hegemony, it refers to groups that are structurally incorporated within the polity through the moral and political authority that the elite exercises (or have constituted). So, a degree of institutionalization and consent is implied in the relation of power. However, in more recent literature, say, in the work of the Subaltern Studies Group, the subaltern is ever ready to become an insurgent group, that is, to act as agency, so that authority is never secure but must remain vigilant. Subalternization would be the attempt by a dominant power, recognizing the agonistic situation in which differences in power are authorized, to maintain the conditions for subordination.

2 A comparison with Japanese modernization discussed in Chapter 2 is worth making. The main element I would highlight is that Japanese modernization took the form of a strategy developed by the Japanese governing elite to establish Japan as, economically and militarily, an equal of Europe/the West, but in order for Japan to remain culturally Japanese. The difference from the implantation of modernity in colonized countries is that modernity there was initiated by the European colonizers and meant equating modernization with Westernization, both for the colonizers and the colonized, whereas in Japan the two remained distinct, mediated by ideological goals that allowed cultural translation to be at the same time a mediation and an appropriation. Clearly, it is worth keeping in mind that mediations and appropriations are mechanisms that operated in colonialism as well – for instance, because of various forms of resistance – but the power relations are different, and the question of sovereignty or of domination needs to attend to the specific relations of force in the particular case.

3 I would draw attention to the Enlightenment sources of modern governance, and thus to the functioning of a specific notion of reason, and of the state in its apparatuses, even when these have become invisible in the way the apparatuses operate.

4 The implication for psychoanalytic theory is that it is not just the either/or of good and bad objects, but dynamics that already diffract subjectivity into the ambivalence of and/and while filling with content the liminal and sublime dimension of beingness; a different theorization of subjectivity opens up here.

5 For those interested in the psychoanalytic debate, it could be argued that it is much more than catching sight of someone's genitals, even if these were to mean anything at all for an infant. But, pleasure being what it is, and given later prohibitions, it is not surprising that sexuality comes to play the role of the dominant relay in the adventures of the gaze, once language

comes into play. I should add to this analysis the point of view of seduction (see Papoulias, 2002), here not reduced to sexuality, but to a particular intimacy, 'performed' in the manner in which an infant and a 'carer' must 'capture' each other's attention and secure attachment to each other if they are to co-dwell in the world as a bonded unit, the parent–child dyad.

6 I should stress that Ricoeur, following Heidegger, understands being to be the entity that questions itself as to its way of being. The importance of this standpoint is that it liberates ontology from cultural particularisms and proposes an understanding of being that prioritizes the temporality of being, as Augustine recognized well before modernity. There are difficult philosophical arguments that need to be rehearsed here, for it is not at all obvious that time is fundamental, or that the idea of consciousness necessarily implicates that of temporality. Apart from the philosophical reflections, for instance as found in Augustine, Husserl or Heidegger, developed in the work of Levinas or Ricoeur, there are arguments that bring into play the point of view of complexity when we think about an entity whose mental capabilities are sufficiently developed to produce self-consciousness. One may well wonder whether other animal species are conscious of themselves as specific entities and can imagine themselves as an element in the scheme of things. It is not simply a matter of memory either, for other animals remember, as shown in their action premised on a past knowledge. There is no evidence though that nonhumans have the means for keeping records or memories; this requires collective techniques and agreements, a complex language, involving the communication of the past and crucially, the communication of temporality. We could explore what mechanisms are necessary for this to happen, for instance, systems with feedback, which all machines that learn from experience need to have, including the brain. The emergence of human language, in the sense of an indeterminate system of signification, open to newness or creativity, seems crucial in the development of this level of complexity. It is correlated to the development of commensurate complexity at the level of relations among individuals belonging to the group. The determining concept must be that of the future, or rather futurity, that is, the ability to or the possibility of imagining or anticipating a state of affairs without precedent, the ability to imagine in the present a situation in which newness comes in the future. One key concept to think through here, in relation to ontology, is finitude: the fact that we know in advance that we must die.

7 There is always the temptation to limit the indefinite character of the process of articulation, and thus the anxiety of uncertainty it provokes, by attempting a 'fusion of the horizons' (Ricoeur, 1988: 221, following Gadamer) circumscribed by the space of experience and the horizon of expectation. The implication for the analysis of subjectivity is that, on the one hand, there would be a notion of a subject-in-process, open to rectifications conditioned by unexpected forces, and, on the other, the fusion of horizons that prescribes their coincidence or correspondence, so that identity is no longer abandoned to the undecidability of futurity but is always-already reinscribed and contained within the horizon of the already-determined. It is, as we know, the point of ideology to produce closure through the fusion of horizons, for instance in the form of the functioning of a totalizing doctrine or discourse, or a metaphysics of transcendence.

8 I should point out that although history takes the form of a narration, it is important to avoid reducing history – the history of a community or that of a particular self – to a species of fiction, and thus abolish the question of truth, for instance, regarding the Holocaust or colonial oppression or an individual trauma. Ricoeur insists on maintaining the polarity between the two, using the notion of debt to make visible the responsibility which history owes to those who have been, namely, the responsibility to ensure that historical narrative does not fictionalize the dead, thus, killing them twice over, but must 'return their "having-been" to them' (Ricoeur, 1991: 186).

9 The sublime, it could be said, is a passional experience of the thrownness of being. Equally, one can understand it as an effect, at the aesthetic-expressive level, of the apprehension of the ungrounded aspect of being. To that extent, the sublime is an intimation of the 'there is', in the Levinasian sense. It relates at another level to what one tries to bring to presence in/through the arts, that is, a dimension and a space that opens being to its strangeness (for itself and for others) (Santner, 2002), so that the new may appear and be welcome.

10 The notion of the other as host opens up a relation to history and to the inter-subjective such that it is possible to imagine the body as the monument in which the time of one's life and the time of the community are inscrypted, that is, we can propose that the body functions as both text and crypt, the site of inscription as well as of burial, the at once legible yet secret place in which are recorded the events and experiences of a life. So, like narrative, corporeity too is a guardian of time in that it is the field (or 'clearing', to use Merleau-Ponty's – *pace* Heidegger's – terminology) in which space and time interpenetrate to produce 'a historical landscape and a quasi-geographical inscription of history' (Merleau-Ponty, 1968: 259).

11 The mechanisms involved in this process of change clearly cannot be accounted for within the model of the self-steering mechanisms which the discourse of self-management describes, or within the model of social construction alone. The former, although it posits the folding of an outside within the subject – for instance, to constitute a 'soul', as in Nikolas Rose's (1989, 1996) work – does not make a place for the unaccountable, liminal element in the process of formation; the latter model does not deal well with the psychic and spiritual dimensions of subjectivity, thus with affect, or, besides, with the question of embodiment.

12 A question about who may speak or act for whom could be raised here, relating to the debate in postcolonial studies about voice and address – for example, the accusation that those working in Euro-American academic institutions cannot speak for indigenous/native peoples or make claims that appear universal since these claims are specific to particular theoretical (mostly 'Western') standpoints. If the question is: did/can Fanon claim to speak for black people?, I would argue that readers of Fanon (and other activists and theoreticians), have so far been able to draw their own lessons for politics and theory from his reflections, without having to ask for his credentials. One must remember too that in circumstances in which the oppressed are denied the right to tell their stories, others must bear witness to what is happening; it is a question of responsibility for what is done to one's fellow beings. Of course, there is no reason to heed any particular author/speaker, even if issues of authority get, rightly, entangled in the debate. The problem is bound up with the constitution of intellectual elites, and the effects they can have in spite of the negligible proportion of the population that actually reads any theory. A wider problem about intellectuals and power is at stake here, and a problem about the kinds of material that may feed into a critical politics, irrespective of its provenance.

4

Towards a Postcolonial Political Economy

> Let's begin at the beginning. What does privatisation really mean? Essentially, it is the transfer of productive public assets from the state to private companies. Productive assets include natural resources. Earth, forest, water, air. These are the assets that the state holds in trust for the people. In a country like India, seventy per cent of the population live in rural areas. Their lives depend directly on access to natural resources. To snatch these away and sell them as stock to private companies is a process of barbaric dispossession on a scale that has no parallel in history. (Roy, 2002: 136)

The place of political economy

This chapter adds the concerns of political economy to the agenda of postcoloniality established in the course of the previous chapters. It aims to bring to light the apparatuses that have been put into place in the form of assemblages and technologies to constitute the current state of the world, and to interrogate the values and assumptions that underlie the practices of domination and exploitation they authorize. A vast literature has emerged, epitomized in Roy's unequivocal condemnation of neo-liberalism in the quotation above, that exposes the ravages of global corporate capitalism and impugn the new forms of creating 'accelerated poverty and accelerated wealth' (Joxe, 2002) that is being institutionalized through the neo-liberal extension of the rule of the market to the public sphere and the domain of the social. This intensification of disparities in the distribution of wealth and capabilities coincides with a shift in the process of globalization from a long period characterized by extension to a period characterized by intensities that one can detect in a diversity of forms, for example, the compression of time/space in relation to communication and exchange (Harvey, 1989), the speeding-up of flows (Virilio, 1986), the production of 'superprofit' driving economic strategy (Sassen, 2000), the amplification of risks and insecurity (Beck, 1992; Boltanski and Chiapello, 2000), the exponential growth in technologies of 'hyper speculation' (Arnoldi, 2004; Lee and LiPuma, 2002), the growth of complex mega-cities (Koolhaas, 2002; Sassen, 1999), the privatization of culture (Canclin, 1998, 2001), and the current intensification of surveillance and violence alongside accelerated exploitation. This knowledge adds to the growing conviction that alternatives to prevalent disordered empires are both possible and absolutely necessary. In that context, the focus on a dissident political economy has a strategic value for postcolonial critique.

The most obvious reason for rethinking political economy within the frame of postcoloniality is the recognition that the transformations in the world economy that have taken place in the course of the past 30 years or so have left no country in the world outside their loop. The diversity of terms deployed to make sense of the changes, for example, global corporate capitalism, finance capitalism, neo-liberalism, glocalization, Empire, cultural economy, new world order, information age, stands as an index of the complexity and scope of the forces that now operate across the globe; they pose a challenge for theory that I have tried to address through the conceptual vocabulary that I have been establishing in the book. It could be argued that radical theorizations already exist in the early critiques of 'development', mostly established from a Marxist perspective in the period of the cold war, for example in the analyses elaborated by those who have addressed the question of the economy within the framework of imperialism and neo-colonialism, for instance, in Samir Amin (1974, 1976, 1998), Gunther Frank (1967), Giovanni Arrighi (1972), Paul Baran (1959), or in the approach described as world systems theory, notably developed in the work of Wallerstein (1974, 1980, 1989).[1] What unites these critiques, written in the wake of decolonization, is the conviction that the state of the economy in what was located as the 'Third World' could not be understood outside the perspective that regards asymmetries, uneven development and global economic inequalities to be the combined effects of forces and tendencies inherent in capitalism that European colonialism had unleashed upon the world, generating geo-political relations of power that systematically (re)produce or reinforce these effects. While this influential work remains in the background of any analysis of the global economy, the search for alternatives must account for the changes while opening up new theoretical and political agendas for the critique of the present.

In what follows, I will broaden the scope of the postcolonial critique of the economy, taking as point of departure some of the themes that have appeared in the important work that directs attention to the dynamic and reciprocal inter-relationships of the economy, politics and culture. This explicit rejection of the demarcation of these categories in conventional political economy in underlined in Robert Cox (1987; Cox and Schechter, 2002) who has elaborated a neo-Gramscian position in terms of three categories of forces, namely, institutions, ideas and material capabilities – in other words, natural, technological, and organizational resources – that operate as a 'dialectical triad' in shaping the world order. These capabilities, institutions and meaning-making practices – Cox points to the centrality of communication technologies and communicative practices – together determine ways of being and doing in any specific space. Cox emphasizes the importance of the social context of production and of relations of authority in shaping the social relations of production. Together with the internationalization of the division of labour and the integration of the labour force within the capitalist organization of society, these changes point to the accumulation of social power in correlation to the asymmetrical accumulation of the rewards of production. It is an approach that re-inscribes the centrality of power in the processes involved, thus opening them up for the kind of analysis I have been developing in preceding chapters. This means moving away from the perspective of inexorable laws of development or from the point of view of invariant structural determination. It also allows one to move towards the examination of conditions of possibility, genealogies, assemblages, flows, dispersions and turbulences, that is, the natural and social technologies of worlding a world, historically specific, that have constituted existing ways of making and being, a different, if related, project.

At the level of practices of production of culture, Canclini (1998) has examined the case of the reorganization of culture through the Multinational Agreement on Investment (MAI) proposed by the Organization for Economic Cooperation and Development (OECD) to reveal the intricate workings of the financial, legal, technological, ideological assemblage that ensures the 'constitution of a unified world economy', as the director of the OECD candidly expressed it. The measures, that show clearly the intent behind the agreements and legislations, include putting an end to the right of governments to limit the acquisition by corporations of public companies being privatized, new rules to extend deregulation to transnational investment in films, television, publishing and cultural sectors, granting corporations the right to claim compensation for damages and curtailment of profits arising from government policies, the curtailment of the ability of governments to take action against any damage that corporations may inflict on the environment. The shift in power towards the mega-corporations is clear in this policy of 'liberalization'; for Canclini, the effect for artistic creation and for the kind of cultural works produced is an homogenization that is bound to 'narrow the very possibility of integrating and discussing what emancipation, renewal, expansion and democratization might mean' (ibid.: 5), precisely the aims he says are inscribed in the radical ideals of modernity. However, artistic output over the past few years shows that spaces for dissidence and critique still exist in the postcolonial/postmodern world, sometimes in the most forbidding conditions, as in Iraq today.

With regard to the question of hegemonic and counter-hegemonic discourses and practices implicit in Cox's approach and Canclini's analysis of global culture, it is worth juxtaposing Derrida's (2002) assessment of the relation of truth and trust, and thus of stratagems seeking either consent or else pacification, to the current functioning of the 'tele-technosciences' in constituting worlds. His remarks appear in the context of the discussion of the relation of faith to knowledge against the background of the 'return of the religious' and its figures – 'tele-techno-media-scientific, capitalistic and politico-economic' machines (ibid.: 78). The economic here enters into a complex network of relays that obliges one to question its functioning by reference to its location within an order, and an ordering, of technoscientific interventions and technical performativity that conform to a basically capitalistic rationality. He says: '[T]oday, there is no incompatibility, in the said "return of the religious", between the "fundamentalisms", the "integrisms" or their "politics" and, on the other hand, rationality, which is to say, the tele-techno-capitalistico-scientific fiduciarity, in all its mediatic and global-izing dimensions' (ibid.: 81). The agenda for political economy that this juxtaposition of Cox and Derrida makes visible is the fact that the systems of thought that establish the rationality and authority of the current post- and neo-hegemonic orders increasingly operate, on the one hand, through discourses with a claim to scientificity and truth and, on the other, through new technologies that performatively stage these truths, and that have a relay or dispositional function with regard to them, serving politico-economic power. The crisis in the form of judgement about the good relates to the self-referential nature of this machinery for fabricating truths. Therein too lies the question of faith. I shall establish in the course of my develop-ment of a postcolonial political economy the affiliations of neo-liberalism with a fundamentalist faith or trust in the rationality of an order that in effect reconstitutes existing relations of power and capabilities. A problema-tization of the question of hegemony is indicated in Derrida's reference to the effects of an ensemble of apparatuses hinged by relay concepts. For, these are machines that manufacture consent-distraction through tele-technologies, and manage security through a military–police–surveillance assemblage. It is a war machine (see also, Curtis, 2005).

One could contrast the problematic of political economy indicated above with the 'capabilities approach', which elaborates another vein critical of conventional economic theory, but from a different (radical liberal) pers-pective, developed by Amartya Sen (1985), Sen and Nussbaum (1993) and Martha Nussbaum (1995, 2000, 2002) in their attempt to establish differ-ent grounds for judging the performance of the economy and realign social policy. The approach rejects the criterion of utility that underlies economic calculation of cost and benefit regarding state policy, and emphasizes instead human well-being and agency. It rests on the grounds that human beings have an intrinsic worth, and should be the ends of economic devel-opment and not the means. This shift turns attention to issues of participa-tion, thus of power, in the shaping of the freedoms that enhance the ability of human beings to enjoy the things that make life worth living and fulfill-ing; it points to disparities in the distribution of capabilities among nations and groups, based on gender, race, and so on. The implication concerning the just society is that economic development should address problems of the more equitable development and distribution of human capabilities beyond the contractarian paradigm that circumscribes neo-liberalism as well as old-school liberalism.

In proposing a postcolonial political economy, I want to shift the grounds of the debate towards the kind of ethnography of power and ecology of culture/cultural ecology that the terms I introduced earlier indicate. There are several components to this task, beginning with the critique of the cur-rent world dis/order that makes visible the co-articulation of economic and geo-political interests at work in shaping that order. Part of this critique will

125

return to the analysis of occidentalism that I have established in the course of the book regarding the triadic relationship between rational capitalism, the Western form of colonialism and instrumental or positivist modernity, particularly the emergence of a militaristic logic alongside the predatory thrust of capitalism and the universalizing drive of modernity understood as a Manichaean civilizing project. I will use the case of the development of 'big dams' to show the co-articulation of the networks of inter-locking socio-technical apparatuses, cultural values and discursive formations that in their specific combination determine what happens on the ground when one speaks of modernization and development.

My argument is that, in any culture, over the years values and beliefs become hard-wired in the substantive logics inscribed in the institutions and knowledges and the specificity of their ordering or arrangement that constitute practices of the everyday. This means that although the conditions of possibility of any specific practice are historically contingent, they also have a cumulatively structurizing effect, limiting what can be thought and done at any particular time, at the same time as they make possible the constitution of a world (see also, De Landa, 2002). I illustrate this through a thematically organized account of the global economy in postcolonial times. One of the aims here is to show the disparity between theory and real economies as a way of further undermining the assumptions and calculations that frame strategies of development and social policy. It will become clear in the course of the analysis that the autistic and inhuman tendencies in capitalism have become intensified with global corporate and finance capitalism. The ongoing colonization of the public sphere by the language and practices of neo-liberalism therefore presents a moment of grave danger for ideas of the public good and human well-being grounded in ethical considerations. In the light of this, I return to the issues of justice and ethics in my concluding section, where I suggest an alternative ontological and ethical foundation for a concept of justice to guide the move towards transmodern and transcolonial forms of sociality that would be non-oppressive and non-exploitative.

In order to clear the ground for establishing the parameters for this critique, I shall begin with an examination of a number of interrogations of the economy in relation to globalization and world order that have appeared recently. These interrogations have been developed from a diversity of standpoints, ranging from liberalism, which acknowledges that there are serious problems with capitalism but believes that they can be fixed (Stiglitz, 2002, or Gray, 1998), to post-Marxism where it is argued that it is only through the supersession of the current order can the problems that beset the contemporary world be resolved (Hardt and Negri, 2000; Joxe, 2002). Other critiques direct attention to the transformations that have reshaped the economy, technologies, identities and societies in the past two decades or so and propose a new analytical language. One can mention, as indicative examples, Castells (1996, 2000) studies of the information age, Sassen's (1998a, 2002) interrogation of the hypermobility of people and money in generating hyperprofits in the global economy, Featherstone et al.'s (1995) analysis of the dynamics shaping the mutations of global modernities, Tomlinson's (1999) examination of cultural imperialism and global cultural mediations, Sen's (1985) macro-economic and historical arguments for sustainable development and Mann's (2003) analysis of the 'American empire' in relation to the new form of militarism that sustains it. They establish a background of knowledge against which one can understand the efforts of dissident movements to elaborate a global political culture capable of initiating change, many of which are documented in the accounts of the World Social Forum by Fisher and Ponniah (2003) and Jai Sen et al. (2004).

Prolegomenon to critique

The broader historical and postcolonial perspective against which the critique of political economy can be located includes aspects of occidentalism that I indicated in earlier chapters, particularly the values inscribed in colonialism and technocratic modernization and the co-articulation of capitalism and militarism, operating at different levels, at first strategic but that has increasingly become systematic and ideological in scope. My examination in Chapter 2 of the emergence of imperial governmentality and of disciplinary systems of subject formation and social regulation pointed to the resilient effects of imperial governance and capitalist expansion on the technologies of the social that were invented in the nineteenth century, institutionalized at the level of state apparatuses and law. In relation to the mutations of capitalism and globalization since then, there are several phases that are worth noting when thinking about corresponding attempts to analyze the relationships from the point of view of political economy. It is taken for granted now that a form of globalization emerged with European colonial expansion, shaped by the context of the universalizing, world-transforming project of modernity, that differs in significant ways from other cases of global expansion such as those pursued by the Chinese or in relation to Islam. What is striking about the modern phases of globalization is the correlation of global economic reorganization with global war and universal 'progress', and the extent to which the colonies, and from 1955 the 'Third World', have been drawn into these transnational grand stratagems of power.

I want to draw attention to one aspect of the genealogy of globalization that throws a different light on the question of the worlding of the present world and its underlying order, namely, by reference to the apparatuses and technologies, the 'dispositif', that enact globalization. My focus concerns the relationship of the economy, ideology and militarism looked at from the point of view of shifts in the conditions of possibility. My periodization of the processes distinguishes four phases following on from the great expansion of Europe and the construction of the West since 1492. The first relate to the First World War, tied to the 'second industrial revolution' and imperial rivalries – European, American and Japanese – on a world scale, then to the Second World War involving the clash of totalitarianisms and the different economic strategies corresponding to them. Both phases saw the drafting of the colonies into the conflict, with significant consequences for decolonization, and the emergence, as part of post-war settlement, of new apparatuses that frame world governance, for example, the (now defunct) League of Nations after the First World War, the United Nations and its various bodies, the World Bank (with the US Treasury holding a 51 per cent controlling share), the International Monetary Fund, the World Trade Organization and other international organizations regulating trade and international law, and new military alliances like NATO. One should add to this the emergence of a global culture (Featherstone et al., 1990) at the level of new tele-technologies and cultural forms that actively produce the sense of inter-connectedness and co-presence at the international level that reconstitutes a global imaginary in the first half of the twentieth century – the spread of the cinema and technologies of telecommunication such as cable and radio, new forms of world transport such as the airplane, world sport instantiated in the Olympic Games and world championships in various sports, the spread of a cosmopolitan urban architecture, the re-articulation of modernity and consumption, for instance, exemplified in the emergence of the department store in many cities throughout the world, 'vernacular cosmopolitanisms', that nevertheless share common elements. They are the technologies and apparatuses that worlds the global in the period up to the cold war.

From a postcolonial point of view it is important to see the cold war as the next phase, in the form of the Third World War, namely, the struggle for hegemony between liberal capitalism and communism, that has largely been fought on colonial and postcolonial soil, involving most of the countries of Africa, Latin America and Asia that formed the tri-continental alliance in the shape of the Third World. The latter was set up by the non-aligned states at the Bandung Conference of 1955 precisely to avoid being forced to opt for either the Soviet or the Western blocs, with the limitations such options imposed about the possible direction of development. Yet the reality is that the global economic and military stakes in the Third World War has meant that no country, from Vietnam to the Congo to Bolivia, has been able to avoid being positioned as one domino in a line of dominos, to recall the doctrine formulated by the American Secretary of State, J. F. Dulles, and so escape being drawn into the strategic calculations of the major powers. The result has been the systematic and relentless destruction of socialist routes to development in the Third World, through a long series of coups, military interventions, wars, destabilizations, assassinations and ideological struggles.[2] They have utterly distorted decolonization (Venn, 1998).

My line of analysis suggests the world has entered a fourth phase, characterized by a global 'war on terrorism' and extremism and by universal surveillance; it puts in place the institution of a permanent state of emergency; it is intolerant of dissidence and alternatives; it seeks a 'society of control'. This ongoing Fourth World War is motivated by the colonization of the lifeworld and all productive activity by neo-liberal practice and values, in alliance with Evangelical Protestantism. The stakes in this war concern the emergence of a 'new world order' constituted through new apparatuses and networks of world governance, alterations in the relation between states, control over international law, shifts in geo-political power relations, the development and dissemination of new technologies, the formulation of new political goals and new forms of enclosure enacted through the transfer of wealth from collective to private holdings. Although mediations by local forces and circumstances have markedly altered the effects, it is clear that the history of the postcolony makes no sense outside the context of these global conflicts.

A postcolonial political economy, thought within this broader perspective, makes visible the stakes fought over in the internationalization of socialist and liberatory struggles that developed with these different phases of globalization: the Russian Revolution of 1917, the emergence after the First World War of organizations and movements such as the India Congress Party (1922), the Chinese Communist Party (1922), the Congress of the Peoples of the East (1920), the Pan-African movement (1919), Brazilian and Mexican radical artistic and political initiatives (1924), the Harlem Renaissance from the 1920s; then the upsurge of decolonization after the Second World War, followed by the violent liquidation of socialist projects in the 'Third World' in the period of the cold war. Today the stakes focus on the imperium of corporate capitalism and the global intensification of pauperization as a consequence of liberalization and marketization. This genealogy of the present, configured in terms of the correlated imbrication of militarism and capitalism, makes it increasingly clear that neo-liberal globalization attempts to bring to completion, and naturalize as 'the end of history' (Fukuyama, 1992), the institution of an inhuman capitalism.

The postcolonial intervention in political economy is further motivated by the fact that too often experts in poor, that is, pauperized, countries, often trained in the 'West' or on the basis of Western knowledges inscribed in programmes of study that are a legacy of imperial governmentality and occidentalism, implicitly accept the authority of these knowledges when they argue for policies of 'development'. Often they and national leaders rely on, or are persuaded to accept, the advice of experts about 'development' and 'modernization' that assume the validity of particular paradigms, for instance, the 'liberalization' of public utilities and markets, that are in fact disadvantageous from the point of view of redistribution and autonomy. Liberalization makes it legitimate for corporations and firms to acquire publicly owned utilities, lands, enterprises and resources; in other words, it allows the conversion (a new form of embezzlement) of collective wealth into private property, abolishing the absolutely vital distinction between wealth and property that Arendt (2000) emphasized. The extent to which the indigenous and the global experts share a vocabulary of action, and thus agree on calculations regarding what is to be done – and, besides, share a common cosmopolitan cultural capital – predispose the two sides to circumscribe the problems within the same conceptual space. An ironic recent case of this form of epistemological imperialism is that of countries including Palestine and South Africa which have sought advice from precisely those who are intent upon a restructuring of the world's economy which is intensifying the transfer of wealth from the poor to the rich, in this case, the Adam Smith Institute, a well-known neo-liberal bastion keen to privatize publicly owned assets of all kinds everywhere as part of a strategy of total marketization (*Guardian*, 2 January 2004: 23). Another pertinent case concerns Structural Adjustment Programmes, foisted upon struggling economies, but sometimes freely adopted, as in Pakistan's current Five-Year Development Plan on the assumption that they actually provide the right solution for 'imbalances' in the economy or for redressing the 'inefficient' allocation of resources. Such expert discourse empties the economy of politics (Teivanen and Wallerstein, 2002), thus ideologically naturalizing the established system of power by converting the question of the common good into decisions about a choice of techniques for managing change towards pre-established ends. Yet, the new phase of pauperization that is in process is transforming societies and politics in ways that raise fundamental issues of value. It is the central task of postcolonial theory to open up to a critical gaze the machinery of pauperization, depoliticization and disenfranchisement which has been put into place in the new world order, in the hope that different theorizations would authorize alternative courses of action and alternative ways of being. I can but outline some of the issues within the scope of this chapter.

My analysis of modernity and modernization in earlier chapters has shown that conventional approaches within the social sciences, when limited by paradigms that inscribe the disciplinary, as opposed to critical, relations of power/knowledge, neglect too much the processual and conditioned character of the dynamic interactions between the social, the cultural and the economic. The latter focus brings into visibility the fact that processes of formation of the social and of subjectivity operate on the basis of the hybrid assemblages made up of strings and networks of mechanisms that are pragmatically put together through grafts, syncretic mixtures, creolizations and borrowings that accompany the diasporic movement of peoples, techniques and ideas. Similarly, the approaches that theorize these domains in terms of 'levels' insufficiently account for the mechanisms that constitute specific ways of being and thinking, for instance, regarding the imbrication of culture and the economy in the processes constituting identity as I examined in the last chapter. This separation is very much an aspect of the positivist methodology still dominant in the social sciences; it is echoed in liberal political discourse that disaggregate the political into relatively autonomous segments rather than theorize their co-articulation (Lefort, 1988). While, admittedly, the subdivision and disaggregation of social phenomena have analytical advantages, especially from the point of view of governance based on the concept of the nation-state, to treat them as separate and distinct kinds of activities, without history, has the consequence that the historicity and complexity of actually existing societies are inadequately theorized.

Furthermore, the approach here is informed by the conviction that in order to ask how people live, what they aspire to, how they describe their identities, what values they support, what preoccupies them, what future they envisage, what world they wish to live in, it is vital to recognize the dynamic interactions between the economic, the social, the political and the cultural in the making of the conditions that determine the means of existence and ways of being in the world. This suggests a pragmatics of everyday existence that attends to the inter-subjective institution of the lifeworld, (Castoriadis, 1987) and the interpenetration of culture and the economy at the level of actors' understanding of the situation and their assumptions about common worlds that frame situated judgements about action (Cox, 1987, 2000; Boltanski and Thevenot, 1991). Culture, of course, is a meaning-making activity; it inscribes norms, values, knowledges, ways of being, and social imaginaries that are performatively instantiated in the everyday world and that constitute appropriate subjectivities. In the new global economy culture itself has become productive, (Lash and Urry, 1994; du Gay and Pryke, 2003) and is increasingly commodified (Canclini, 2001). The implications for the analysis of culture, bearing in mind the standpoint of tele-technologies that I introduced above, puts on the agenda a complex problematic of power that must recognize the multi-dimensional play of knowing, being and desiring in determining social action. Additionally, the framing of the colonization of the domain of the political within the gestalt of commodity makes this colonization more total than in previous periods of modernity, obliging theory to rethink the nature of the social order which is being established. It is worth remembering that the co-articulation of culture and the economy, and the dynamic and shifting form of that relationship, are something that has been persistently asserted or implied in the writings of 'postcolonial' activists and theoreticians such as Amilcar Cabral, Kwame Nkrumah, Che Guevara, W.E.B. Du Bois, Mao, Mahatma Ghandi, sub-commandante Marcos. The location of their thoughts and action is intimately bound up with the fact that, as 'organic intellectuals', their struggle to change history had to draw on living history, inscribed in the everyday, to refigure the anticipation of a better future that connects with people's experience of oppression. These are all reasons for breaking with conventional political economy.

Liberal interventions

So, what points of departure enable one to map out the outline of a new space for the critique of political economy? In the interventions I mentioned above, one encounters at one end of the scale liberal thinkers who, alarmed by the widening inequalities and imbalances in the global economy, advocate restructurings and reforms that nevertheless will leave capitalism intact. For example, Gray (1998) sees 'global *laissez-faire*' as the culprit when he claims that the project of organizing the world's economies into a single universal market is a utopian nightmare, beholden to a vision promoted by Enlightenment ambitions, that creates all sorts of instabilities and produces fundamental disruptions of cultures and economies that are bound to make the whole system unworkable. Instead of totalizing homogenization, Gray argues that one should allow varieties of market capitalisms to co-exist within some flexible regulatory framework.

Another denunciation of excess comes from Mann (2003) who uncovers incoherence at the heart of America's attempt to establish a new world empire, arguing that America's vision of world domination, detected by the left, liberals and conservatives alike, is driven by a militarism that is economically irresponsible, politically schizophrenic, ideologically confused (ibid.: 13). Yet there is planning and intent: 'Do not think that US policy toward Kyoto, land-mines, Star Wars, Iraq, Iran, or the Southern Philippines are *ad hoc* or unconnected. They are all part of the grand strategy for a global American Empire, first envisioned as theory, then after 9/11 becoming reality' (ibid.: 2). He lists the developments and the key figures that over the past 15 years have put together the policies and strategies that determine US action today. The policies have their origin in neo-conservative thought, documented in the declarations of people like Rumsfeld, Cheney, Wolfowitz, Perle, Bolton and others, argued for in papers such as the 'Defense Planning Guidance' in 1992, and 'Rebuilding America's Defenses' in 2000 sponsored by the Project for a New American Century. These documents favour the development of new weapons of mass destruction, they reject treaties that curb US autonomy; they scorn the United Nations and propose unilateral military action to defend American interest.

It is clear in Mann's account that the programme for 'world domination' is directed by veterans of an implacable war against every form of socialism, welfarism, and everything that stands in the way of total pure market and corporate sovereignty. So, there seems to be a case for claiming that an ideologically recognizable position underlies the US economic grand plan, indicating in principle a connection between the economy, ideology, military power and political strategy, although, as I have noted, Mann argues that the present articulation of these aspects reveals incoherence, due partly to the historical complexity of the multilateral relations of power established in the real world and partly because of the one-tract mindset of the American militarism that imagines it can bring about a new unifying order through overwhelming force (ibid.: 266). However, the events of 9/11, its brutality and unexpectedness, provided a trigger to implement the aims of the Project, allowing the American government to recast them in terms of a war of 'good versus evil', itself a re-coding of the connection between the Project's goals and Christian (Evangelical Protestant) fundamentalism that betrays the twinned effects of religious dogma and the mythical narrative inscribed in the Project's military scenario. An interesting twist is that the rhetorical political spin rewrites the European imperial notion of a civilizing mission in the language of the 'humanitarian rescue' of indigenous people from 'despotic rulers' or from those who threaten mass destruction in the pursuit of a war against 'Western civilization'. America it seems promises perpetual peace so long as one accepts its 'benevolent hegemony' (ibid.: 10); this means accepting that she is 'the economic engine of freedom, opportunity and development' (US Trade Representative, 2001, cited in Mann, 2003: 49). It announces the institution of a new 'manifest destiny' (see Chapter 2).

I have introduced Mann's thesis of an 'incoherent empire' because of his emphasis on militarism when surveying the current global scene, although his focus on America tends to obscure the role of 'America' as signifier in neo-liberal, corporate capitalism. Yet, while he catalogues so well the decisions and policies that have shaped the contemporary geo-economico-political map, he limits the analysis to conventional approaches when it comes to ideology and the economy, for example, seeking evidence of 'hegemony' in, among various sociological factors, the relative popularity of American media in the world (a declining share as it happens), rather than in underlying narratives and scenarios of the good life, the good society, desirable identities and lifestyles and the values inscribed in them. Similarly, he points to the business-driven interests in American economic policy-making, concerning the setting of tariffs, the distribution of aid, investment strategies, the settlement of debt, and so on, without questioning the presuppositions of development or the structural forces that determine the direction of policy. His focus on American imperial plans obscures the role of the signifier 'America' as a node and 'point de caption' in the totalization of the neo-liberal corporate capitalist doxa. My point instead, or in addition, is that the colonization of the domains of the social and of the political by forms of communication deriving from advertising (Mattelart, 1994), and by forms of calculations originating from accounting practice invented within the framework of capitalist interests, means that critique must address the fundamental assumptions and substantive logics, hard-wired into key institutions, thus having structural effects, that are at work in perpetuating existing power relations. Significantly, Mann's conclusion that a possible change of government in the USA would avert the catastrophes being created by the neo-conservatives fails either to question the status quo or to recognize the longevity of the processes that condition the present distribution of power, opportunities and liberties in the world.

A pertinent economically-informed analysis is that of Joseph Stiglitz (2002) who has been on the inside (as the former chief economist at the World Bank, awarded the Nobel Prize for economics in 2001) and is therefore able to speak from the point of view of one who once was instrumental in implementing policies in principle designed to spread the benefits of globalization but which he acknowledges have had the opposite effects of causing 'devastation' for 'developing countries' (2002: ix). He blames the 'ideology' of the 'Washington Consensus' wedded to older, market fundamentalist economics, and the 'politics' of those in power, as well as the IMF's faith in the neo-liberal doctrine that asserts that 'markets, by themselves, lead to efficient outcomes' (ibid.: xii). However, his abiding trust in the capitalist economic system produces a reformist analysis, grounded in the supposed insights of 'new economic theory' (ibid.: 221). Nevertheless, in the course of his critique, he catalogues the disastrous policies pursued in the name of the market and of adjustment programmes, occasionally balancing the story with claims that for many people 'low-paying Nike jobs' are better than 'growing rice on the farm' (ibid.: 4), or that 'opening up the Jamaican milk market to U.S. imports in 1992 may have hurt local dairy farmers but it also meant poor children could get milk more cheaply' (ibid.: 5). No mention is made of the frequently reported cases of firms using these policies to dump out of date stock, or the hidden costs of these structural changes. The liberal paradigm framing his analysis prevents him from understanding the present reality in terms of a genealogy of exploitation and oppression that retraces their conditions of possibility in the soil of colonialism and imperialism, conditions that have become institutionalized in the apparatuses of global governance and trade and in the authority of dominant knowledges; they over-determine that power and capital operate in the way that he has so convincingly unmasked.

A recent case to illustrate this point is that of Vietnamese coffee, encouraged by investments from the World Bank to expand production in the areas deforested by the use of 'Agent Orange', used as a weapon of mass destruction during the Vietnam War. This unsafe coffee, produced by cheap labour, itself one of the consequences of the war, now dominates the global market and has led to the collapse of the price of coffee beans and the unemployment of millions of people throughout the world. The crisis has been created by the combination of deregulation caused by the abolition of marketing boards, promoted by the US government and the IMF, and the policy of corporate power in forcing the price of commodities to its lowest level (Wild, 2004). The analytical failures in Stiglitz are offset by his recognition that deregulation of the financial sector generated the Asian financial crisis, that Mafia capitalism and asset stripping in Russia were the result of hasty privatization without the establishment of institutional and legal structures to manage transition, that privatized monopolies are worse than state monopolies, that the marginalization of the role of government at the expense of the market have often allowed the interests of profit to prevail over social and environmental concerns or the securing of public goods (2002: 220ff.). I shall examine a range of cases later to show the inadequacy of limiting analysis to a survey of 'preventable' failures while keeping faith with the view advanced by Stiglitz that new improved modern economics could deliver the solutions if only policy-makers would follow its recommendations (ibid.: 221, 222).

Before turning to Hardt and Negri's thesis, it will be salutary to focus on the tragic case of ex-Yugoslavia to make absolutely clear the weakness of liberal reformist critiques. Here is an example of the sustained and planned destruction of a rival economic model carried out in the name of the neo-liberal corporate grand plan of a 'unified world economy' with stunning disregard for human suffering. In his study, Merefield (2004) argues against the explanation of the disintegration of the region in terms of the idea of 'Balkanization', that is, the claim that the eruption of ancient ethnic conflict is the result of the failure of the socialist model. He focuses instead on the arguments developed by Magas (1993) and Chossudovsky (1996) that the strategic interests of Germany and the USA had laid the basis for the disintegration of Yugoslavia, helped along by the role of external creditors and global finance institutions. These arguments point out that up until 1980, Yugoslavia had managed to run a successful market socialist economy that combined policies of multiculturalism with self-managed labour, which meant that the labour force was not open to casualization or flexibilization and the economy could not be penetrated by global market forces. Chossudowsky (1996) points out that throughout the period from the 1960s to the 1980s Yugoslavia had become a regional industrial power with annual GDP growth of 6.1 per cent; it had free medical care, high literacy rate and high life expectancy. Far from being a 'failed state' it represented an alternative to the model and policies advocated by the global market economy.

American policy under the Reagan administration pushed for a 'quiet revolution' or 'regime change', as it is now known to bring this non-conformist state within the fold of market capitalism. From 1980 the US and international creditors began to impose several macro-economic reforms regulated by the IMF and the World Bank, aimed at destabilization. A new financial aid programme was negotiated in 1989 to include the devaluation of the currency, a wage freeze, large cuts to government spending, the elimination of worker-managed companies and the liberalization of foreign investment laws. Merefield notes that 'By 1990 industrial sector production was declining by 10 per cent per annum, and the decade-long dismantling of the welfare-state neared completion. In addition, debt-restructuring had increased the level of foreign debt, and mandated currency devaluation had hit hard at the living standard' (2004: 7). Furthermore, IMF Central Bank's monetarist policy greatly reduced state finance for economic and social programmes, the money being diverted to debt financing instead. These measures hastened the crisis of the state so that Yugoslavia's federal fiscal structure collapsed, boosting secessionist tendencies along ethnic lines, driven by the wealthier republics of Slovenia and Croatia. From 1989 to 1991, Western consultants completed the scuttling of Yugoslavia by advocating the forcible bankruptcy of 'failing' businesses, the eradication of social banking replaced by profit-oriented new institutions. By 1991, 'real wages were in freefall, social programmes had collapsed, and unemployment ran rampant. This dismantling of the industrial economy was breathtaking in its magnitude and brutality. Its social political impact ... was tremendous' (Best, 2003: 369, quoted in Merefield, 2004: 8). The consequent ethnicide, inept military interventions and the criminalization of the army of refugees

(Merefield, 2004) have become tragic chapters in the history of neo-liberal globalization and liberalization. What is interesting is the evidence that calculations and strategies directed by macro-economic framing of objectives, and merciless will can set in motion and coordinate a combination of apparatuses, institutions, laws, subjectivities, technologies to ensure capitalistic restructuring takes place, whatever the human cost. The complexity and sophistication of the assemblage put to work, and the militaristic logic guiding its conduct, make talk of the 'right theory', as in Stiglitz, or appeal to modernist humanist ideals as in liberalism look either wishful or naïve.

Towards alternatives

At the other end of the scale of theory, there is no question that the system as a whole, and capitalism in its various mutations are to blame for the economic problems and the many cultural and environmental disasters that have beset the world. Hardt and Negri (2000), for instance, speak in terms of the emergence of a new Empire and a new form of rule, announced through the ruptures and shifts that they detect in globalization and in the reorganization of production and labour. In their, albeit problematic, analysis of the new postmodern world order, Hardt and Negri claim that what characterizes the emergent Empire is a new form of sovereignty, distinguishable from the previous imperialism in that it is de-centred, de-territorialized, machinic in the mode of its operation, sustained by the 'multitude' across weakened nation–states, and able to manage 'hybrid identities, flexible hierarchies, and plural exchanges through modulating networks of command' (2000: xii, xiii). Global capitalism has made possible the integration of economic and political power into a single power that over-determines them in a 'unitary way', combining them in 'a new inscription of authority' (ibid.: 9). It is establishing a new model of the production of normative and juridical instruments to establish 'pacification' and a universal order. The authority of Empire derives from the claim that it has the capacity to bring about a just order. A new form of sovereignty is being organized, with America as the exceptional state. Yet, Empire produces its counter-empire in the forces of the multitude; the latter is a constituted yet disparate force, 'immaterial' and 'living labour' in all its forms, its energy now increasingly deriving from intellectual and affective labour (ibid.: 208, 209); they resist incorporation. We are, it seems, far from the model of sovereignty that emerged with the post-Westphalian (1648) European imperial project that was centred on the concept of the nation–state and was concerned with inter-state respect for territorial boundaries (in Europe) as part of establishing territorial rule. Its authority was founded by reference to a governance applying to bounded constituencies, although, as I have shown in the last chapter, the European imperial ambition, incited by capitalist accumulative and appropriative expansion and the universalizing scope of the project of modernity, was driven by an inherent globalizing impulse.

One of the chief merits of Empire has been to direct attention to a longer timescale, or *longue durée*, thus the succession of slow and rapid sequences of change and the complexity of the conditions of possibility, and to cultural factors in the developments whereby capitalism and the modern form of sovereignty had become hegemonic in the period of modernity. The **genealogies** that the authors reconstruct include what they call the 'dialectics of colonial sovereignty', which they analyze in terms of its constitutive effect for the discourse of the Enlightenment and for the foundation of the European nation-states. Hardt and Negri claim that the postcolonial world is still kept in a state of subordination, subsumed under capital in the process whereby 'the outside is internalised' (ibid.: 226) and integrated in the global order of capital. Their analysis links the genealogy of capital and that of the state from the modern phase to the postmodern/hypermodern phase, citing Braudel's (1977) argument that 'capitalism only triumphs when it becomes identified with the state, when it is the state' (in Hardt and Negri, 2000: 236); this, they argue, is being realized with the emergence of a 'disciplinary society'. In the latter, a 'factory-society' is instituted and the 'civil society is increasingly absorbed into the state' (ibid.: 243), with implications for the kinds of subjectivity that are constituted for it.

I shall return to some of these themes at the end of this chapter. It is clear from the range of analysis that I have noted that the economy cannot be understood within the paradigms of economic theory but must be relocated within a broader canvas encompassing at one end the standpoint of complexity, flows, creolizations, and translations in the constructions of the assemblages that constitute the contemporary world, and at the other end turbulences and alternative narratives of becoming, thus the implications of a radical, non- or post-liberal ontology. To that extent, although this chapter imports some material from the territory of Development Studies, it remains attached to that of a critical cultural analysis, as the discussion of method in Chapter 1 indicates. Additionally, the inter-disciplinarity of critical postcolonial analysis, together with the complex reality of the postcolony, condition this shift in focus; it suggests a different theoretical approach to the analysis of the present, informed by the kind of departures I summarized and knitted together in the first chapter in terms of a critical phenomenology. In that context, the focus on a dissident political economy has a strategic value for postcolonial critique.

The greater common good?

I began this chapter with an epigram from Arundhati Roy's exposé of the catastrophe which developments such as 'big dams' inflict on countless people because it encapsulates the many problems that afflict postcolonial countries, connecting them in its narration in such a way that a different questioning of the present begins to emerge that goes beyond the economic level of the problem. The most salient feature which her account reveals is the inhumanity inherent in the neo-liberal capitalist mindset that today is able to objectively ordain the elimination of whatever and whoever stands in its way, and thus appear as surplus to requirement or as negative costs in its calculus; it is the evidence of its autism. Roy fixes our attention onto the appropriative impulse in the neo-liberal strategy of privatization, particularly the transfer of public, collectively owned and established wealth into private ownership. As my discussion later shows, it is a form of dispossession more total than that undertaken by the 'enclosures' in seventeenth-century England or in France in the early modern period (Braudel, 1977, 1981–84), for what is erased in today's episodes of dispossession is the cultural and material landscape that sustains particular ways of being, their places and regimes of memory (Nora, 1984–93; Radstone and Hodgkin, 2003), and the conditions of their possibility. In cases like the big dams projects, it amounts to a form of cultural genocide, reminiscent of the (partially successful) colonial destruction of cultures through the combined forces of evangelization, modernization, and Westernization.

However, my arguments and those of Roy are not about a choice between the 'modern, rational, progressive forces of "Development" versus a sort of neo-Luddite impulse – an irrational, emotional "Anti-Development" resistance, fuelled by an arcadian pre-industrial dream' (2002: 47). In any case, 'traditional' peasant or village life in 'developing' countries is not exactly a haven of gender and ethnic equality, and is far from an existence untroubled by varieties of exploitation, and by illnesses and hardships. The stakes are elsewhere than in this knee-jerk conventionalized position-taking that re-inscribes the modernity versus tradition divide, or the technoscience versus indigenous customary knowledge split that obstructs a serious interrogation of the present reality, as I have tried to demonstrate in previous chapters. The fact is that the reshaping of societies worldwide, which has begun, implicates a new phase of pauperization, with lasting far-reaching effects that a postcolonial political economy must attempt to open up to a critical gaze.

First, in order to tease out the intertwined threads, let us take a closer look at Roy's account in which these threads are woven into a story of unequal exchange and distribution, of appropriation, mismanagement, profiteering, of cultural, human and environmental disasters, of global NGOs' doctrinaire machinations, and of course resistance or turbulence – it is in the habit of the natives to be turbulent. It starts with a bird's eye view of a doomed community in the Narmada Valley, or better, a community whose doom has been foretold in corporate boardrooms and law courts, in government committee meetings, in countless gatherings of engineers, experts, bureaucrats, consultants, all pooling knowledges (excluding indigenous knowledge) and amassing all kinds of data to make the decisions and draw the plans about the building of the Sardar Sarovar dam, calculations that have set in process the tragedy that Roy depicts. Curiously, it seems that the World Bank offered to finance the building of the dam two years before these calculations had yielded a decision either way (2002: 68); later it was forced to withdraw because of local resistance and reports highly critical of the project. Strategies about 'development' tend to be keen on such projects and the loans necessary to carry them out are readily offered. The small print in Development Aid reveals other stories. For instance, the World Bank Annual Report of 1998 shows that India between 1993 and 1998 paid the Bank $1.475 billion more than it received. In the end there are some simple questions: Who pays? Who benefits? Who profits? Of course these questions may become as complicated as one wishes, depending on whose side one is on, and on how many points of view one is prepared to credit.

The title of Roy's account 'The greater common good', with its trenchant irony, places the exposition alongside a history of transformations and changes that were, or are, also meant to be in the interest of the majority or for the benefit of future generations, usually abbreviated in the unimpeachable slogan: The National Interest. The history of the greater common good tells good and bad tales: New Deals, the welfare state, liberation struggles, as well as Stalin's murderous social engineering, the Khmer Rouge's Cambodian social and cultural reconstruction through extermination, great public engineering projects like the big dams or nuclear power undertaken in the name of progress and development that multiply the risks of accidental catastrophe; more recently we have the tale of neo-liberal privatization, or what is more innocuously called 'remodernization' by some of its advocates, that is, another form of 'progress'. Often the disputes get overwhelmed by technical matters, and one is supposed to let the experts decide; or one's representatives. So, concerning the common good, democracy, mostly of the procedural variety, gets to play a hand, as dummy, in this game; and, somewhere down the line, justice appears, calling for accounts.

Roy's narrative of the Narmada Valley gives us a glimpse of the community, 'older than Hinduism' (2002: 43) about to be washed away apparently for the worthy sake of bringing irrigation and clean water to the whole people. But, as the story unfolds, we find some serious discrepancies in this tale of 'progress'. Dams do not work, as the experience in the 'First World' has shown – they cause floods, spread diseases, get silted over after a time, destroy existing habitats while producing new ones that may not be as rich or diverse. A worrying consequence is that the land becomes waterlogged, which causes salinization when salt levels reach over 1 per cent, a toxic level for plants. So, the land needs extensive drainage systems, a cost left out of estimates of the cost of building dams, because otherwise these would be 'too expensive'. And they displace large numbers of people. As Roy points out, in India, in spite of the claims by development agencies, big dams have produced irrigation disasters and floods and have not greatly benefited those meant to benefit, as the disappointments with the Green Revolution shows (ibid.: 53). It is a fact that more food has been produced since independence but no government-sponsored studies exist to show the part played by new dams in this; one estimate works it out at 12 per cent, more or less the amount of grain consumed by rats in the storage facilities where India's 'surplus' grain is kept (ibid.: 59–61). It appears too that land cultivated using water from wells and appropriate technologies are more productive.

The displaced have not benefited, do not benefit. Roy describes the lives of the inhabitants before and after eviction from their land in terms that recall the kind of de-traditionalization and dis-embeddings that have happened elsewhere in the wake of marketization. A cultural ecology of the way of life of these people shows the inter-relations of geography, environment, nature, culture, historical memory and sociality that structured their existence and was lived as the durability of the world that grounds ontological security. They once had the rivers and forests and pastures to give them everything they needed: crops, food for their herds, a wide variety of fruits from the woods, fish from the rivers, thus a great deal of what they needed that was free, recovered from collectively available resources. The important separation of wealth from property, underlined in Arendt (2000: 207), is exemplified in the everyday existence of the inhabitants of the Narmada Valley (and other regions such as the forests of the Amazon or Africa or in the Australian outback). The villagers existed mostly outside a monetary economy, in communities actively constituted in the networks of labour and the inter-relations and dependencies, at once cultural and economic, which sustained their way of life. Significantly, they are politically and economically weak ethnic minorities, Adivasis and Dalits, mostly small farmers with no title to the land they cultivate or graze, forming a small percentage of the whole population but a majority (60 per cent) of all those displaced by the 3,500 big dams that have been constructed in the past 50 years in India, numbering a conservative 30 to 50 million people. They have largely been paid a cash compensation (males only) and left to swell the cities with cheap labour, unable to cope with or acquire quickly enough the new knowledges and skills they needed to survive in their new environments. Many eventually ended up in the sex industry or as the quasi-slave sweated labour producing goods for the global commodity culture. Their bondage is the price they pay for the modernization programme carried out in the name of 'development' and the greater common good, the inevitable collateral damage of 'progress'. Clearly, some people, in India and elsewhere, do benefit. Roy gives ample evidence of the opportunities and rich pickings that become available in the wake of these development programmes; she notes the vast sums earned by consultants, including experts on Environment Impact Assessments and resettlement programmes, contractors of all kinds who advise on 'development' in former colonies.

The story does not end with the dams, for it has become clear that a bigger strategy is at work in these schemes, as transnational corporations like Enron, Bechtel, General Electric, Rand move in for a share of the assets, through acquiring power plants and other utilities – immediately increasing prices, as Bechtel did, by 300 per cent, in Bolivia in 1999, with obvious political fall-out – and selling generators and other heavy plants for which there is no other market (Roy, 2002, section on power politics). In India, the deals made with Enron involved scrapping agricultural subsidies and increasing the price of water to 'realistic' levels; it will destroy small farm agriculture along with countless lives, and it will cost the state and the people billions, one way or another.

The logic of the new economy

The case examined by Roy is interesting because as one unravels the threads one finds that it reveals in microcosm what seems to have been happening more globally in postcolonial countries. It would be too easy to invoke a worldwide conspiracy to account for these regularities and trends, although enough evidence exists to point to the networks of agents, agencies and institutions – for instance, Davos, the Adam Smith Institute, the IMF, the Brookings Institute, the Project for a New American Century, plus an army of experts and consultants, networks of power/knowledge, government departments – that purposefully create the conditions and the ground rules for the acquisition as private property of the common wealth of people and the hyper-exploitation inherent in neo-liberal capitalism. Furthermore the workings of finance capitalism, now the dominant sector of the global economy (Arnoldi, 2004), mean that the drive to acquire assets to underpin the share value of corporations is relentless.[4] However, one is entitled to wonder if particular logics are at work here, inscribed in a conceptual framework and in institutionalized practices, working through interlocking routines and vocabularies of action as well as in the manner of a political or cultural unconscious, that is, inscribed in habits of thought, regimes of familiarity and conceptual categories that routinely structure the gaze and circumscribe action (Boltanski and Thevenot, 1991). In this regard, one can point to two sets of scaffolding that structure these situated and pragmatic logics.

On the one hand, one finds the apparatus of a globalized economy, put in place in forms of ownership, financial institutions such as banks and stock markets, the structure of conglomerates, management practices, trade arrangements and agreements, legal structures, agencies of regulation like the World Bank that together ensure that transactions between the parties take place within particular limits and according to particular rules (Harvey, 2003). In other words, when one examines the framework within which practices that in their combination determine the economy, from the licensing of products and patents, the servicing of debt, the distribution of risks, the determination of intellectual property, to the allocation of resources, one finds the assemblages describing a modern techne. Its genealogy would reveal the mechanisms and apparatuses, the technologies of production, distribution and regulation, contingently constructed in response to specific circumstances and interests, that work according to the substantive logics inscribed in them, rather than the logic of an abstract rationality. They combine instrumental and theoretical calculations and specific appropriate subjectivities apprenticed into their articulation in practices. For example, the assemblages or 'dispositifs' that exist make it possible for the USA to allocate to itself the right to bypass the patenting laws, as happened with the drug Cipro after Sept. 11th (Klein, 2002) and so use generic drugs by defining its situation as 'a state of emergency'. By contrast, the USA (initially at least) vetoed the option of African countries declaring a state of emergency that would have enabled them to use generics to combat the AIDS crisis. My point is that the apparatus does not exist that would allow South Africa to veto the USA's use of Cipro. An incidental but vital aspect of the episode is the confirmation that the USA can declare itself to be the exception, the only state not bound by the laws applying to all others, a mark of its current sovereignty (Agamben, 1998; Harvey, 2003; Venn, 2002); it is a gesture that has been repeated in the American refusal to sign international treatises, even including the Convention on the Rights of Children, and recognize the jurisdiction of international law courts over its own action or citizens.

I should emphasize both the processual character of the practices, combining the dynamic interaction between the level of structure – say, the system of banking – and that of the experiential – say, the performative aspect of tasks and communication involved in banking, to do with technical skills, codes, gender and other relationships – as well as the constitutive character of the interactions that take place, open to the effects of power, and changing according to the grafts, creolizations, and translations of ideas and practices that are part of the initiation of change. Interestingly, subjectivities are in some sense framed into the setting to work of the aggregates of technological and human apparatuses, lived as lifeforms by participants, as Knorr-Cetina and Bruegel's (2002) studies of the relationship of traders and markets demonstrate. The assemblages form inter-locking networks through nodes or hinges or knots that function as relays for the flow of decisions, agents, technologies, objects, money, values. For example, the IMF acted as a relay in the Narmada Valley project, connecting technology transfer with the circulation of funds, correlating the flow of technosciences with banking and finance capital so that they conditioned each other at the level of process and effects. The IMF is an exemplary case for clarifying the picture of the inter-locking mechanisms involved in global governance, and for illustrating the methodological apparatus that I began to develop in the first chapter. Its genealogy shows a mutation in the form and scope of its operation from its initial role from 1944 to the 1970s of intervening in the economy of the industrialized member states in order to help them achieve their goals. As Pahuja (2004) has argued, from the 1970s its regulatory and financial functions shifted to three aims: that of coordinating loans to the 'South' from other states; the enforcement of conditions attached to these loans (conditionality); and the shift from 'hard' to 'soft' powers of enforcement, using the internal laws of recipient states as part of the mechanisms. This latter shift brought 'matters considered to be domestic concerns within the legitimate purview of the IMF' (ibid.: 163). Interestingly, these developments' 'coalesce around an "informational turn" taken by the Fund' (ibid.: 163). What this account shows is that globally the IMF functions as a knot connecting strings of financial institutions to other kinds of strings, namely, those relating to international and trade laws, to knowledge flows, to diplomatic lines of communication, to informal links connecting powerful players on the world scene that in their combination form the networks of economic and other activities operating within the frame of assemblages – relating to the political, to knowledges, to cultures, tele-technologies, to the law. Together they perform the tasks of global economic governance.

The historicity of these assemblages and flows is something to bear in mind, that is, the fact that they arise from already existing conditions, including resistances or turbulences, that shape the shifts and mutations and inventions that produce new devices or dispositifs for subsequent developments; they are at once rhizomatic (Deleuze and Guattari, 1981) and structural, depending on whether one is focusing on the micro or the macro level of the processes. Thus, in examining existing postcolonial economies, the reality of colonial legacies at the level of the material and social worlds, that is the equipmental level in the Heideggerian sense, cannot be left out. Equally, the turbulences that disturb the flows, provoked in the case of the Narmada Valley by the movements against the big dams and the environmental destruction they cause (Roy, 2002), enter into the analysis, here forcing the withdrawal of the World Bank.

On the other hand, at the level of authorizing narratives and legitimating devices, one needs to examine the discourses and shuttle concepts, and the appropriate subjectivities and their know-how, that now operate in the calculations that order the circulations and exchanges between the different sectors and 'scapes'. These rely on material as well as immaterial factors, namely, specific discourses, say, about how the economy works, or about what modernization means in pragmatic terms, the perceived interests of groups and thus the force of ideologies and their effects for specific subjectivities positioned in institutional settings and expert practices. Thus, in terms of the embedded logics in contemporary culture, it is important to underline the fact that they rely on the authority of quite specific concepts about the economy and society that are consistent with a particular worldview, so that their analysis directs attention to the standpoint of hegemony (and counter-hegemony and disorder and multiplicity) and, further along, to ways of being, thus to issues of an ethos, issues that are outside the economy as conventionally understood. The constitution of this world-view relates to the epistemological and ontological principles that came to circumscribe the discourse of modernity, discursively organized into an episteme in the course of the institution of modernity. I have shown in Chapter 2 that this interweaving into congruent networks occurred in part because of underlying homologies or affinities, in part because of contingent but contemporaneous emergences, in part because of calculated rationalizations, through the apparatuses of modern governance driven by the shifting interests of power, in part because of the effects of the sciences of the social and new technologies of disciplining subjects and populations. I highlighted the gradual privileging of the cognitive over the affective and ethical dimensions of human existence, in affiliation with the notion of a self-sufficient, autonomous, rational subject who is positioned as the agent of history and knowledge. This privilege is consistent with the logic intrinsic to capitalism whereby relationships between people are expressed in the impersonal, dehumanized and abstract language of the relationship between things (what Marx had analyzed in terms of reification and alienation). The post-modern re-articulation of the violence of abstraction is expressed in the discourse of economic and technological efficiency and progress that self-referentially operationalizes the legitimacy of goals in the technical and performative specifications determined by the discourse itself; this self-referential foundation of legitimacy over-determines the institution of the system as a closed system since every feedback reflexively maps into the system itself, as Lyotard (1984) has shown (see Chapter 3). One increas-ingly finds this totalizing cognitive mindset or gestalt at work at all levels of corporate management structure and government and administrative orga-nizations, expressed in the mantra of new management.

The hinges of capital: property, accounts, instruments

A crucial concept within the conceptual framework of capitalist techno-cratic reason is that of property, specifically in the assumption that every-thing is alienable in the form of property and can thus be exchanged through a market (Waddingham, 2004).[5] Furthermore, the market operates to instantiate the equivalence of objects and other entities at the level of value, with money as the common denominator of value. This idea of property has now become common sense, functioning as a central element of capitalist doctrine, in spite of the fact that the basis of ownership invokes principles that have been constantly contested in the history of colonialism and in rad-ical political theory. We need to bear in mind here that wealth, in the system of classification used by governments and global organizations, is measured according to norms and criteria that apply to money economies, an approach that implicitly discounts non-monetary arrangements, for instance, common ownership of land, or customary use and systems of barter which do not translate into a monetary value or do not conform to a market economy. These qualitative aspects of 'traditional', or rather non-monetary and non-capitalist lifeworlds, count for nothing and do not compute in the language of the World Bank and the IMF, although they sustain countless communi-ties and are worth a lot more than the outrageous 'one dollar a day' bottom line used in NGO-speak. I shall call this wealth, invisible to capitalist accounting practices, unless and until someone wants to acquire it, 'collec-tive capital'. In the Narmada Valley case, it was the wealth that sustained hundreds of villages and secured the way of life of their inhabitants, however inadequate that might have been from the point of view of 'development', modernization, social security and, indeed, equity and justice.

If we were to apply Locke's principle that one may own as private property anything with which one has 'mixed one's labour' (Locke, [1690] 1963), it is hard to see on this principle alone how most of what is given in common and exist naturally such as rivers, mineral resources, air, forests, and so on can be appropriated by individuals or companies. Locke, we know, added the principle of making efficient use of resources, as sign of rationality, an argument deployed to justify colonial dispossession; but it is a circular argument, given that the criterion of efficiency at work in the argument re-inscribes the presuppositions that found the capitalist and rationalist discourse of property (Venn, 2000). It could, of course, be argued that if one has a legal right to own land, then one owns *ipso facto* the riches that go with it. But that ownership right universalizes principles that rest on culturally incompatible ontologies, for instance in the case of Native Americans and Aborigines who do (did) not regard resources held in common such as land as something that can be bought and sold at all (see also Patton, 2000). The case of the Narmada Valley dams brings up the question not so much of who 'owns' the rivers and the forests and communally constituted 'wealth', as to the ontological and legal status of common and social wealth and thus the form of its 'ownership', and the legitimacy or illegitimacy of its sale.

A further point must be considered here, relating to the legal status of the corporation. For some time now, the invention of the incorporated company with limited liability in the shape of the joint stock company has resulted not only in the separation between ownership and control, but more importantly, in the institution of a new legal entity with a legal persona of its own, independent of the owners of stock. As Neocleous has argued, 'the development of company law had produced a new form of legal subject, the private corporation, and a new from of property, the share ... Capital had become a fully fledged "person" in law' (2004: 4). There are important consequences from the point of view of allocating responsibility, as is shown by the consistent failure in the UK to secure compensation from corporations for accidents at work in spite of the many legal cases (ibid.). The matter of responsibility covers greater ground, for the corporation owes legal responsibility to the shareholders alone and not to workers, let alone 'society' at large. The working of the stock exchange, particularly the shift in the ownership of stock and shares to financial institutions and funds, mean that the corporation is driven by the need to maximize profit and thus secure the best return for the shareholder. This logic relies on calculations and accounting practices that have no place for the human. A study of the market in derivatives, and its generation of hyperprofit from 'financial assets derived from (the futures of) financial assets' (Arnoldi, 2004), shows the extent to which capitalism has entered a self-referential stage, creating markets out of markets on the basis of informational technologies of the virtual that enable values to be created on the speculation about future values (Venn, 2006). When we consider that the turnover of exchange-traded derivatives in the first quarter of 2003 was $197 trillion, compared to the annual turnover of global GDP of $47 trillion (Janneau,

2003, in Arnoldi, 2004), we must acknowledge that a new scale is emerging that is now driving capitalism, with consequences for the value of the share which is now subject to these new forces. The virtualization of the notion of property through new informational technology makes it all the more urgent to reconsider the foundation of the notion of property.

The displacement of the issue of property onto the terrain of ontology triggers another set of questions, particularly concerning responsibility and the idea of the just society. To begin with, one must recognize that the idea of property trails in its wake a prior question about the status of entities that may be considered as property at all, and thus bought and sold or exchanged. Already it is generally recognized – but for how long? – that there exist certain parts and elements of the world that must remain collectively 'owned' or available to all, for example, the open seas, the air, the Arctic regions, the great national parks. They are an intrinsic part of the common good to the extent that free access to them is a basic condition for life (the air), or because private ownership would deprive others of the means to sustain the idea of community at all or would so impoverish the quality of life that a situation of fundamental injustice would be created. It is interesting that neo-liberal discourse, in privileging private property and its understanding of freedom in terms of individual right to property and its private benefits, acknowledges that the issue of responsibility, especially in the sense of social responsibility central in liberalism, must be relegated to a subsidiary problem of political economy (Friedman, 1962; Nozick, 1975; see also Ryan, 1987). For all these reasons, it could be argued that any transfer of ownership from the common or social wealth to private holding is illegitimate (and often amounts to theft, as any study in detail of the actual transactions would reveal, *pace* Roy 2002; MacIntyre, 2003).

Clearly, some concept of natural right and natural justice operates in these arguments, and related to it, the problem of different traditions that found these concepts and authorize differences in conduct. The capitalist discourse of property is one such tradition; feudal relations in their different modes (European, Asian, African, Arabic), some sadly still operating, constitute another, though the former has become universalized and globalized as the rational and authoritative position. A genealogy of such discourses would reveal the historical conditions and the processes whereby an originary violence underlie major instances of the acquisition and unequal distribution of wealth. The legitimation and institutionalization of such originary violence through legislation are evidenced in, for example, the dispossession of Aboriginal and Native American lands or that of tribal lands in the Amazonian forests. Other cases of an originary violence that institutes or enlarges private property include the many instances of mis/appropriation: enclosures in Europe, enslavement following military campaigns, 'carpet baggers' in the USA; Kleptocracies and neo-feudalisms; biopiracy today.[6]

The point about legitimacy becomes clear if instead of rivers or oil we think about the sale of human beings in slavery, in the past and today, or the fact that not so long ago wives were seen as the property of their husbands;

in some parts of the world, children and women are still treated as property and sometimes sold into capitalist forms of slavery. The massive traffic in child labour in what amounts to forms of bondage is made possible only on condition of the existence of a market for such labour and the assumption that children can be reduced to the status of property. No one would regard such practices as ethically acceptable. It follows that if one were to alter the ontological status of the earth, what is regarded as common sense or natural today may well be thought of as inhuman and barbaric in the future. This is why I tried to show in Chapter 2 that the specificity of modernity depends on the particular character of the discourses – concerning property, the rational unitary subject, the status of the state, the rationality of the sciences – founding the modern period and its political economy. This particularism about legitimating discourses applies equally to all other periods and cultures, so that it is not possible for any culture to hide from the need to confront the founding principles of its mode of existence, for example, by claiming either exception, or the universality or superiority of its own beliefs. The thrust of my argument is that an incommensurability exists between the neo-liberal and capitalist language of the market and property and that of the communal good which asserts instead the primacy of the relation to the other and the primacy of the social, with implications for the question of value.

An important aspect of the new authorizing narrative is the determining role of instrumental rationality in governance, including in the constitution of appropriate subjectivities for the functioning of the apparatuses of production. The disciplinary techniques involved in this process have developed through the co-articulated emergence of technologies of the social that connect the barracks with the schoolroom with the factory with the family with the law courts to establish the machinery of normalization working to form and regulate subjects and citizens (Foucault, 1976; Bhabha, 1994; Henriques et al., 1984). This constitutive assemblage has entered into the discourse of nation building; it is seen as the superior rational means for defining and instituting the 'common good'. Within its perimeter, the signifiers of modernization, of development, of the national interest, and of economic and technological efficiency have gradually acquired a metonymic force, united under the signifier of the common good that has amplified their authority (see also Pheng Cheah, 2004).

Instrumental technocratic rationality, also, acts as a conceptual relay for the military spirit of corporate capitalism. The corporate mode of calculation operates a non-human, non-zero-sum game that has intensified the inhuman character of the older variety of capitalism. Accounting practice completes the erasure of the specificity of human values, reducing them to a profit and loss, private/privatized cost and benefit balance sheet measured according to monetary criteria within the frame of the market. Accounting practice enables the market to function as the neo-liberal embodiment of Hobbes' Leviathan, operating as Law and principle of Sovereignty.

In short, corporate strategy and language cannot consider human and humanitarian factors – except as input in its calculations or in the fabrication of an advantageous corporate image, that is, as propaganda. Quite apart from the long history of the co-articulation of capitalism and militarism, exemplified in the processual consolidation of European colonialism as I have shown in Chapter 2, and more recently repeated in the militarism described by Mann (2003), this form of institutional autism relates to the fact that it has to deal with forces and factors that appear as aggregate entities that are not in the control of any one agent or agency: raw material supply, interest rate, labour supply, technological innovations, demand, the vagaries of fashion and taste, rivals' strategies, natural processes and events, the operation of the stock market, and so on. The language and tropes of corporate and capitalist market practices – terms and expressions such as win/lose, strategy, logistics, making a killing, take-over, capture, price war, aggressive bid, lean and mean, bear and bull market, and many more – establish an **imaginary** which is thoroughly imbued with the values of aggressiveness and violence. Corporate goals are the defeat of the enemy/rivals/obstacles in win/lose situations; there is no room for care of the other, except as part of a 'war of words' to win a pay-back in terms of approval rating, or as a tactical investment in symbolic capital. The affinity between the mentality of war and aggression and business practice is instantiated in the technology of formation of managers, for example, through training processes that draw upon the vocabulary of military thinking including team-building and leadership, and on the 'toughening' courses based on military training that have become part of normal practice. In this way social actors are formed that inscribe an aggressive, militarist, bullying, egocentric form of subjectivity encountered in business practices and, increasingly, in political and social institutions. An important point is that they also privilege and constitute a specific form of masculinity (Johnson, 2004). The 'revolving door' practice facilitating the exchange of personnel between the military and business reflects the affinity that actually exists. In short, for the capitalist corporation, business is war in another form.[7]

In terms of a world-view in relation to hegemony, one must point out the convergence of the hegemonic discourse of modernity and of the West into the standpoint I have called occidentalism. It sets Europe up as the centre and model for the development of the rest of the world. Not only has occidentalism provided the basis for legitimating colonialism and given exploitation an ideological cover in the guise of the civilizing mission, it accrued to itself the signs that lent the project of modernity its historic significance and 'rightness', and, in tandem with it, gave Europe and the West their specific meaning as the model and initiator of the 'progress of humanity', expressed in Kant's (1884) view about the historic universal role of Europe (see also Derrida, 1997a). The legacy of occidentalism as a mindset in the form of the paradigm of 'development' still benefits the 'West' and disadvantages the rest.

Regularities in the exercise of power, and coordination at the level of the substantive logics operating in the apparatuses of power that have effects that could be called 'hegemonic' are constituted in this discursive and socio-technical complex in which the norms of occidentalism and of capitalism have become normative. But is consent thereby assured? In his discussion of power and authority, Joxe recalls the Hobbesian view that 'consent creates power but power also creates consent' (2002: 122) in order to tease out the basis of the legitimacy of sovereignty in the concept of the protection of the multitude. Protection is needed from disorder and from the conflicts that arise from class and gender, and one should add, ethnic, antagonisms. The authority and legitimacy of a hegemon – the Market, an authoritarian state, the Leader, the totalizing doctrine, an imperial power – rest on its ability to protect all its subjects. In the *Empire of Disorder*, Joxe argues, power relations 'have become increasingly asymmetrical ... rights are violated everywhere' (ibid.: 152), while the hierarchy of violence instituted in the nation-state has been transformed into a generalized threat of terror embodied in the form of para-military forces that assassinate in the interests of global financial interests and mafias. The political regime of global Empire for Joxe has become an unstable hybrid of sovereignties punctuated by the shift in power towards corporations whose leaders exercise considerable power in politics. This process is not as new as Joxe makes out, although the question of sovereignty has come to the forefront, since the colonization of politics by corporate capitalist interests, dominated by the concentration of capital in financial institutions, subverts the public good by prioritizing the interest and sovereignty of the corporation over those of the people. Together with the production of asymmetries, through what I call the new machinery of pauperization, characterized by the redistribution of wealth from the common and the poor to the rich, this shift in sovereignty undermines the legitimacy of the state as a democratic institution. The tendency inherent in these displacements is for the appearance of despotic regimes, including those hiding behind the veil of procedural democracy. This is already happening in many parts of the world – for example, Afghanistan, Columbia, the Democratic Republic of Congo, Zimbabwe, Philippines, Haiti – where mafia and narco-capitalism, state terrorism and institutionalized insecurity combine to maintain machineries of exploitation and oppression (see also Sassen, 1998; Strange, 1998).

An important point is that although the new economy is organized, it is also disordered, producing asymmetrical effects that create and recreate divisions of rich and poor (Joxe, 2002). For Joxe, the attempt to stabilize these effects proceed through another central aspect of what he calls the 'empire of disorder', namely 'the equivalence between the organized form of military violence and the organized form of the economy' (ibid.: 189), enacted in the frequency of 'sub-contracted massacres', as in South America, dictated by the implications of global economic strategies (ibid.: 10). To that extent, it could be argued that 'politics is the space where the relationship between violence and the economy is managed practically' (ibid.: 193). The violence underlying the militarized economy is expressed in forms ranging from biopiracy to the forcible displacements of people resulting from development strategies and global 'liberalization', as we have seen in the case of 'big dams' or regarding the speeded-up conversion to capitalism in Eastern Europe and Russia.

If one understands military violence in the sense given to it by Clausewitz ([1832] 1968), that is, as a form of the pursuit of politics by other means, then the form of global capitalist economy that one encounters today, besides the changes in the machinery for extracting surplus value, re-inscribes the imperial governmentality that I described in the last chapter. I noted the uneven mix of sovereign and pastoral power that characterized it, sustained by a clear correlation between economic interest and military objectives, that became instituted in a disciplinary apparatus relaying the barracks with the schoolroom with the law courts and the administrative compound. One must note here that the existence of more than 360 American military installations across the globe adds the necessary 'big stick' to the economic muscle built up by corporate interests. This form of governmentality now operates via states – many reduced to the status of client states, that is, without autonomy or sovereignty – through its re-embeddings in the apparatuses of global governance such as the IMF, the WTO, 'aid' organizations, and through the international legal system regulating transactions of all kinds from trade to the cross-border movement of people and the ownership of inventions, products and knowledges. Aspects of governance have mutated in the form of the regulatory devices that manage the 'scapes' described by Appadurai (1996) (see also Strange 1998; Sassen 1998), to which one should add an infoscape that would correlate the different scapes into a complex whole at the level of calculation, thus facilitating global surveillance.

However, against the loose alliance of organized crime, bandit and narco-capitalism, financial and corporate conglomerates and their institutionalized forms of intimidation, stand local popular creative sovereignties; for instance, the thousands of movements represented at the World Social Forum is evidence that counter-hegemonic initiatives continue to find (contested) space for pursuing emancipatory goals. The problem of what informs and motivates them, and the problem of the different grounds for imagining alternative futures for postcolonial and transmodern socialities belong to the political economy I am exploring.

Actually existing postcolonial economies: circuits, networks, turbulences

Before addressing these issues, I would like to provide a glimpse of the state of the world today that establishes the evidential base to support and extend the theoretical claims made so far. Let us start with the uncontested balance-sheet of 'liberalization' and 'marketization' in the global economy. It is now taken for granted that the gap between rich and poor, winners and losers, almost everywhere has widened in the past 20 years or so.

One needs to take account here of the point I made earlier about wealth held in common, irreducible to monetary value, that nevertheless sustains countless communities; indeed, one could extend this notion of wealth to construct a different account of sustainable economies and socialities. In spite of this, even in terms of current measures, a gap exists – a telling fact when it comes to buying, say, medicines at the exorbitant price that drug companies charge – confirmed by every survey and report of global economic trends, of world poverty, health care provisions, income distribution and so on. For instance, the World Economic Forum at Davos in Switzerland, the think-tank of 'globalization from above', reported that in 2001 the top 20 per cent of earners globally received an income 86 times more than those making up the bottom 20 per cent of earners. In 1997 it was 74 times, and in 1960 30 times. To translate such statistics into meaningful quantities that would give a measure of the scale of disparity, one should look at the distribution of actual incomes per capita worldwide, when it becomes clear that the richest countries enjoy massively disproportionate incomes compared to the poorest. The World Bank survey of 2003 reports that per capita income in the 56 richest countries was over $9,000 while for the 64 poorest, it was less than $735. In many countries the income of the poorest is less than '1 US dollar per day', applying to over 300 million people globally. Another aspect of the 'big picture' is the decline in the share of world trade in many parts of the 'Third World'. For instance, while world trade has expanded by 17 times in the past 50 years, the Latin American share has reduced from 11 to 5 per cent, and the African share from 8 to 2 per cent. One would need to add to this statistic the fact that in Brazil, for example, in the past few years, the effect of policies advocated by the IMF and the World Bank has meant a 600 per cent decline in the purchasing power of the Rial compared to the dollar or the pound sterling, with the result that agribusiness in the USA has been able to pick up Brazilian assets incredibly cheaply, representing a net transfer of wealth from the poor to the rich, managed and legitimated through the accounting system. One may well ask: is this simply coincidence? Or should one look at the effects of trade agreements such as the WTO, NAFTA, OPEC and the tendency of global forces to push poor countries down the spiral of a 'race to the bottom', reflecting what Joxe refers to as accelerated poverty and accelerated wealth (Joxe, 2002: 43; see also Klein, 2000).

Similar stories characterize the effects of 'liberalization' in other countries. For instance, a recent report (UNCTAD, 2004) details the worsening economic position of Africa in the world, highlighting the following factors: the worsening terms of trade since 1980, the stifling effects of agricultural subsidies in the USA and Europe while structural adjustment policies have forced African countries to dismantle marketing boards that provided support services to farmers, and guaranteed minimum prices, debt servicing (see George, 1988, classic study; the cost of debt servicing worldwide in 2000 was $68 trillion), and the vulnerability of commodity-dependent economics subsisting on one or two products like groundnut, cotton, cocoa. The inequality is repeated across health measures, literacy levels, educational opportunity, mortality rates for children and life expectancy, access to electricity, clean water, telephone, health provisions, and so on. And, in the background is the unavoidable problem of the debt burden; even the World Bank recognizes that the 23 'least developed' countries have an unsustainable debt burden whereby income from export and aid funds are used simply to service the debt. In that respect it is worth noting that when the World Bank was being set up at the end of the Second World War as part of the Bretton Woods (1944) global institutions, J.M. Keynes, one of the key advocates of the need for an apparatus to regulate the economy globally, predicted that the level of interest that was being proposed for borrowers from countries with weak economies would mean that the debt burden would reach the kind of proportion that has since become all too real. He proposed an alternative that the Americans vetoed.[8]

A picture emerges of gross, increasing and long-standing disparity between the rich and the poor, the 'North' and the 'South', increasing in most countries. Interestingly, all the countries that fall in the category of the poor or struggling or 'developing' are former colonies. As one would expect, many approaches and paradigms have emerged to explain the systematic disparities of wealth and opportunities among nations. Colonial discourse, often resurfacing in the common-sense understanding of 'underdevelopment' or 'failed development', accounts for the disparity in the idea of historical 'backwardness', implicit in the discourse of modernity and its racialized temporality, rewritten as 'lag' in the discourse of development, as I examined in Chapter 2. Some versions add the differential effects of technology and modernization to this 'backwardness', and so propose strategies of technology transfer as part of 'aid' packages. Other explanations propose the view that the social structure and cultures in specific societies make them incompatible with and inhospitable for modern capitalist values, and so produce 'underdevelopment'.[9] In contrast, one finds explanations that relate the continuity of systematic inequalities to another continuity, namely, that of the underlying power relations and machinery of exploitation established in the period of colonialism and capitalist expansion. These narratives point to the consequences of the 'underdevelopment' of the 'Third World' by Europe, for example, in Walter Rodney's studies ([1972] 1989), that is to say, the systematic and planned pauperization of the colonized through pillage (Jalée, 1981) and through the colonial form of the restructuring of the economy – producing monocultures, dependencies, 'banana republics' – that serves the interest of the colonizers (Amin, 1976).

It is important also to stress the effects of kleptocracies (Appiah, 1992), that is, the theft of the national wealth by local elites, during and after the period of colonial occupation as part of imperial governance, often an ethnically distinct group (Chua, 2004). Their self-serving activities collude with corporate capitalism to prevent a more equitable distribution of wealth, and deny many countries the chance of attaining economic independence and prosperity at all. This too has a venerable history, as Litvin's (2003) study of multinationals at work shows; he establishes that the main similarity between colonial firms like the East India Company and today's corporations is a model of business practice based on the interweaving of profits, politics, theft and self-deception about motive. Kleptocracies, then, are encouraged and kept in place by states and multinational corporations because they function as middlemen in the process of the expropriation of the people's labour and resources. The emphasis in my analysis is to keep visible the historical dimension through genealogical approaches, so that the effects of colonialism and imperialism remain visible in any theorization, for instance regarding 'uneven development' (Amin, 1976; Arghiri, 1972), or the mechanisms put in place in the period of imperialism, and their mutations in the post-independence period, that reproduce the global relations of capitalism. It is important therefore to locate the economy as an integral part of complex assemblages that one can theorize in terms of processes of glocalization (Robertson, 1994) and of the dynamic and mobile character of the interaction between the economy and political, social, cultural and technological processes. In what follows, I will introduce a number of accounts, grouped in clusters and abridged, to illustrate the complexity of the assemblages and networks in terms of their operation in practice, and to provide a number of parables for grounding a dissident political economy.

Agribusiness and farming have a symbolic value in the analysis of the postcolony, although today an increasing percentage of the population in tri-continental countries live in urban environments, for instance, 40 per cent of Africans live in cities (Enwesor et al., 2002; Simone, 2001). Perhaps this is because agriculture remains, on the one hand, the most vulnerable sector for the economic and technological power of the corporation while, on the other hand, it still inscribes the possibility of self-sufficiency and a space for resisting capitalism through the development of appropriate technology and alternative ways of being. One of the new social movements to emerge in the past few years that enable one to raise a range of issues about political economy, globalization and agency is that of the Landless People's Movement (LPM). It includes the significant Movimento Sem Terra in Brazil, which since 1986 has liberated millions of hectares of underused land and redistributed it to small farmers, groups in Africa such as the Indaba Social Movement, and the Via Campesina network of farmers in Europe. The Ford Foundation is (surprisingly, but perhaps not so surprisingly) one of the organizations, alongside War on Want, which subsidize LPM in Africa. LPM has been very successful in Brazil. Against this one must consider related facts and developments. Small farmers produce 70 per cent of the world's food. Yet they do so against enormous handicaps, increasingly well-documented and publicized. In a report, *Rigged Rules and Double Standards* (2002), Oxfam describes how trade policy advocated by the rich countries, for example, 'liberalization' in 'developing countries' – that is, reducing tariffs and opening the country to market forces so that corporations can acquire utilities and other assets – and trade rules, for instance, the high tariffs imposed by the USA, Canada, and Japan on imports from 'developing' economies, and the subsidization of farming in Europe, amount to the robbery of the poor of billions of dollars each year. Subsidized exports drive prices down while prohibitive tariffs force poor countries to compete on unequal terms. In the countries of the EC, each cow is subsidized at the rate of $803 per year (World Bank and Action Aid, in *Guardian*, 8 Sept. 2003), and in the USA it is $1,057, a figure one should set against the '$1.00 a day' on which millions of poor people in the 'developing' countries 'survive'. The irony is that the World Bank and the IMF impose liberalizing trade conditions on poor countries as conditions for 'aid'/loans. A salutary case to reflect upon is that of rice production in Haiti, one of the poorest countries in the world. From the 1980s, driven by the IMF and the WB, the import tariff on rice was cut from 50 to 3 per cent, with the consequence that cheap US imports flooded the country. At the beginning of 1990 Haiti was almost self-sufficient in rice; ten years later, production had halved and subsidized imports from the US had secured more than half of rice sales. The effects on farmers and the rural population have been catastrophic. The World Bank, it should be noted, has praised Haiti as a leading trade liberalizer.

Another case concerns the plans to 'rationalize' farming methods in Andhra Pradesh in India through the integration of small farmers into large farms, the replacement of local seed varieties with GM seeds, the use of tractors and other heavy machinery instead of bullocks. It is estimated that about 20 million farmers will lose their jobs or their land (*Guardian*, 2 April 2002: 15). Clearly, some people, namely, the already wealthier and more powerful landowners, will benefit, as was the case with the 'Green Revolution' some years ago. Small farmers protested but were overruled on the grounds that corporate interests were also in everyone's interest, in spite of reports that judged the project had 'major failings' and 'provided no alternatives for those displaced' (Monbiot, 2003).

In both cases, what immediately becomes clear, apart from the power of corporate lobbies and the quasi-religious hold of neo-liberal dogmas on those decision-makers, is the network of relationships and institutional hinges (Bishop and Phillips, 2002) that connect local developments to global forces to institutional practices in trade and finance to general policy pursued by global regulatory bodies to economic paradigms – currently dominated by varieties of market capitalism – to historical patterns in geopolitical relationships and to forms of power and resistance.

A second cluster of activities, relating to war and the armaments industry, reveals the same networks of inter-relationships and their historical conditions of possibility. I noted in my analysis of imperial and colonial governmentality in Chapter 2, the stratagems of power and the contingent formation of colonial states whereby social groups divided by religion, ethnic belonging, and geography were arbitrarily aggregated into administrative and military units in the form of colonial territories, with disregard for the cultural and historical coherence of existing communities. In the postcolonial period, economic, political and other pressures arising from local as well as global trade and manufacturing interests have reconstituted old hostilities in many such territories.

One consequence is that for decades now, since the ending of the older form of colonialism, vast regions in the formerly occupied territories have been devastated by continuous wars. In Africa, for example, civil wars or ethnic conflict in the post-independence period have ravaged countries such as Angola, Congo, Ethiopia, Eritrea, Rwanda, Namibia, and parts of Nigeria; many other places have been affected by wars that have been more sporadic. In most cases one finds that older divisions and differences, sometimes intensified in the course of colonialism by the divide and rule stratagems, have become split along the lines of economic interest. This is especially so where critical material in involved, for example, oil in Nigeria – the land of the Ogoni people is one of the territories involved (see below) – diamonds in Angola, or the classic case of coltan (colombo tantalite) mined along the Congo and Rwanda border. Coltan is used as a coat in electric components in mobile phones, military aircraft, games consoles; 80 per cent of the world's reserves are in the Republic of the Congo; the Rwandan and Ugandan armies are funded from the pillage of coltan, while the continuous conflict in the region is driven by the knowledge that whoever controls the territory and the reserves will be sitting on a colossal fortune. Of course, the weapons used in all the conflicts are sold by the rich countries, often as part of a so-called 'aid' package, often secured through bribery and corruption involving players across the global landscape. It is worth pointing out that the top ten arms manufactures are based in the USA (7), the UK (2) and France (1); their trade, added to that of Russia, accounts for over 95 per cent of 'legal' trade, estimated at $111 billion in 2002 (*New Internationalist*, no. 330).

The way in which armed conflicts in the old colonies directly benefit corporations is illustrated in the case of the plunder of the Congo by more than 80 multinational companies detailed by a UN report (21 October 2002; *Guardian*, 22 October 2002: 15). Some of the named corporations, like Anglo-American plc, that holds a 45 per cent share of De Beers, operate across several sectors including mining, financial services, explosives, forestry, so that profits are made right across the diverse activities. Many of the individuals accused of benefiting financially include top military personnel from African countries. It is an elaborate modern system of pillage.

The inter-locking agencies of corporate capitalism and kleptocracy is starkly revealed in the case of Nigeria, where their combined predatory activities have demonstrated that even when a country is apparently producing vast wealth, escape from poverty and repression depends not so much on wealth creation alone, but on a range of factors and forces, some local, such as ethnic and older class divisions, and some global such as the interest of the oil cartel. Nigeria today is one of the poorest states in the world in spite of the billions of revenue that oil has generated. It has been ruled by military regimes for 30 out of the 39 years of the post-independence period; it is a deeply divided country split along ethnic, religious, class and gender lines, repeating the divisions that led to the civil war after independence.

Amidst the chaos, the power of Islamic fundamentalists has grown among the Muslim population, with many people supporting Sharia laws. Those who oppose the dominant elites are hounded with extreme cruelty as in the case of the Ogoni people on whose land, the Niger delta, the oil reserves are to be found. From the beginning of the discovery of oil in 1958, the Ogoni and other small groups living in the Niger region have been left out of all negotiations and agreements, while their homeland has been transformed into a wasteland through pollution and disregard for health and environmental concerns. Since 1958, an estimated US$30 billion has been extracted by Shell Petroleum Development Company, the Nigerian National Petroleum Corporation, Chevron, Mobil, Texaco and other oil corporations (Shell withdrew from Ogoniland in 1993). But the Ogoni still live without basic amenities and cannot cultivate the land, though fortunes have been made by those in the Nigerian establishment. The struggle of the Ogoni people for justice and a share of the wealth illustrates not only the brutality of repression but the interweaving of transnational capitalist interests, local corruption, geo-political calculations and military power. Their suffering is iconically represented by the fate of the writer and environmentalist Ken Saro-Wiwa who, along with eight other activists, was executed by the Nigerian military government in 1995 for fighting for the rights and interests of the Ogoni. The inadequacy of the response from international bodies and the difficulties encountered in the pursuit of redress and meaningful changes in the power relations in the region is further proof that at this stage in the development of the forces of resistance globally to neo-liberal corporate capitalism, the bottom line is reduced to the power to witness and testify, and in that way make visible the injustices that cry out for radical change in our way of being. (see *Interventions*, 1 (3): 430–8, for a summary of details).

The case of the Congo brings to light the longer history of the relationship of economy and brutality that remains as a backdrop to ongoing brutalities in the region. King Leopold II of Belgium appointed himself King of the Congo in 1883 (which he sold to the Belgian state in 1908) and proceeded to enrich himself by forcing countless numbers into slave labour in the rubber plantations and in the ivory trade. Hundreds of thousands died of exhaustion, starvation and barbarous punishments, such as the cutting off of ears, noses, limbs – sent as trophies or evidence to Belgium. The population of Congo halved to 10 million between 1880 and 1920 (see Adam Hochschild, 1999). In the post-war period, wars have ravaged the country leading to partitions (eventually forming the Congo Republic and the Democratic Republic of Congo). In East Congo in 2002, seven armies have been operating, including Rwandans and Zimbabweans. They attack each other and the civilian population, raping and killing with a casual brutality that has become an everyday terror for civilians caught up in the chaos. One may well wonder what scars run through the psyche of the population that connect the present to the colonial past in this century of violence. A case study of Unita would be salutary here, pointing to collusions with economically interested parties, including the armament industry, and political constituencies. So, in each case we find that the strategic interests of the developed world are not far away from the underlying sources of conflict. The flows of weapons, aid packages, funds, valuable products, military personnel, 'inducements', establish networks and circuits that point to the underlying inter-connections and patterns, with relay points that may be economic, cultural, political, military, or administrative, depending on the specific conjuncture at particular points in time. These relays or hinges are worth further exploration from the point of view of their functioning as enabling and mediating agencies and shuttle points.

But, it would distort the picture if one were to simply point the finger at the 'West' and 'neo-colonialism' or corporate capitalism, even when one knows that many existing rivalries and conflicts have an origin in colonial policy, as in the case of the Hema and the Lendu tribes in the Democratic Republic of Congo who now fight the most pitiless war over the oil in the Ituri region (*Independent*, 26 March 2004: 26, 27). Colonial legacy cannot be invoked to enable indigenous groups to disavow responsibility for inhuman conduct. In Rwanda, the genocide of millions – about a million Tutsis were exterminated by the Hutu in 1994 – was carefully planned; it was then carried out by a combination of military personnel and civilians with a brutality and ruthlessness that stun the imagination. The briefest investigation of the details reveals a catalogue of murders, mass rape, torture, carried out by neighbours as well as strangers with a level of callousness that makes it difficult to understand how human beings, whatever the circumstances, can cause that kind of suffering to other human beings. This applies equally to events in ex-Yugoslavia, for the inhuman knows neither frontier nor period. Once more the problems point to the need to find an analytical framework that does not collapse back into old dichotomies or reinscribe existing power relations and the socialities they sustain.

Another central aspect of the real postcolonial economy relates to exploitative practices that constitute women as a separate category, suggesting the need for a gendered political economy. As one would expect, a great deal of literature exists (for instance: Anthias and Yuval-Davis, 1989; Beneria, 1985; Jackson and Pearson, 1998; Kandiyoti, 1991; Marchand and Runyan, 2000; Mohanty et al., 1991; Nussbaum and Glover, 1995; Rai, 2002; Sangari and Vaid, 1993; Visvanathan et. al., 1997) that has demonstrated the centrality of gender in all questions to do with development and the economy generally. To start with, one could look at a rather obvious example for a politico-cultural-economic analysis, namely, the sex industry (boys too are involved here) which includes sex tourism, prostitution and the pornography industry. It is now well established that in several South-East Asian and African countries there operates a prostitution industry in which the workers are virtual sex slaves, sometimes bought as indentured labour, sometimes sold to cancel a family debt or else recruited through whatever devious means, then inserted in the global circuits of the sex industry generating billions of dollars.[10] Alongside this gruesome trade, one

157

could add the growth in the global service sector that has seen the migration of an army of women from poor countries or poor families going abroad – but not just to Euro-America – to work as servants, nannies, cleaners, house-keepers, and so on, exporting most of the money earned back to their families. They are often the subject of physical and sexual abuse, they have little legal or employment protection, although they are an important part of the diasporic economy in which circuits of labour and money are inter-connected into networks of loosely regulated exchanges. The overall picture revealed by the stories of bonded female labour across this range of activi-ties make visible the networks connecting poverty with the sex industry, with the drugs industry, with trafficking, with pornography, with mafia cap-italism, each sector accounting for billions of dollars a year. Thus, the global flows associated with the 'shadow economy' (see Nordstrom, 2000) in every country trace homologous circuits of money and people, goods and services that gives a measure of the tragic fall-out from 'development', liberalization, ethnic and civil wars fuelled by profit. Of course, economic theory gener-ally, including the economics of development has little to say about these activities in terms of accounting for their substantial effects on the 'official' or visible economy.

A postcolonial gendered political economy should include the institu-tionalization of female oppression in customary practices; these are sus-tained by the systematic exploitation of women through an unequal, or unequally valued, division of labour, and in terms of everyday iniquities arising from the inscription of gender oppression in customary practices. As examples of iniquity, one could consider the practices associated with the bride price – for instance, the countless tales from India of suffering inflicted on women whose parents fail to meet the promised dowry – or with sexual mutilation in many regions of the Muslim world, or with the 'payment' of a daughter in compensation for a debt incurred or an injury inflicted. A recent case is that of four men convicted of murder in Pakistan who tried to escape punishment by giving their young daughters in marriage to elderly relatives of the victims, in line with the *vani* tradition of com-pensation. Similar practices exist elsewhere, for example, in Ghana, Togo, Benin, Nigeria (*New Internationalist*, 337, 2002). One might be tempted to examine these practices purely in terms of culturally embedded differences, and the different performative instantiations of belonging. My aim, how-ever, is to avoid the politically and ethically disabling relativism of absolu-tizing difference. I argue that it is more fruitful to relate the practices to the broad concerns of a revised political economy, and to a view of a critical or radical transmodernity that would disrupt the tired dichotomy of the 'West' versus the 'non-West', and so politicize them according to principles that would refigure the relations between the local and the global within the problematic of a cosmopolitanism defined in terms of (non-ethnocentric) universal values and rights. The ethical stakes, for example, from the stand-point of responsibility for the other, would then be less obscured by parochial disputes.

Against these stories of abuse and oppression one could cite the case of SEWA, the Self-Employed Women's Association, set up in 1972 in the Indian state of Gujarat to syndicalize poor women workers, working in the streets of cities, in the fields, or from home as hawkers, vendors and makers. They are the weavers, potters, embroiderers, bidi rollers, basket makers, shoe makers, carpenters, and so on, whose work link the urban economy with the rural and the global. These women, unprotected by conventional syndicalist organizations, have brought together diverse occupations and needs in a form of organization that not only ensures collective strength in negotiating fair deals for their labour and products, but extends the benefits of solidarity to support for obtaining credit and loans, and to the provision of training and legal help. Importantly, SEWA's membership cuts across ethnic as well as occupational divisions. It is an interesting example of indigenous modernization and appropriate development, whereby tradition, modernity, economy, culture and gender and radical politics reconfigure diasporic or creolized worlds (for details, see K. Rose, in Visvanathan et al., 1997).

My next case introduces an element of the global economy that is ignored by conventional political economy yet reveals some deep-seated characteristics of capitalism and everyday reality that should incite us to see the world we are in without blinkers. I will rely on Carolyn Nordstrom's (2000) studies of the invisible, shrouded world of economic activity outside the legal confines of states, concerning the ways and the semi-institutional mechanisms whereby quite large groups are able to sustain themselves outside the state and generally produce sufficient wealth to buy arms, maintain a whole range of services like health and education and monetary services. These activities connect with the more visible, 'legitimate' apparatus of the global economy in intricate ways, operating through nodal or relay points that throw a very revealing light on the more visible and theorized aspect of the economy. As Nordstrom notes: 'gold, diamonds, drugs, precious metals, human labour, sex workers, timber and even seafood move out of war zones into world markets to purchase everything from AK-47s and M-16s to satellite-linked computer communications and weapons systems, from antibiotics to basic grains' (Nordstrom, 2000: 36). She notes that the point of the study of these shadowy networks is not so much the glimpse into a secret world as the fact that existing states and these shadowy organizations exist side by side. Their activities illustrate how economic, political, social and cultural assemblages and practices are woven into each other to performatively constitute the plural, disordered, yet regulated worlds of the black economy and how the latter is spliced into the wider transnational network of institutions and rules of operating. We are led to recognize that they 'are not marginal to the world's economies and politics, but central' (ibid.: 37); indeed, these networks employ millions of people and generate (even some years ago) more than a trillion dollars a year. In her summary of the bare facts, Nordstom highlights the following: 20 per cent of the world's financial deposits are in unregulated banks and offshore locations; the value of illicit drugs and weapons sales together exceed a trillion dollars;

in many ex-Third World countries like Peru, Kenya, India, or Thailand, about half the economically active population are employed in the black or informal economy. These activities also demonstrate the linkages between corporate capitalism and narco- and mafia capitalism; money, laundered in one way or another, is the hinge.

My final example concerns the emergence of special industrial and technological zones or 'growth triangles' that operate as sub-regional economic zones differently regulated from the rest of the countries in which they are located. They are a more sophisticated development of the earlier free industrial zones set up to encourage investment in 'developing' countries through incentives like tax holidays, the state construction of appropriate infrastructure, export allowances, cheap non-unionized labour, and so on. The growth triangles make use of existing corporate, inter-firm alliances to establish hierarchized networks of technological expertise, management skills and cheap labour, for example, the Indonesia–Malaysia–Singapore (Sijori) zone close to the Singaporean capital and command structures (see Ong, 2000). They basically provide infrastructure facilities, cheap labour and technological and managerial expertise for global capital investments and represent an improvement in flexible production techniques (Harvey, 1989). An important part of the package includes granting foreign capital a large degree of sovereignty and autonomy over the territories, with the state relinquishing obligations and responsibilities towards its citizens working in the zones. For instance, policing is carried out by security personnel answerable solely to corporate power according to quasi-state administrative and legal practices aimed at securing social stability in the zones conducive to the production aims of the corporations. In any case the population in such zones are drawn from several countries so that it is a new kind of cosmopolitan mix, segregated according to gender and nationality. Ong (2000) gives the example of young Indonesian women, supervised by male technicians and managers from Singapore, unable to appeal to their own government for protection. New forms of sovereignty and authority are emerging in these developments that challenge older modern forms of state sovereignty and lead analysis to reconsider the relations of economic and political power in global corporate capitalism.

Thus, we begin to have a picture of actually existing economies in which a significant proportion of the world's population live an existence confined within a complex made up of non-state-regulated networks of exchange and arrangement that constitute everyday socialities for many communities. Huge sums of money are acquired through these activities, involving all manner of smuggling and criminal operations – of people, oil, drugs, precious metals, weapons, money, and so on – which are dispersed throughout the 'official' economy. These cases show that the relationship between state and non-state, legal and illegal, orderly and disorderly is much more fluid than assumed by conventional theory. Castells (1998) too makes the point that academic analyses ignore the reality and effect of criminal activity at the heart of the global economy.[11] This interpenetration of narco- and mafia capitalism and the 'official' economy, operating through a complex network of relays leads one to view corruption not a matter of a few dishonest executives but as the inevitable outcome of a logic intrinsic to economic conditions today, instantiated across the diverse sectors of the economy: in the workings of the stock markets, in accounting practices, in oligopoly situations, and in the opportunities for theft and fraud that deregulation and the lack of effective regulatory bodies have introduced. Far from being a rogue corporation, Enron was simply a typical if 'unlucky' case. The point is that the interpenetration of the 'shadow' networks and the 'official' networks have important implications for rethinking political economy, as well as for the analysis of governance and the critique of neo-liberalism; more generally, there are lessons that challenge the social sciences' understanding of everyday social reality. Clearly, quite a different view of the location of the postcolony in terms of the global politico-economic power relations follows from the reality I have brought into focus.

Translating the future: diagrams of possible worlds

When thinking about transcolonial and transmodern alternatives to the 'world order' being put into place, the major problem that arises concerns the principles that could guide both critique and political action. Anti-capitalist and anti-globalization movements throughout the world have instinctively turned attention to the activities of transnational corporations and global regulatory bodies such as the International Monetary Fund and the World Trade Organization. By targeting neo-liberalism and corporate capitalism as signifiers of exploitation and iniquity, these movements have reconstituted the global in terms of the apparatuses of world governance and the new forms of imperial power that are now reconstituting the social according to the dictates of the market. Fundamental issues about sovereignty, legitimacy and the social good are implicated in all these struggles. This is reflected in the aims of the World Social Forum as an organization that brings together the range of oppositional and reconstructive movements that are united in their call for more democracy and rule by civil society, for the respect of human rights, for greater accountability, for the shift to production for people's needs rather than the needs of profit, for the promotion of cultural and bio diversity in the spirit of plurality and conviviality, and for an end to corporate rule and to the process of deregulation and liberalization that extends its hold. This stance is reflected in the Charter of Principles declared by the World Social Forum (in Sen et al., 2004).

The Charter shows that ideas of justice, and the principle of responsibility and respect for all human beings, as well as a commitment to care for the planet, motivate the wide range of activities that these movements undertake; these activities demonstrate that the question of political economy relays the question of the theoretical and philosophical foundation that promote alternative visions of sociality. This recognition is expressed in de Sousa

Santos' (2004) analysis of the anti-globalitarian project of WSF when he argues that the possibility of a 'movement of movements' poses basic theoretical problems to do with creating a 'global consciousness', for the latter must be able to translate into a common vocabulary the diversity of goals inscribed in the different political languages and different forms of organization of the movements. This, he says, implicates the need to make explicit the basis of common ground and to invent new forms of agency, different from those that operated in the liberal and the Marxist versions of modernity. He proposes a theory of translation, related to a 'negative universalism', that would allow for 'mutual intelligibility among the experiences of the world' (ibid.: 341). Underlying his analysis, and the WSF documents as a whole, one may detect the dream of a new, non-Eurocentric, Enlightenment, informing a new emancipatory project.

I will now address the question of alternative worlds by way of the concept of translation as trope, for it brings up the question of the transformations, appropriations, misappropriations and retranscriptions that take place across differences – from one tradition to another, from one language to another, from one context to another – processes that relate, on the one hand, to the impossibility and necessity of translation, and, on the other hand, to the issues that have been examined, from a postcolonial standpoint, in terms of transculturation (Kraniauskas 2000, in Brah and Coombes, 2000) and hybridity, and that I have addressed through a revised concept of creolization. Equally, the problematic of translation brings into view the fact that the process of colonization and appropriation involves a translation into the language of the colonizer that transfers authority to the latter. At the philosophical level, it raises the problem of what resists transposition from one language or register to another, that is, the problem of the proper name: 'Any signified whose signifier cannot vary nor let itself be translated into another signifier without loss of meaning points to a proper name effect' (Derrida, 1985: 312). While the issues of creolization and of difference relate more straightforwardly to a politics, since relations of power are played out in them, the problem of the proper name triggers both political and ontological questions. This is because the proper name – Auschwitz, Hiroshima, Biko – makes a requirement both of untranslatability and translatability, that is, it requires, on the one hand, that one respects the irreducible specificity and singularity associated with the proper name (say, Auschwitz), which exceeds representation and would lose meaning in translation. Yet, on the other hand, the proper name, because it stands as testimony to a debt, summons one to attempt to translate the experience into a common idiom, as a response to suffering and fragility, and as a sign of solidarity. It can therefore be argued that the scene of translation is inscribed 'within a scene of inheritance and in a space which is precisely that of the genealogy of proper names, of the family, the law, indebtedness' (ibid.: 104). This line of argument enables fundamental questions relating to an ethics to appear, for instance, regarding the place of translation in the task of a (non-forgetful) forgiveness and of anamnesis as conditions for the possibility of dialogue and the reconstitution of community torn by conflict (Ricoeur, 1996; Venn, 2005). Another implication is that one must phrase translation from the position of the addressee: the stranger, the refugee, the homeless, the minor, the other, so that the problematic of hospitality is seen to be central to the issues. Clearly, the latter needs to be grounded in a postmodern ontology, that is to say, one which rejects the presuppositions of the self-sufficiency and autonomy of being and instead promotes as fundamental the idea of heteronomy, that is, the more-than-one character of being, indicated in the idea of being as being-with and being-in-the-world that I have shown in previous chapters. (See also Curtis, 2001.) Additionally, the problem of translation across cultures and differences of interests and goals is repeated at the political and ontological levels in terms of the tension between universalism and particularism (Sakai, 2001: v), suggesting an undecidable character to translation – besides the implications that arise because of the insufficiency of the signifier and of heteroglossia – and thus an openness to multiplicity and heterogeneity alongside the search for common ground.

Derrida's analytic of translation enables one to uncover other aspects that widen the scope beyond the standpoint of dialogue and exchange. For instance, the point of view of universalism hides yet also reveals the temptations of total or pure translatability, thus of the tyranny of a common idiom that would be sovereign in relation to signification across different domains. In any case this temptation must assume a transparency and literal correspondence between signifier and signified that do not obtain in real situations (because of the economy of *différance*: Derrida, 1982: 6–11). Every language, every culture is impure, made up of several tongues relating to class, gender, region, geography, and so on, so that every language and every culture are open to a double disruption of their claim to speak for a unified community or to force a consensus: on the one hand, it is open to the critique of the assumption of unitariness and homogeneity – of language, of culture, of the subject; on the other hand, the demonstration that the instability of the signifier arises from the effects of the plural forces that determine its mobility makes possible the disruption of the authority vested in the authenticity or originariness of the signifier/culture. The point of view of translation, it can be seen, trails many of the issues that belong to the agenda of a critical postcoloniality.

The link with political economy becomes clear when one interrogates neo-liberalism from the point of view of its colonial or imperial ambition. I have underlined the extent to which its values and assumptions, its calculation of means and objectives, its determination of efficiency, its dogmatic faith in the market have been imported into the public domain, restructuring the goals and practices in fields as diverse as education, health, research, social services, cultural provisions, and governance generally. Its language is being promoted as the universal language, which means that its monolingualism is made to write off alternative practices and narratives of becoming, so that it can impose the tyranny of its values. This process is systematic and calculated, proceeding according to a rationalization – so-called (re)modernization – that does not tolerate critique.

A central part of this process is the privileging of a particular language, that of new management, that doubles both as the normative, (would-be) hegemonic, discourse and as cultural capital, the acquisition of which functions as the basis entitling the 'owner', that is, the managerial class, to appropriate (through differential pay) the value created by the labour of others. A study of the strategies employed to transform the public domain indicates the systematic manner of the translation taking place, leaving no space for other voices or narratives. This imposition of its 'genre of discourse' over all other genres erases or marginalizes any 'differend' that exists (Lyotard, 1988); it makes it impossible for differences to be expressed or to be admitted as legitimate, except if expressed in the language of consumer choice. Furthermore, the subsumption of the different strategies applying in different spheres of activity to one homogenous model of justification eliminates the plurality of interests that have historically existed between different components of the social and thereby eliminates the ability to make judgement between competing needs (see Boltanski and Thevenot, 1991, and Ricoeur's discussion, 1996). Thus, to take the case of education, the translation of its purposes and interests into the language of management and capital and the privilege of the latter in allocating resources or in judging practice not only effectively delegitimizes alternative narratives of education, it obliges practitioners to rephrase their activity in the monolingual idiom of neo-liberal economic management and reorganize them to fit with its organizational demands – for example, in prioritizing targets set in response to the interests of governance and accounting practice – or else be marginalized and excluded as regressive or obstructive.

Furthermore, the law is made to operate as instrument for normalizing the new practices and norms, making them normative: a classic ruse of power. This strategy whereby only one genre of discourse or language is made admissible institutionalizes a form of political terror (Lyotard, 1988). One finds these strategies at work at the level of new governance as well as in organizations like the IMF and the WTO. It is well to remember that the authority to name is after all the prerogative of the powerful and the index of a dominating force. In other words, neo-liberalism's conceptual and discursive colonization of the social and public sphere follows the pattern of every colonization, in particular, the Western or occidentalist form that must pathologize the other/the alternative and proclaim its necessary superiority. In the neo-liberal world order, the complicity of monolingualism, monotheism and corporate capitalism is completed in the fundamentalism of Evangelical Protestantism and the market. A similar pattern, combining monolingualism, a monotheist doctrine, and an economic system into a homogeneous totality can be detected in every fundamentalism and totalitarianism. Neo-liberalism undertakes the Talibanization of the political: you shall speak our language or disappear.

An important aspect of the neo-liberal colonization of the public sphere refers to the corruption inherent in the tactic that imports private interest into the public interest, as Arendt (2000) has perceptively argued (notwithstanding the problems in the separation of public and private). In other words, the colonization through privatization of public services and functions inevitably distorts public interest by forcing it to be at the service of private interest. It is a move that even Kant, that most liberal of thinkers, counselled against, on the grounds that reason (and judgement) then could not be free or objective, that being a condition for rational governance to operate at all. My points earlier in discussing property in the light of the legal status of the joint stock company and its limited liability and responsibility, as well as the effects of new informationalized practices of trading on the stock market, particularly the futures and derivatives market, adds a completely new dimension to the issues of the public good that Arendt addressed.

This hyper-capitalism makes even clearer the incommensurability that exists between the language and values inscribed in contemporary capitalism and that which pertains to the common good. In short, the notion of the public good does not compute in the language of the capitalist corporation, it cannot translate it, except for contractual agreements that transcribe the values underlying public goods, say, good education or sound health, into its own terms, as measurable quantities and as 'value for money'. On the evidence so far, the excesses and hyper-exploitation that have followed privatization fully bear out the Arendtian prognostic.

Excess and corruption, besides, are consistent with the fact that capitalism, particularly in its neo-liberal incarnation, is in itself amoral, since its discourse is devoid of ethical principles that properly belong to it. Such principles, for example, concern or responsibility for the well-being of one's fellows, the happiness of the majority, respect for liberties and rights, are borrowed from elsewhere, outside capitalism. That is, it must appeal to ethical principles and codes outside itself to legitimate its existence, specifically by relying on vestiges of Enlightenment humanism, or on values that appeared with the discourse of modernity or have mutated from Christian ethics. Shorn of this imported/translated veneer of moral values, it reveals itself to be fundamentally unethical and amoral. The convergence of mafia capitalism and multinational corporate practice is simply a development of the autistic undercurrent in capitalism into an institutionalized criminality. At least, radical liberalism and its regulatory apparatus, enshrined in the idea of the welfare state or welfare capitalism, managed to keep capitalism in check; the insurantial technologies it put in place delivered the contractual obligations and undertakings that found the legitimacy of the modern democratic state. Importantly, the concept of welfare, affiliated to the idea of pastoral care and pastoral power, acknowledges universal values and rights – expressed, for example, in Beveridge's principle of freedom from the 'five ills' (idleness/unemployment, ignorance, squalor, want/poverty/insecurity, disease/sickness), that beset the citizen – applying to all subjects and that it was the duty of the state to guarantee through a machinery of redistribution and an insurantial technology. A commitment to a notion of justice motivated this pastoral power of the state.

By contrast, with neo-liberalism, social justice is rewritten in terms of provisions for maximising choice and in terms of legal entitlement; the citizen is reduced to the status of the individualist, rationalist consumer of services and goods, s/he buys into a political project, an ideology, a way of life or an image, or otherwise is cast out as the 'remnant', outside the concern of the state (Agamben 1998, 1999), and categorized as a threat to its order that must be contained. This category of the excluded, the stateless and the refugee, as well as those now labelled terrorists and extremists, often find themselves in situations where they are denied the 'right to have rights' (Arendt, 2000: 37), and thus placed outside the human, certainly outside responsibility. The space of the political is itself totalized, completing the militarization of both politics and the economy so that both come to occupy the same space, as Joxe (2002) has argued.

I have introduced the issues of universalism and justice in the course of the discussion of translation and colonization because they are central for rethinking the principles that could underlie postcolonial/postmodern alternatives. They appear in the documents and debates at the WSF gatherings and in relation to other terms such as recognition that have become central in debates about the question of justice (Calhoun, 1995; Fraser and Honneth, 2003; Habermas, 1996; Shapiro, 1999; Taylor, 1994; Young, 1990). The issues revolve around the injuries and hurts that arise because of systematic differences in the allocation of power, wealth, liberty and recognition that are made on the basis of categories such as gender, class, race, religion, body, culture. My insistence on the polyglot, heterogeneous, diasporic and mobile character of cultures and the implicit rejection of any attempt to fix or essentialize the kinds of differences I have mentioned means that I can bracket approaches that assume the boundedness of these categories, for instance, in Taylor's discussion of multiculturalism (1994). In formulating an alternative, I will approach the problem of universalism and justice through a detour via Rawls' (1971) theory of justice since it represents the best liberal position informing redistributive justice, and thus provides the contrast for the different foundation I want to outline.

Rawls proposed two principles or counterfactual devices for determining a just distribution of power and wealth in a community. The first is the 'veil of ignorance' principle whereby it is assumed that all participants in the decision as to what social arrangement would be desirable do not know in advance what their position is in the society in the beginning (the 'original position'). The assumption is that this principle guarantees that people will decide to choose an arrangement that will not disadvantage them should they be in the worst position. In other words, the assumption of basic self-interest is all that is necessary for people to calculate their least risky option in devising a system that appears in principle equitable. The second principle is in fact a proviso, given in the rule that any arrangement must be such as to benefit most the group who are the least advantaged. To take a simple case, it could be argued that a universal tax rate for all incomes unfairly burdens the least wealthy group since they can least afford the reduction in income, whereas a graduated system would redistribute the burden more fairly. The second principle, though reasonable from the point of view of equity, is presumably introduced because of an assumption that the same self-interest that works in favour of the first principle, if left without check, would, after a time, result in an unjust distribution, and so work against the first principle; furthermore, self-interest alone would incline the wealthier to argue for a uniform tax. Rawls' theory, relying on a version of a 'rational choice theory', in effect provides a contractual basis for justice. This is because the redistributive element is grounded in the supposition of self-interest as primary, and eliminates the need for an ontologically grounded ethics. Furthermore, it uncouples justice from obligation, responsibility and recognition, though it retains a redistributive element that relies on appeal to a liberal notion of social justice outside its own framework.

It is clear that, even when limited by the provisos of Rawls' two principles, self-interest produces problems that require constant vigilance because of the conflict of interest it essentializes, and because relative advantages accumulate over time. Joxe (2002), in his discussion of conflict, reminds us that the original Greek version of the Lord's Prayer in the Christian religion, close to the Latin version, appeals to God to cancel our debts in the same way that we also cancel the debt of those who owe us. This version was cited by the Pope in 2000, who uses the Italian translation of the original prayer, to call upon the rich countries of the world to mark the beginning of the millennium by cancelling the debts of the poor countries, to the bafflement of the vast majority of Christians who do not know the original Greek version of the Prayer and do not realize that it makes no mention of forgiveness or sin, added later. Joxe uses the example to make the point that the context of the Greek version was Greek democratic polity and the knowledge that debts tended to accumulate and lead to conflict that had to be defused, precisely through the periodic cancellation of debts. The preservation of Greek polity and democracy depended on this annulment of debts (ibid.: 114–16). A similar, less frequent, annulment of debt operated in Jewish cultures to restore the political community and re-establish the brotherhood of the faithful. It could be argued that the foundation of any polity in self-interest cannot avoid conflict and fundamentally undermines democracy. It is interesting that at some point in the history of democracy, the cancellation of debt was replaced with the forgiveness of sin, a political act by an individual psychology and a moral judgement. Today the emasculation of the public sphere and the 'fall of public man' (Sennett, 1976) is completed in the elevation of the market and money as transcendent entities in neo-liberal doctrine; they have emptied the political of the meaning of freedom – in the Arendtian sense of freedom as the condition for the initiation of action that instantiates being as potentiality – and replaced it with the coinage of capitalist accounting practice.

Self-interest is of course consistent with the presupposition of the self-sufficient, autonomous, unitary subject, constituted in the discourse of modernity and in modern law. The individualism it supports is deeply ingrained across the contemporary cultural landscape: in consumer culture, in child-rearing practices, in a wide range of pedagogies and therapies, in strategies of governance, in political discourse, and in the cult of celebrity. My search for a different basis for grounding universalism and justice requires a gestalt switch to a different ontology, one that I have intimated at several points in the book. This critical or heteronomous ontology prioritizes the relation to the other and the relation to world; I have also argued that world and being, following Merleau-Ponty (1968) are inter-dependent, forming a chiasm, a position that supports the view that cooperative and collective activity in the world form the basis of sociality, as radical Enlightenment thought assumed, and as the neglected work of Tarde established. It draws on the elaboration of a non-Cartesian–Freudian problematic of the subject that one can find in the post-Heideggerian theories of Levinas, Derrida, Lyotard, Ricoeur and that, following Curtis (2001), I have discussed in terms of heteronomy. The argument knits together several discursive strings. To begin with there is, contra Cartesianism, the recognition that a subject by itself does not exist (Ricoeur, 1992). As I elaborated in the third chapter, one comes to be human through a process of identification whereby the other/significant others and a culture as a whole are interiorized through an inter-subjective choreography and an apprenticeship; in this way an essential plurality of the subject is inaugurated. This plurality or more-than-one character of the subject, indicated in the concepts of being-with and being-in-the-world, is lived both at the level of the psyche and that of the social (Venn, 2004).

Furthermore, these processes are anchored in being's recognition of its fundamental temporality, particularly of the within-timeness of being whereby being is a node in the passage from the having-been, the making-present and the coming-towards that describes the temporal space in which being appears, indeed, the space in which one questions oneself as to one's way of being which is a defining characteristic of what it means to be human.[12] I have noted in the last chapter the manner in which this experiential apprehension of time is expressed in the form of narration, and the centrality of narrative for the formation and location of the self. Narrative binds the human being to a culture, that is, to an inter-subjective space, and to history. It also binds the subject to the material and durable space of culture, collectively constituted over time, existing in the form of the technology, the habitus, the spaces of memory, the equipmental aspect of the world upon and with which one acts. It is important to draw attention to the neglect of the non-visual and non-linguistic senses in these processes of apprehending time and of being-in-the-world, for example, regarding the sonic dimension, a neglect which the focus on the materiality and embodied density of being-in-the-world should overcome (Ettinger, 1995; Henriques, 2003, Silverman, 1988; Venn, 2004).

The implication of the point of view I am sketching is that the relation to the other and to a world is primary in the emergence of the self. Capitalism in its various forms sunders this mutuality and solidarity upon which it nevertheless parasitically depends. I would connect the standpoint of indebtedness to both this historicity and this plurality of the self. Indebtedness brings up the question of responsibility for the other, both as a response to what is owed, but equally as a response to suffering, to fragility and to finitude. These existential conditions of the human being are grounded, on the one hand, in the recognition of the temporality of being, and, on the other, they relate to the other in me who is interiorized in the process of emergence of the self as a singular entity. In the Levinasian problematic of being, finitude, fragility and suffering are symbolized in the 'face relation', that is, the proposition that the relation to the other is epitomized in the unconditional response to the demand of responsibility that the other makes of me. The logic of the proposition is that the existential fact of ontological suffering and vulnerability and the singularity of the other expressed in the face command that I respond by the gift of responsibility. As Derrida (1995) has argued, it is a gift of time. The fact that capitalism, and all exploitative forms of sociality, undertake, in one form or another, precisely the appropriation of the time of the other, and the fact that it is now busy speeding up time, for instance, through cybernetic technologies, to accelerate the rate of appropriation of living-time and to intensify the efficiency of its accumulation in the form of money, is an index of its fundamentally unethical nature. The relation to the other and responsibility for the other – bearing in mind that I am an other, for the other – enjoins an ethics of care which is in opposition to the paradigm that prioritizes self-interest and the ego-centric morality of individualisms. This ethics clearly must oppose any form of exploitation and oppression, any system in which the well-being of some depend on the suffering and misery of others, that is, on the theft of the time of the other.

The heteronomous ontology I am sketching provides the basis for considering two other grounds for demarcating an alternative basis for a transcolonial future, namely, a post-Rawlsian polity and a cosmopolitical universalism. Concerning the liberalism of Rawls' theory of justice, my argument is that it is not the counterfactual ignorance of one's position in the scheme of things that motivates a just arrangement of social goods, but precisely the knowledge, on the one hand, of what has happened in history and, on the other, of what is done today in the name of efficient production and fair distribution. My critique of the realities of the capitalist world and neo-liberalism has shown that existing inequalities and exploitations, and the despoiling of the earth, are not the dysfunctional or incidental fall-out from 'modernization' and from strategies for more 'efficient' resource allocation and use. They are inherent in the forces and apparatuses at work in the economy and culture that frame dominant occidentalist notions of modernization and efficiency and/or continue in mutated forms more archaic systems of exploitation and oppression in the postcolony; they are the consequences of their substantive logics. For example, to pick an exemplary case of vulnerability and responsibility, one could consider child labour as a source of cheap production and for sexual slavery. It is clear that it does not just happen. It takes planning and organization and precise calculations of both corporate and private costs and gains, and it depends too on cultural practices and values, 'traditional' and otherwise, constituting the status and role of children. Collusion at multiple points conditions the possibility of this injustice – within families, in the service sector like tourism, at the level of state institutions, banking, transnational flows of money, and so on. One puts an end to it by dismantling the economic-cultural assemblages, globally dispersed, that produce it and inscribe the values that sustain it. Justice therefore is not conditioned by ignorance but must refer to judgement on the basis of knowledge, including knowledge of the underpinnings and consequences of one's action. We know much more about the world today than we ever did before: concerning its cultural and material ecology, that is, the processes and mechanisms that constitute it as an experiential reality, concerning the different cultures in the world and their history; we know too about the injustices that have been done and are inflicted today, we know how and why they happen, we know the terms that are used to justify them: modernization, tradition, religion, efficiency, class, gender, race, sexuality, genetics, and currently 'good versus evil'. The post-Rawlsian injunction to 'be just' is made in view of this knowledge, which is not to say that it is therefore a simple matter reducible to the application of clear rules (Curtis, 2001).

Implicit in the arguments I have presented is a question about universalism. To begin with, it is important to maintain a distinction between the global and the universal, between a cosmopolitanism of the right that abolishes alternative socialities and a critical cosmopolitanism that imagines a future founded on respect for the singularity of the other to whom I am answerable (see also Santner, 2002, arguments that ground responsibility for the other/the stranger in the essential strangeness of every human being). I have started to develop this position through the alternative ontology I have outlined, for in the end the claim to universal rights or to universal principles that would apply to all irrespective of cultural differences must assume a commonality that transcend particularisms. My grounding of this ontology in existential conditions tries to show that questions about universalism are not posed in abstraction or as simply a metaphysical issue, but on the basis of the common experience of fragility, finitude and loss that derives from the recognition of the temporality of being, and on the basis of an archive of debates and knowledges that have made the stakes visible. For instance, we know the objections that have been raised against cultural imperialism on the grounds that it universalizes the validity of norms and values pertaining to a particular culture through the mechanisms of power it sets up, operating through practices of regulation and disciplining such as the law and ideology. The opposite tendency is that of cultural relativism whereby the appeal to principles and norms outside a culture in order to judge conduct within that culture is deemed invalid. Both positions handicap judgement, either reducing it to the application of a rule or subjecting it to forms of tyranny, namely, by declaring inadmissible genres of discourse and arguments that would establish the injustice of particular dominant practices or normative conduct. This tactic has often been deployed to rationalize sexual mutilation, for instance.

We know too that the globalizations and transculturations that have taken place over the centuries have produced cultures that are irreversibly heterogeneous and diasporic. Furthermore, the universal and cosmopolitan ambitions in the project of modernity and the Enlightenment have diffused across cultures notions of universal rights and principles, formalized in human charters and in the United Nations Charter to which all states subscribe, even if nominally. Already then, in principle at least, a 'strong universalism' (see Cronin and De Greiff, 2002) exists that asserts the intrinsic worth of every human being. One version of 'strong universalism' advocates a commitment to a transnational redistributive policy, defended through the concept of capabilities, as I have discussed above. This kind of approach to universalism accepts that the global is both a political and an economic order, and that all states must be answerable to universally applicable imperatives of justice. This principle of answerability to some notion of justice is acknowledged even by corporations when they claim that they are committed to social responsibility. My analysis, however, has shown that corporations and neo-liberalism are unable to respond to suffering or to the other's call for solicitude: they are basically amoral; they have no place for justice or the duty of care that it implies.

The universalism that I am proposing must be established prior to the discussion of the issues in terms of, say, redistribution and recognition, as in Fraser and Honneth (2003). It rests on an ontology that prioritizes both commonality and singularity, indeed, that theorizes their inter-relationship in accomplishing being as potentiality. Recognition of the other within the framework of being-with, of 'oneself as another' (Ricoeur, 1992), entails responsibility for the other or 'heteronomous responsibility' (Levinas, 1984: 63); this responsibility takes the form of solicitude and hospitality as the way of expressing indebtedness. The sociality that arises is secured on the basis of bonds of love: the intimacy of lovers, friendship, filiality, conviviality, and on the basis of common or social wealth as the practical ground for constituting community and fellowship. The choice therefore is between an inhuman and perhaps uninhabitable world and a world in which 'one lives well with and for others in just institutions' (Ricoeur, 1992: 330). The postcolonial critique of the present that I have outlined opens onto a new emancipatory project, one that aims to bring about transcolonial and transmodern ways of being in a just world.

Notes

1 I should reiterate the claim that the development of capitalism was conditioned by the consolidation of colonialism, a claim I discussed in Chapter 2. One could add the many studies – Jalée (1981), Rodney (1989), Hobsbawm (1987), Williams (1964), and so on – that

point to the essential contribution of colonial enterprise and slavery to the success of capitalism. It is worth noting that some studies, e.g. Bayly (1989), reject this claim, arguing that there was a net debit to the (British) Exchequer arising from the costs of empire. But such studies use conventional accounting practices and models and do not seem able to calculate the dynamic effects on the metropolitan economies of demand and trade directly affected by the requirements of colonialism and imperial expansion, or the effects of a relatively permanent war economy, that is, the contribution due to the vast increase in manufacturing and supply and demand arising from new resources and objects of consumption, military procurements – say, regarding the ship building industry – the permanent mobilization of a vast personnel for war and colonial administration, as well as the technological pay-offs arising from the introduction of new raw materials and their processing, and the armaments industry (for example, developments in navigation, steel making, explosives). The proper way to estimate the contribution of colonialism, economic and otherwise, is to imagine its absence: what would have been the fate of Europe and/or capitalism had European colonialism not happened? This is a complex issue, beyond the scope of conventional political economy, since it is irreducible to the economy alone, as my arguments in Chapter 2 demonstrate. Additionally, there are questions of the kind (and this may appear mundane until one works it through): what would have been Europe (or the West) without the dozens of products that at first the 'New World' then the ex-'Third World' made available to Europe, such as, at first: potato, tea, tobacco, tomato, sugar, chocolate, rubber, quinine, spices, then: oil, many metal ores, and other critical raw materials? There are, of course, other such counterfactual questions that throw a different light on the matter of the costs and benefits of colonialism.

2 A list of proper names, by no means complete, of military and economic invasions, destabilizations, assassinations, will stand as testimony of the merciless war that was waged to ensure the failure of the Left in the 'Third World': Korea, Vietnam, Cuba, South Africa, Nigeria, Mozambique, Angola, Chile, Algeria, Brazil, Argentina, Bolivia, the Philippines, Panama, Burma; Che Guevarra, Mondlane, Lumumba, Biko, Allende, Cabral. There is of course another list of proper names, from Prague to Malcolm X, that would refer to the war in the West.

3 An astonishing case is that of American relations with Bangladesh, one of the poorest countries in the world. Bangladesh in 2002 paid $331 million in import tariffs alone to the USA, more than France does, while it received $84 million in aid (*IMF Finance and Development*, vol. 39. no. 3, Sept 2002, cited in Mann 2003: 59). American aid itself is a mere 0.2 per cent of American GDP, half of which goes to Israel, and most of the rest to those able to do a favour for the Americans (70 per cent of American aid goes to NGOs).

4 The role of financial capitalism as a force in driving the need to acquire assets through privatization is central. Finance capitalism operates through the speculative stratagems of the stock market. These are at the mercy of arcane knowledges, expert prognostics, whims, hunches, the swings in mood of the market, risk-taking in, for example, betting on the future price of commodities and future movements of prices. Banks, investment companies, insurance firms have grown to be the dominant sector of the economy in terms of value (on the stock market, of course). But the ratio of corporate assets to quoted value has been diminishing. This makes it imperative that corporations acquire some much-needed assets to restore their stability and reduce their vulnerability, precisely by acquiring the treasury held as common and social wealth – water, minerals, oil, gas, utilities, health, education and other services, indigenous knowledges – in order to maintain their attractiveness for the finance sector, or else suffer a crash in their share prices – the dot.com scenario. This drive for yet more assets is endless. It is trying to colonize time itself, a counter-Enlightenment move in tune with the 'end of history' project.

5 I am grateful to Sally Waddingham whose doctoral research – 'The question of the social responsibility of the corporation in the age of neo-liberal capitalism' – establishes the centrality of property in the discourse of neo-liberalism.

6 Biopiracy has become the classic case of the commodification of knowledge alongside its privatization, the theft of the common wealth of indigenous peoples. Randeria's (2005) study of the neem tree is an exemplary illustration of the combination of law, expertise, technology, local resistances at play in this process.

There is also a problem of what would be fair restitution or new arrangement, in cases where later generations of owners have improved through investment of labour and capital the resource acquired through colonization, and so on, for example, land. The problem is not about the legality of the transactions, for as the law stands, a corporation or state could claim ownership of particular planets on grounds of discovery or first landing on unclaimed 'real estate', and offer them for sale as soon as the claim has been admitted or registered; it is a problem about principles that transcend the law, concerning ontology and ethics.

7 A point could be made here about strategic colonialism, that is, the development that saw the colonial occupation of territory as a factor in the use of their resources and their strategic deployment as a staging post, so that colonial domination directly entered into military calculations at the level of logistical thinking. Said (1993) and Bishop and Phillips (2002) cite several cases of British colonial troops being deployed in further colonial conquests. The interesting departure from other historical examples of the strategic deployment of colonies in the case of other empires – say, the Chinese, the Roman, the Moors – is the dovetailing of military and commercial goals at the level of conceptual framework that has continued into present times; I developed this in Chapter 2.

8 I would not want to invoke 'American imperialism' too readily here, for although the Americans have shown a remarkable degree of consistency in putting their interest first in global economic policy, the idea of imperialism, though it is an important factor (see Harvey, 2004), draws attention away from the logic in forms of capitalism; it is this logic that needs to be foregrounded, though imperialism instantiates it. Clearly American vested economic interest overrode issues of fairness or humanitarian concern, but that interest was over-determined both by the logic of capitalism and the position of the USA in the world economy, including the dollar as reserve currency that resulted in its economy operating as the node in the circuits of capital.

9 This chapter is not the place for a serious comparison of the merits of the competing analyses. My approach implicitly rejects accounts that rely on concepts of lag, or cultural incompatibility. The success of countries like the Asian Tigers, for example, South Korea, Malaysia, Singapore, now China and important sections of India, in competing with the 'developed' West on its own terms, that is, as modern capitalist economies shows that capitalism can develop in a variety of soils. Clearly, it requires specific subjectivities and values for it to operate efficiently, for instance, individualism, rational discipline, and selfishness, the meanness of spirit one associates with Puritanism nationalism, insecurities of all kinds.

Today, for corporate capitalism, a puritan ethic no longer drives the process of accumulation, as Weber had argued by reference to the driving motivation structuring the 'work ethic' and predestination. One aspect of this ethic was an individualism premised on the idea of the calling and the chosen, inscribed in a lifestyle. The legacy of an indifference to the communal good persists in corporate thinking, except when the perception of this indifference harms the commercial interests of the corporation so that the latter is led to represent itself as the paragon of the caring, sharing enterprise, whose driving ambition is to help humanity. The idea of corporate social responsibility has become integrated as part of the cultural capital of corporations, transmutable into profit. It must be pointed out also that variations exist that add fuel to the argument that there is no inherent coherence to the capitalist system, e.g. in the 'Japanese model' where a sense of loyalty and mutual obligation thrives, giving a different sense, perhaps of neo-tribe, to the notion of the 'corporate man'.

10 From the point of view of the conditions of possibility of the sex industry and its role in the economy, it is worth pointing out that in the case of Thailand, the Americans decided to develop Bangkok as a base for R&R for American soldiers during the Vietnam War. After the war, the World Bank encouraged sex tourism as part of Thailand's economic development plan. One needs to take account too of indigenous cultural conditions as a factor in the development of the sex industry (see Bishop and Robinson, 1998). A study on money laundering estimates that just in the case of Thai women smuggled into Japan, Germany, and Taiwan, the prostitution rings earned US$3.2 billion a year (Phongphacit, cited in Nordstrom, 2000).

11 One could add the 'discovery' that corporations – Enron is just one of many – routinely engage in fraud/'creative accounting' on a vast scale, lying about their profits and sales to

sustain their share value on the world market, and make fortunes for insiders, or simply to prevent competitors from appearing to be doing much better; for the constant risk that corporations face in the global economy is to lose ground through a decline in market value and the return on investment, and thus be left vulnerable to take-overs and being broken up – a parasitism that has endemic and institutionalized.

12 The recognition of being as a being in time is itself a development that one could correlate with the increasing complexity of the human mind and culture, relating to language and memory, and developments in tool-using capacity (Venn, 2000).

Glossary

The first occurrence of a word in the Glossary is shown in bold in the text.

Abject

· The term derives from the work of Julia Kristeva (especially, 1982) in psycho-analysis, particularly the description of the process of separation of the infant from its mother which is a founding moment for the institution of the ego. This process of splitting establishes for the child the boundaries of the inner and the outer, I and not-I, self and other. Because of the association with what is expelled from the body, and the traumatic process of separation itself, what the child separates from is experienced as an abjected entity. Besides, the threat of the abject re-entering the ego and undermining its integrity is always present in phantasy, so that thresholds and boundaries of the self and other become marked by the trope of purity and danger. In cultural analysis, the notion of the abject and of abjection is therefore used when an other is denigrated in discourse and associated with negative feelings, as in racisms, and when the person so positioned in discourse experiences herself as an abject subject (through introjection of the bad feelings of the other). Psychic ambivalence is another aspect of the process, for at the level of affect, the other/mother is also the object of desire.

Aporia

The term refers to a problem which does not appear to have a solution, like the chicken and egg case. Often the problem arises because of the way the question is posed in the first place, or because of a basic undecidability in the way a concept is used. Thus because angels are both material and immaterial, it is impossible to decide how many would fit on the head of a pin (giving underemployed scholars ample room for debate).

Archaeology (see also genealogy)

The term is associated with the work of Foucault on the history of the social sciences and the formation and mutation of discourse. One central point about the concept is the recognition that the history or narrative of specific ideas, say, about Galileo's work on planetary motion or the discovery of the structure of the DNA, presents or records successful experiments and findings, neglecting errors or unfruitful research or discussions with colleagues or influences that do not quite fit the rationalist model of the history of ideas. So, in terms of the reality of the emergence and mutation of ideas and practices, much is forgotten or disavowed or buried under a history of progress and thus remain invisible that would otherwise lead us to understand the emergence quite differently. Archaeology aims to excavate the archive, maybe to reconstitute it, certainly to make visible aspects of the historical process that are crucial yet absent in conventional accounts, for instance, in finding that Galileo's inadequate theory of inertia undermined his explanation of planetary motion or that Crick and Watson's account of DNA 'forgets' the contribution of Rosalind Franklin's X-ray radiography studies. A case in postcolonial studies would be the archaeology of resistance in slave plantation and its contribution to the emancipation of slaves, or the contribution of Native Americans to the survival of the early colonizers. From that point of view, archaeology helps to raise questions of the effect of power on knowledge.

Archaeology is also part of the approach to history that emphasizes conditions of possibility, and thus searches for evidence in adjacent discourses and practices; it pays attention to the neglected, it searches for the traces of what has been buried.

Assemblage (complexity, autopoiesis, flow, turbulence, emergence, process)

The concept of assemblage has emerged as one of a series of new concepts, alongside those of complexity, chaos, indeterminacy, fractals, string, turbulence, flow, multiplicity, emergence, and so on, that now form the theoretical vocabulary for addressing the problem of determination, of process, and of stability and instability regarding social phenomena. As with the previous set of concepts in the social sciences, notably the notion of structure, they derive from developments in the natural sciences and mathematics. Their introduction signals an important shift at the level of theorization and methodology, opening analysis to the recognition of the complexity of cultural, social as well as 'natural' phenomena, for instance, concerning sociality, diaspora, the living organism, mind and elementary particles.

Structure in the natural and social sciences grounds causal determination within a logic of stability and linear causality. It is a central epistemological element in the work of the 'grand theorists' of social science such as Marx, Durkheim, Weber, and Parsons. The notion of discrete and nomological determination, which positivism and various forms of structuralism support, has clear pay-offs from the point of view of homogenizing and predicting social phenomena, and thus for the possibility of intervention and rational governance. However, the limitations of approaches based on this notion of determination have been demonstrated in their failure to account adequately for change, resistance, agency, and the event, that is, the irruption of the unexpected or unpredictable. The limitations relate also to their inadequacy from the point of view of co-relating phenomena across different fields, for example, between the psychic and the social, the affective and the cognitive, and between matter and form. The problem for theory is that of thinking structure as well as multiplicity and indeterminacy within the same theoretical framework.

The concept of assemblage has appeared in the wake of these critiques and questions. In the recent literature it is mostly associated with the work of Deleuze and Guattari (particularly *A Thousand Plateaux*, 1988) and clearly explained in DeLanda (2002). One can also retrace its emergence by reference to developments in the physics of small particles, in topology, in molecular biology and generally in the interface between the theorization of emergence and becoming (say, in ontogeny and phylogeny), adaptation, autopoiesis and cybernetic systems (that is, open systems with feed-back), and post-structuralist mathematics (e.g. of chaos, complexity, string). They all emphasize adaptivity rather than fixity or essence, the formal properties of the system rather than the specific instance or individuation, the spatio-temporal dimension rather than quantities, co-articulation and composs-ibility rather than linear and discrete determination, multilinear time and the temporality of processes such that emergence and irreversibility are brought to the fore, for instance, in embryonic development (Bateson, 1980; Prigogine and Stengers, 1984). Deleuze and Guattari translate these themes into a vocabulary that re-codes emergence and becoming, namely, (de/re)-territorialization (relation to topology), the machinic (relation to the cyber-netic, autopoiesis), multiplicity (relation to differentiation, compossibility).

In the light of the foregoing, assemblage can be seen as a relay concept, linking the problematic of structure and regularity with that of change and far-from-equilibrium systems. It focuses on process and on the dynamic character of the inter-relationships between the heterogeneous elements of the phenomenon. It recognizes both structurizing and indeterminate effects, that is, both flow and turbulence, produced in the interaction of open systems. It points to complex becoming and multiple determinations (Ong and Collier, 2004). It is sensitive to time and temporality in the emergence and mutation of the phenomenon; it thus directs attention to the *longue durée*. While Deleuze and Guattari suggest desiring machines as exemplar, one could instead refer to weather formation and the genome, or for that matter, to the formation of identity and of diasporic cultures; in other words, assemblage opens towards the question of emergence and becoming.

Nevertheless, it is important to distinguish between the level of abstract general theory – say, the mathematics of string, topology – and the level of concrete material and social life, and the singular or individual entity. For human beings the meaning of social action and of existence adds a dimen-sion to analysis that cannot be reduced to or derived from the general theory. In any case, intermediate concepts are needed for the analysis of concrete social and natural processes and mechanisms. Thus, theory itself can be con-sidered as an assemblage that operates as specific conceptual combinatories in addressing specific problems. The coherence of the particular combinatory would be grounded in the respect for the general principles outlined above. Assemblage is one of the terms that today signals the emergence of a new episteme.

Co-articulation

The term is used to indicate the dynamic interaction between two or more discourses or practices such that the outcome or state of affairs in any one of them at any particular time is the result of their reciprocal effects. The discourses and practices or processes are inter-connected by way of relays, hinges or nodes that may be specific concepts or institutions or mechanisms. For example, the genealogy of the discourse of mental measurement (IQ) and that of the development of statistics – specific tests or correlation – show that they are co-articulation in relation to social policy and the concepts of population and of the normal.

Colonialism (decolonization, imperialism, neo-colonialism, postmodern or neo-liberal colonialism)

Colonialism is the conquest, territorial occupation and subjugation of a population; it has occurred throughout history, involving most countries on one side or other of the process, for example, the Aztecs, the Vikings, the Romans, the Chinese. When colonialism spreads across several countries and is relatively lasting, it has often been organized in the form of an empire, say, the Mughal in India or the Ottoman in (what the Americans call) the Middle East and Eastern Europe. Imperialism is an administratively and militarily coherent apparatus of control directed from a centre of power, say Rome or Istanbul. European or modern colonialism adds specific ingredients to the process that marks it as a distinct form: its model combines appropriation-as-dispossession with the reduction of the colonized to the status of a lesser being – an other – according to epistemological and ontological discourses that claim the knowledge, culture, beliefs, way of life of the colonizer to be superior and that fix the colonized in the position of an inherently inferior being. In other words, European colonialism adds ontological and epistemological violence to military domination and economic exploitation. It is correlated to occidentalism. In its imperialist form, from around the beginning of the nineteenth century, it attempts to 'civilize' the colonized (a process which ideally was meant to include Christianization) by means of processes of assimilation and integration operating through technologies of formation and regulation of the subject – an imperial governmentality – and through processes of subalternization whereby the colonized are recruited into the apparatus of empire as part of its infrastructural supports. One's understanding of colonialism has been altered as a result of the active process of dismantling it through oppositional strategies and liberation struggles, that is, decolonization.

Neo-colonialism refers to the continuation of colonial domination and exploitation after formal independence. It operates through different economic, legal, political, administrative apparatuses of domination, relying on institutions and attitudes instituted or developed in the period of colonialism, for instance, the World Bank, the IMF, the WTO, regional trade agreements, investment strategies, values inherent in the notion of development, a culture of debt.

We are perhaps now seeing the emergence of new forms of colonialism, outside the frame of intelligibility of modernity, and thus postmodern in orientation. They would relate more directly to transformations that have happened in the course of the struggles over the past 30 years and that have gradually seen the emergence of globalization in terms of networks, flows, de-territorialized processes that appeared relatively chaotic or fractal, and that are being reorganized in the form of a 'new world order' or Empire. Such new forms could perhaps be called total or postmodern imperialism, or Empire (Hardt and Negri, 2000) that is, the idea of a de-territorialized, global system of hegemony and domination; we could even detect the emergence of neo-feudal imperialism, characterized by feudal relations of power that do not require direct control over territory and the polity, but operate through relays or hinges so that economic, military, political, cultural, technological activities can be correlated in terms of an overall worldview such as neo-liberalism, and global institutions and international laws that inscribe neo-feudal Empire; military intervention takes the form of a policing directed by the interest of security. In the light of all this, one could understand colonialism to designate forms of dispossession and subjugation founded in the homogenisation of a centre, an origin, a sovereignty or a world-view; when they all combine in one form of rule, one has the total or pure form of colonialism.

Creolization (creolite, diaspora, hybridity, mestizaje, syncretism, transculturation, translation)

My usage extends the dictionary definition that applies it to a native of a colony of European descent, or to the French, Spanish, etc. 'patois' spoken in some former colonies, or to a 'mixed race' inhabitant of the Third World, particularly in the Caribbean. If we look at creolization as a process, what happens is that an indigenous people appropriates some elements of a foreign language, mixing it with their own and other elements to create a vernacular or indigenized form of the language; thus, the creole French used in Martinique or Mauritius. In the latter case, it has been established as a language in its own right, for obvious political goals relating to the decolonization of the mind. But language is not neutral. It inscribes struggles and a whole culture; it is a memory, carrying tales of what has happened in the history of a people, and connotations that keep the trace of the community's existence and deeds. For that reason, throughout colonialism, it was the target and symbol of power struggles. Thus, the Spanish Conquistadors do not consider the language of the Native Americans as a proper language – Caliban was not supposed to be able to speak at all, until the arrival of the colonial masters – the English outlawed the Celtic language in Scotland, and successful colonization can be measured by the degree to which a language is implanted in a colony. Creolization therefore is the result of a cultural struggle. It is also the result of the encounter of cultures brought together through the diasporic (diaspora means dispersion in the original Greek) melange of peoples that colonization, migration and displacement produces.

Indeed, looking at it as a general process, one can detect forms of creolization in the English language, made up as it is of elements of French, Latin, Anglo-Saxon, Norse, and so on. Similarly at the level of cultural practices, there are countless examples of the admixture, 'hybridization', syncretism, mestizaje, transculturation, cross-overs (as in music) that every culture has experienced: in artefacts, everyday practices, beliefs. Religion such as Christianity, Judaism and Islamism share so much that one could speak of each as the creolized form of the other, bearing in mind the historical order of succession as well as subsequent reinterpretations of the founding texts. Of course, fundamentalist and doctrinaire accounts would argue against the idea of borrowings and admixtures, since purity is central to the strength of the doctrine. Creolization assumes cultures cannot but be heterogeneous and polyglot (perhaps small tribes that have remained isolated for very long periods of time may remain culturally the same for generations).

Read: Sarah Ahmed (2003).

Deconstruction

The practice of deconstruction starts with the idea that texts, discourses are the result of multiple determinations, so that what is said is shaped by conditions of possibility and a process of constitution that include factors that are not visible yet are 'present' in the text as effect or about which the speaker or author is not conscious. The term refers to the work of Derrida, in particular, his critique of logocentrism and structuralism and the closure of meaning they differently produce. Deconstruction is meant to make visible how a text has been constructed, and throw light on the present-but-invisible aspects that structure it or circumscribe its meaning. One of the aims of deconstruction is to challenge taken-for-granted self-referential frame of intelligibility and bring to light what they conceal or what they normalize. Thus, the black/white divide not only inscribes stereotypes, it produces as effects what they name/assume.

Furthermore, the practice of deconstruction invokes a whole problematic of signifying practice that puts to work notions of trace (for example, in the idea of an absent-presence) and of *différance*, of discursive formation and archaeology, of metaphor and metonymy, tropes generally, that is to say, all the ways in which discourse, whether in speech or writing, attempts to 'represent' or bring to presence or communicate a world that intrinsically differs from the system of sign that refers to it. Meaning thereby is deferred to a practice of interpretation that is itself a provisional point of correlation of sign and referent. Thus, the concept of postcoloniality has been the object of deconstructive analyses from the beginning. Deconstruction, as in the case of the postcolonial, has its stakes. The political pay-off is that the challenge to hegemonic and legitimating discourses through deconstruction and other devices opens up these discourses, say, about 'race', to other accounts, particularly those that make visible the erased or hidden or taken for granted process of production of discourse, thus the effects of power inside them: deconstruction, additionally, makes visible the ideological functioning of discourse. To that extent, it could be said that it is one of the tools, alongside genealogy and discourse analysis, of critique.

Desire (demand, need, wish)

Desire is one of a complicated cluster of terms in psychoanalytic theory which is fraught with problems. Desire – in Lacan, Kristeva, Deleuze and Guattari, as distinct from the term 'wish' or *Wunsch* in Freud (see Laplanche and Pontalis, 1980) – is used in the generic sense, relating to affective economy, and not by reference to a specific desire. Its sense is best understood as one of three terms, the other two being need and demand. Need is applied to the 'individual' as a biological and physical organism; thus the infant's immediate need is for food and comfort. Demand relates to a signifying activity like speech; it assumes an other or Other (say, mother, or the generalized other) to whom the demand is addressed; it expects a response. So, a relation to the other is involved from the beginning in the logic of the demand. The response from the other may satisfy a need, but exceeds it, since the response is itself a token of recognition or of love, the sign of a bond. Already, one can imagine a gap between a need and a demand, since one never knows if a response is adequate. Desire is born in that gap between the appeal to the other in the demand, and the response that is itself anticipated as a gesture that establishes or confirms an affective bond, an aspect of which may involve the satisfaction of a need. Additionally, demand, at the level of the relation to the other, enters into other psychic processes, particularly concerning the experience of loss (say, in the separation from the mother), and thus the problematic of lack. (Note that in Lacan, the concept of lack belongs to both psychoanalytic and philosophical discourse, referring to both Freudian theory and the phenomenology of, say, Heidegger.) One should understand Bhabha's reference to the 'desire for the other' within that conceptual grid, so that issues of recognition/ misrecognition and subjectivity are triggered in the text. Thus, the reference to ambivalence in the relation of colonizer and colonized suggests a dilemma (or aporia) at the level of the mechanism of desire in that relationship: the colonizer refuses recognition of the other as a significant other yet demands recognition from the other, while the colonized demands recognition from the colonizer yet must reject the colonizer as a significant other. This play of recognition and misrecognition, discussed from a different point of view in Hegel's 'master–slave' dialectic and by Fanon, plays an important part in the analysis of identity, identification and mimesis in the colonial and post-colonial context, especially in the context of hegemonic discourses like Occidentalism, and effects of 'cultural imperialism'.

Diaspora

The concept of diaspora has undergone significant shifts in the past few years. Classically it was applied to the dispersion of the Jews, and the earlier typologies reflect this. For example, Safran (1991) describes the ideal type of diaspora by reference to the following characteristics: dispersal of a popula-tion to several territories, the shared memory of homeland, minority status in the host community and the experience of exclusion, the hope of return, connections maintained to the homeland that have effects for identity. While some or all of these characteristics have been shared in the experience of Jews in Europe at various points, this typology could equally be applied to Palestinians and to Caribbean migration to various degrees, depending on the geography and conditions of dispersion. Cohen (1997) in his modifica-tion of this typology points to five types of diasporas: victim, trade, labour, imperial, cultural. Clearly, across time and generations these types slide into each other, so that it becomes difficult to keep to strict characterization. It is increasingly recognized that the process of dispersion and migrancy is more fluid and complex, and applies to more varied movements of popula-tions than conventional approaches have described (see *Interventions*, vol. 5, no. 1 2003, on Global Diasporas). My argument is that a postcolonial under-standing of the term must recognize that migrancy has been endemic to the history of cultures in all periods, clearly evident in cities and the urban centres of empires over the ages. While reference to a history of the Jews has inflected the early conceptualization of diaspora, it is the emergence of the concept of the state as a nation-state that continues to distort one's under-standing of migrancy and dispersion. In particular, the 'imagined community' of the modern state is assumed to be, ideally, ethnically homogenous, and temporally progressive or linear; the implications for the notion of citizen-ship, of belonging, of 'normality' regarding conduct and identity, of rights, have been further determined by the history of colonialism and by racism and the power relations they inscribe. Yet all cultures are polyglot and dias-poric; the evidence for this, denied by ethnic essentialism, is clearly demon-strated in all cultures, genealogies of languages, musics, food, technologies, religions, knowledges, artistic practices and so on. Postcolonial critique shows the extent to which each, in its 'national' characteristics, is the result of appropriations, borrowings, grafts, exchanges, adaptations, creolizations, translation, operating in the *longue durée*, though clearly the effects of colonial imposition cannot be left out of the picture.

Episteme

The term designates the conceptual structure that frames knowledge in particular periods and places. Though admittedly a vague concept, its main fruitfulness for analysis is to point to the intrinsic (spatial and temporal) limits that circumscribe knowledge, and to draw attention to the fact that the epistemological terrain on which one poses and answers questions about the world determines the grid of intelligibility that enables one to make particular sense of the world. It draws attention to the shifts in the epistemological framework that determines the ground rules within which discourses are generated and make sense, for example from the classical to the modern episteme in Europe. Thus, for Foucault (1972) in *The Order of Things*, the episteme in the classical period is framed by the principles of similitudes, analogy, emulation, sympathies that set out the parameters within which one could understand the properties and behaviour of things. They circumscribed the conceptual framework within which the world made sense. All thought in the period maps into the episteme. As a concept it points to the fact that because of these structures of knowledge, one is unable to make sense of the world outside the perimeter of the episteme. For instance, Native Americans, because of the episteme within which their concept of nature and their relation to the earth was framed, could not make sense of the concept of individual, private ownership of the land, and thus of the European laws that legitimized private forms of ownership regarding land.

The episteme operates at the level of a culture as a whole. The concept relates to but is distinct from that of problematic and paradigm. The latter is more specific and 'regional' and should be understood by reference to the usage in Kuhn's (1962) *The Structure of Scientific Revolutions* (though he finds it difficult to pin the concept down in a definite way and there are disputes about its precise meaning and effect on scientific activity and thinking). A shift in paradigm, for example, from Newtonian to Einsteinian physics regarding the absolute character of time and space, does not challenge the broader episteme (though in this case it had enormous implications for the conceptual structure framing our view of the world). The postmodern is supposed to involve an epistemic shift in our understanding of the world though this is far from clear yet since much still rely on the conceptual framework established by the philosophical discourse of modernity, for instance, regarding the criteria for objective knowledge or the classificatory systems in the social sciences that neglect non-European, non-Western modes of knowing.

Genealogy

The everyday use of the term points to ancestry or lines of descent in tracing the blood line of a particular person. In this case we know the process of generation and only need retrace the parental and consanguine relations that lead backwards to reveal an ancestral tree. But genealogy in Foucault's (1984) sense must not be confused with this kind of search; it is an approach to writing the history of concepts. Its orientation is to write a history of the present by reconstructing the conditions that have made possible a current understanding of a concept or a historical situation. In the case of a concept – say, race – or an historical development – the emergence of the nation-state – antecedent events and conditions of possibility are not obvious, or should not be assumed. It is possible to reconstruct different genealogies, since the decision about conditions of possibility depends on judgement of effects as well as archival research to check for factors that other narrations may not have taken into account and to trawl through existing accounts. The work of the Subaltern Studies Group in India covers aspects of genealogical work.

Globalization

It is difficult to avoid the term in any discussion of the state of the world. But interpretation and attitudes vary so much that one can only disengage some broad trends and characteristics from the mass of material (see Robertson, 1994, for a classic examination). From a postcolonial perspective, one could note that globalization indicates: (1) the significant acceleration of flows across the world: of people, images, money, technologies, ideas (as in Appadurai, 1996); (2) the idea of the compression of the world made possible by technologies of communication and transport and the speeded-up and intensified processes of production and distribution that accelerate contact in time and displacement across space, or a time–space compression (Harvey, 1989; Robertson, 1994); (3) the idea of a tendency towards the homogenization of culture, for example, as expressed in the claim that corporations dominated by Western, largely American, interests and world-view have colonized other cultures to produce commodified 'McWorlds'; (4) the recognition that there have been forms of globalization before, for instance, Westernization and occidentalism, and it could be argued that the Arabs and the Chinese had pursued projects of globalization. Globalization is a complicated, complex network of inter-relations and networks that should not be reduced to simple good/bad effects at the level of culture (see Featherstone, 1991; Hannerz, 1996; Tomlinson, 1999), but examined in terms of what is at stake in the specific developments. For instance, increasingly diverse social movements are coordinating their efforts as part of a 'globalization from below' to counter 'globalization from above'. It is true, nevertheless, that, given the extension of imperial and colonial regimes of power in the post-independence period, globalization has had a net pauperization effect on the postcolony, as even 'insiders' such as Stiglitz recognize (Stiglitz, 2002). I would emphasize the fact that globalization does not just happen, or that it only exists in the mind or in discourse. It is the result of specific socio-technical apparatuses and technologies of formation that today include institutions, and *dispositifs* such as the United Nations, the World Bank, transnational corporations like

Time/Warner, Toshiba, Exxon, and events such as the World Cup, the Olympic Games and other international realities organized on a world scale. Globalization is produced by this assemblage.

Hegemony

The term hegemon refers to a leader, a dominant power or state. The concept has mainly been developed by Gramsci (1971). The problem which the concept in Gramsci addresses is this: domination can be sustained for a time by the use of force, but how does a group exercise power without constantly having recourse to force? In history we know that many forms of sociality have existed that are characterized by gross and systematic inequalities or clear differences in power and status. Yet such societies have often been politically stable for long periods, for instance, feudalisms, and capitalisms. The question of power must thus be displaced onto that of authority and legitimation, that is, the means whereby a dominant power assures consent to its rule. There is clearly a role for the state, through the law and other apparatuses where power and the norms of the normative are institutionalized, and through which forms of coercion operate when necessary. But additionally, consent and consensus, for Gramsci, involved mechanisms at work in civil society. These relate to the ways of establishing moral and intellectual authority among a population. The mechanisms are part of everyday action in the social world, they form opinion and values, direct conduct, constitute subjectivities, establish a 'common sense' and a 'good sense', and come to have the status of the taken for granted, what a community takes to be the already-agreed upon. Hegemony and the exercise of power by the dominant group · or 'block' of groups go hand in hand. It is difficult to transform this taken-for-granted world where consent has become part of a way of life, for instance, in today's consumer culture in the rich countries. Gramsci spoke of organic intellectuals, belonging to the class they represent in the domain of thought, who would produce hegemonic and counter-hegemonic ideas and values.

Human rights

The idea of human rights rests on the principle that human beings have a number of fundamental rights by virtue of being human. The better-known rights are the right to liberty, the freedom of worship, the right to strike, the right to free speech. The United Nations Declaration of Human Rights is the document listing the principal rights agreed and ratified by all member nations. Additionally, the UN Convention on the Rights of the Child (not ratified by the USA) is a more recent document that protects children from many forms of abuse and attempts to establish the basic premise for ensuring the welfare of children. We know that most countries routinely break one or more of these rights, for instance, by torturing prisoners, detaining political opponents without trial, denying whole categories of people the right to free speech or to vote, or putting up obstacles that prevent workers from joining unions, and so on.

The idea of human rights has been criticized by some for its universalism, in that it assumes or implies that all human beings everywhere are the same, or should accept the same basic principles regarding rights. This objection is often associated with the Eurocentric or Western character of the particular rights that have become institutionalized as universal. Furthermore, it has been argued that rights such as group rights and customary rights, are not recognized, because the existing universal rights are expressed in a language that, in juridical terms, privileges the individual over the communal or the collective. The debate is quite complex and should be examined case by case rather than in abstract terms, that is, by reference to specific articles in the various conventions and declarations. Also, changes in what may be considered universal rights happen all the time, for instance, the claim that corporation must disclose information to the public on the basis that the public has a 'right to know' (the transparency argument).

The fact is that human rights are often the only appeal that the oppressed have for redress or justice, whether from within-state oppression (for instance, in the case of ethnic and gender oppression) or that arising from external intervention (as the USA in Chile). All struggles for colonial liberation have been motivated by ideas of inalienable freedoms and liberty. The World Social Forum, for instance, set up in opposition to corporate, neo-liberal capitalist pauperization of peoples everywhere, draws support from notions of human rights and declares new ones such as the 'Universal Right to Food Sovereignty'. The problem is: millions of asylum seekers thrown into camps, political prisoners held without trial or tortured, disenfranchised workers, whole categories of people oppressed by the powerful have nothing but the claim to human rights as the only principle of hope, and perhaps the only means to seek redress or justice. So, what kind of intervention is one making when one objects because these rights are Eurocentric or Western or liberal? Should they wait for the emergence of an 'authentic', 'uncontaminated', consensual set of rights? What would those be?

At the theoretical level, the problem brings up the question of ontology, namely, the question of how one is to conceptualize the human being, and whether a discourse about being can be constructed that would have universal foundations and would be universally accepted. My view is that one can and should attempt to produce such a universal discourse, and that it must be based on secular, that is, non-theological (but not necessarily anti-spiritual) arguments (Venn, 2000). This possibility is itself conditioned by the debates about the human being that have gone on for centuries (mostly in theologies and philosophical reflections in all cultures), and in modern times within the discourse of modernity and the Enlightenment. Those who would dismiss the centrality of human rights are confused about the nature of the questions and the historicity of the problem – namely that the specific content may change with time, but the principle of rights does not. Objections have mostly come from those who want to hang on to local, mainly religious, usually sectarian views that support one form or other of oppression and exploitation, and increasingly from corporate and governmental interests for whom particular universal rights are obstacles, although they are quick to capitalize on the idea of rights when it can be made to serve their own interest. Another standpoint in favour of universal rights is to imagine what the human condition would be like without the guarantee, even minimally in principle, of such basic rights. It is important therefore to examine and weigh up what is politically at stake in the principle of universal rights and in the debates about specific rights.

Imaginary

I use imaginary by reference to Lacan's use of the term. In Lacan it is always one of three inter-related terms, the other two being the Symbolic and the Real. The capitals indicate the difference from substantive discrete symbols and the experiential real. The schema in which the Imaginary is elaborated is part of an explanatory model of what, at the general level of a universal process, might be happening in the mind or in the psyche. We have no direct access to the processes involved in the mind, and so can only propose a model, and deduce some consequences from it that can be checked out by reference to people's actual speech, and conduct (or, in models in neurophysiology, by reference to electrical discharges and bio-chemical activity). Even then it is a matter of a judgement about sense that involves other considerations. There is no way for psychoanalytic theory to get out of this dilemma. See A. Wilden ([1968] 1881), Lacan's (1979) *Four Fundamental Concepts of Psychoanalysis*, especially sections 14–17, Grosz (1990). Lacan is difficult to read because in the background to his claims and discussion lie key problems in philosophy – for example, the Cartesian concept of the cogito and disputes in philosophy about it, Heidegger's emphasis on time, the temporal dimension in the understanding of being, the work of Hegel, Husserl, Freud, Merleau-Ponty, linguistic theory, de Saussure and Jakobson. So the difficulty relates to the ability to pick out the often absent references, and so understand the context and the questions that Lacan's arguments address. Many disputes about Lacan arise from this difficulty and the different interpretations that the text opens itself to because of the complex and often invisible background to what he is saying. Additionally, his discourse, e.g., the Seminars, was addressed in an open forum to an audience of peers and colleagues, often well established in their own right, such as Althusser and Foucault, so that he did not have to spell out the references in his speech, since they were taken for granted as part of a common background and formation shared by that audience.

Longue durée

This is the idea, associated with the *Annales* school of history in France that developments in history take a long time to emerge clearly enough, and that historical research should therefore examine shifts and changes over a long span of time, paying attention to the different temporalities that characterize different kinds of historical realities and forces. Thus, one can distinguish sudden events like a revolution, conjunctures that have effects over several decades, and realities that change slowly, such as aspects of everyday culture, for example, religious affiliation in a particular country. It developed in opposition to explanations in terms of facts and their succession or structures and laws of development; instead it emphasizes complex and uneven determination in history. One must be careful to avoid reading back after the event, that is, hindsight reading that many historians fall back upon to point to continuities or precursors when such events owe more to contingency. It is tempting to assume necessary outcomes, especially in the context of scientism, and so retroactively attribute a logic to historical process. The work of Braudel (1949) on the Mediterranean or Le Roy Ladurie ([1967] 1978) on the Montaillou are examples of historical work that are framed within the *longue durée*.

The other (alterity, the Other, the 'other', otherness, singularity)

The term other immediately brings up a two term relation: the same and the other, the 'I' and 'You', identity and otherness. At the most immediate level, there is the recognition that each person exists as a distinct entity, who recognizes herself as a named person, remaining constant as such (as a self and as a legal subject) in spite of changes in the 'personality'/attributes/appearance, etc. of the person (for example, Michael Jackson). This 'singularity' of the subject or 'individual' is the topic of widely divergent theorizations, for instance, in Levinas as opposed to liberalism – that I will not pursue here, though it is vital from the point of view of the foundation of an ethics (Venn, 2000). One theme is relevant though, namely, the universalization of the subject in some philosophies and theologies, specifically in the discourse of modernity relating to the philosophy of the subject as a rational, unitary, self-present autonomous entity. Its canonical form is the Cartesian subject. In occidentalism, that concept is relayed to the Eurocentric ideology that posits the norm of the subject to be the European white male. Within this discourse, the colonized person is positioned as lacking in rationality, less developed, closer to nature, unable to act as an historical agent: she is 'other'. This sense of otherness is implicit in the expression 'Europe and its others' – this is the title of key debates in the early 1980s that interrogated 'colonial discourse' from the point of view of its construction of the other as 'other' (see Barker et al., 1985). The other, within this same Cartesian parameter, includes women (see Bordo, 1986). So, one sense of the otherness of the other is circumscribed in colonial discourse and in masculinist, patriarchal, phallocentric discourses.

Another sense relates to the impossibility of fully knowing one's others, in that I do not know what is in someone else's mind, and I cannot put myself in the place of the other. For example, I cannot die or suffer in the place of a loved one, in order that she may not die or suffer. The term alterity best applies in this case; the alterity of the other remains as an ontological (and psychological) category and barrier. The sense of the singularity of the other arises from this line of thought (Heidegger says we all die alone), elaborated to encompass issues of fragility, finitude, ontological suffering, responsibility for the other, and thus the question of ethics.

Over-determination

One can think of over-determination as a specific case of complex or multiple determination, that is, as situations and occurrences where there is no one simple cause in the form of A causes B. Instead, outcomes are determined by several factors acting in combination where each already predisposes the process towards the outcome. With over-determination, a plurality of the initial conditions leads to the specific outcome or effect. Thus, one could say that globalization was over-determined if one considers that modernity itself as well as rational capitalism have an inherent thrust towards the global, but each by itself may not have been a sufficient determining cause. In psychoanalytic discourse, dreams may be thought to be over-determined in the sense that several unconscious elements and mechanisms may be so organized as to saturate the dream-content. To take an everyday situation, one may well say of someone who works in a crowded institution, is stressed out, and is recovering from an illness, that the fact that she has caught a cold was over-determined.

Paradigm (problematic)

Kuhn (1962) in *The Structure of Scientific Revolutions* addressed the problem of how scientists went about their daily work as scientists: what frames their investigations, what rules guide their practice, what theories shape their thinking. He used the term paradigm to refer to the recognized and universally accepted achievements that for a time provide a particular scientific community with the model problems and solutions that they take for granted in their normal practice. This normal science shapes research programmes until 'anomalies' are increasingly found that shake confidence in the paradigm and incite scientists (usually a younger generation) to search for new models and theories and exemplars. A new paradigm then appears, for instance, as happened with the Copernican revolution (against the Ptolemaic system), or the thermodynamic theory of heat or Einsteinian physics in opposition to Newtonian physics. In postcolonial theory, the idea of development acts as a paradigm, although it rests on assumptions – for example, ideas of the good society, progress, modernization – that indicate other conceptual elements – say, Eurocentrism – at work in constructing its 'normality' or authority. This problem can be better addressed using the wider though related concept of problematic (Bachelard, 1951). A problematic indicates both the positivity of the sciences in the sense of the operating concepts and technical apparatus for producing knowledge, in answer to theoretically formulated questions, as well as the system of unspoken, and often invisible ideas and assumptions that frames how a problem is perceived, what questions one is able to ask and what answers make sense. Africa considered as a problematic refers to the assumptions that enables one to refer to Africa in the singular, a European construction. One finds the problematic repeated in Afrocentrism as the other pole of the denigration and abjection of Africa in racist discourse, since the former remains on the conceptual terrain of the problematic while asserting a different paradigm of Africanness. Similarly, the problematic of subjectivity includes several paradigms circumscribing theorizations of the subject, e.g. as constituted or as constitutive, or as in socio-biology.

The postcolonial

The postcolonial can be understood as a virtual space, that is, a space of possibility and emergence. It is thus also potential becoming; it opens towards a future that will not repeat existing forms of sociality and oppressive power relations.

The postmodern (postmodernism)

This term has become so overused that it is tempting to dispense with it altogether. Yet, because it appears in all manner of discussion about the state of the world today, it is important to establish how it is being used in this book. I will neglect much of the relevant literature for the sake of brevity and clarity, and focus on the differences, or imputed differences, with modernity that the term signals and that locate its place as an analytical concept. To begin with, the postmodern indicates a period after modernity, grounding the break in a particular, usually unspecified, way of conceptualizing modernity, for, without this understanding, one is unable to decide that anything is or is not postmodern. Postmodernism has tended to refer more specifically to the arts and to the arguments in aesthetic theory, in contrast to modernism as a movement or series of related movements in the arts from the end of the nineteenth century that challenged orthodoxies in culture as well as in politics. Modernity in philosophical discourse indicates a period characterized by a secular vision of the destiny of humanity; it is a vision of history in which human beings, motivated by the desire to create more just societies, undertake to transform human condition according to instruments and concepts produced or determined by the application of reason to the problems of the world. Accordingly, its keywords are reason, progress, the subject, but also emancipation, democratization, the maturity of 'humanity'. It is in the name of this project that decisions about legitimate authority and good governance are justified, and judgements about good science, good laws, great art, are circumscribed. It is claimed that consent to government and its provisions rests on the ground that the modern state advances modernity's goals of a progressive and ethical march towards the ideal community of human beings. It is my view that what is significant about modernity, in addition to secularism, is the idea of revolution, specifically, the willingness to imagine and anticipate a fundamentally different social order or state of affairs in order to bring about a more just society, and the willingness to bring it about. Revolution goes beyond dissension, rebellions, uprisings that do not fundamentally alter the system.

Given the promise of the discourse of modernity, it is not surprising that its appeal carried everything before it – in Liberalism and Marxism – and still runs deep (as in Habermas' defence of the continued relevance of the project, against what he calls neo-liberals, and a good deal of contemporary political activity). I will emphasize, as I explained in Chapter 2, that one must understand this appeal within the broader context of ontological considerations, specifically, the need for human beings to anticipate, as a promise, the possibility of better times or the renewal of past pleasures or joys, or the need to imagine the possibility of redemption. This is because human beings exist as beings in time, bearing within them the memory of what has been (in their own lives and in that of the inter-subjective world in which they are inscribed, including the memory of psychically constitutive – thus, liminal, deferred, displaced – loss) and being able to locate the present in relation to an anticipated future. This ontological condition, and its spiritual dimension, have been expressed primarily in the form of religions, that is, in narratives of hope and redemption. Modernity is the only discourse of the human condition that dispenses with God or gods and substitutes 'Man' in 'His' place. In practice – say, in Cartesian narratives of the subject – God remained fundamental (as guarantor, and as the unacknowledged metaphysical presupposition) to the belief that the human being could indeed act as the subject imagined by the discourse of modernity and deliver the promise of the advancement of humanity (hence the force of Nietzsche's declaration that God is dead, and so is 'man', and his advocacy of a 'beyond man').

Before returning to the postmodern, one other feature of modernity must be emphasized, namely, the belief that the arts mediate between the instrumental rationality of means and the ethical imperatives of ends, giving expression in its saying to the hope of something beyond the present (though perhaps inscribed in it as a promise or sign). Thus, the great novel, say Dostoievski's *War and Peace*, a painting like Picasso's *Guernica*, or *The Crucifixion* by Souza, or a film like Eisenstein's *Battleship Potemkin*, are supposed not only to address at the experiential and affective level the deep-seated problems of the time, but, in their way of telling, convey an essential or fundamental but unpresentable quality about human beings, a desire that participates in or even motivates the process of enlightenment. Basically, cutting a lot of corners, the (good) work of art is meant to challenge one's state of being, promoting the questioning of being as to its way of being that is at the heart of the possibility of imagining a different way of being. This applies equally to the postcolonial existential reality, as the Souza painting, and countless more examples of the postcolonial arts of resistance, reveal.

Against this background, one can understand the postmodern as the period characterized by the rejection of the assumptions and practices, the claims and narratives that legitimate or are attributed to modernity. Gone is the idea of a project. Gone too is the 'desire for revolution' that Kant thought decisive. The discourses that supported such a project have been the target of a whole range of critiques: because of their Eurocentrism, their occidentalist presuppositions, their patriarchal presumptions including the phallogocentrism, or because they have failed to deliver the promised enlightened society, indeed, their efforts have resulted in a great deal of inhumanity. Lyotard ([1976] 1984) is the figure most associated with the critique of the postmodern (though many people mistakenly continue to believe he advocates it), although Jameson's (1991) characterization of the postmodern has set some key parameters for analysis. Jameson selects the following as defining differences from modernity: (1) the death of the subject (the subject as agent, and as the subject of responsibility); (2) the spread of works that present the surface of things giving only an illusion of depth; (3) the loss of a sense of historical depth, e.g., works that exist and refer to the now, to the present by closing off reference to other times (say, in the typical blockbuster film); (4) the emphasis on textuality at the expense of reality; (5) pastiche (instead of irony); and (6) the valuing of the copy, the simulacrum in Baudrillard's sense (say, in Damien Hirst's works). What is common to all these characteristics is the idea of 'depthlessness'. Many people would like to attribute them to the products of mass culture (therein another debate). Indeed, a visit at Tate Modern would indicate the difference between modernism and postmodern art, for example, in the work by (most but not all) American artists in which the features highlighted by Jameson seem to be present.

Jameson's own Preface to Lyotard's *The Postmodern Condition* (PMC) ([1976] 1984) repays close reading in the light of what has been said since about the postmodern. In his book, Lyotard analyzes the location of knowledge today in relation to the project of modernity. It is in that respect that the term postmodern is used. In PMC, he begins with the claim that what characterizes modern science is the way in which it is legitimated, namely by reference to a philosophical discourse that it engendered in answer to the question of its own status as the only legitimate knowledge. In this way it appealed to a grand narrative that functioned as master or metanarrative, founded in the Enlightenment notion of a universal Reason and an autonomous rational agent of truth in pursuit of the humanization of humanity; thus it is that 'the hero of knowledge works towards a good ethico-political end – universal peace' (PMC: xxiv). He specifies in a later work (Lyotard, 1988) that the metanarratives to which he refers are those applying to modernity; in particular they envision:

> the progressive emancipation of reason and liberty, the progressive or catastrophic emancipation of labour (source of alienated value in capitalism), the enrichment of the whole of humanity through the progress of capitalist technoscience, and also, if we were to count Christianity itself within modernity (thus opposed to ancient classicism), the salvation of creatures through the conversion of souls to the christic narration of sacrificial love. (ibid.: 31)

The proof of the pudding for this narrative of the progress of humanity towards a more just society on the basis of the progress of reason is meant to be found in the institutions and the achievements that inscribe this ideal or project. Given the history of the project of modernity: wars of colonization, genocide, capitalist slavery, the barbarity of the Second World War and the inhumanity of the concentration camps – Auschwitz as the expression of a very modern inhumanity and thus as signifier of the failure of modernity's grand narrative – Lyotard argues that one must lose faith in the metanarrative underlying modernity's claim be an ethico-political project. This loss of faith in the assumptions and foundations that the discourse of modernity had privileged in legitimating its idea of a project of emancipation is one sense of the postmodern.

Another sense relates to the means invented to achieve the project, and the historical conditions (capitalism, colonialism) that have gradually meant the privileging of instrumental rationality – the power to – and capitalist technoscience in deciding the criteria for accomplishing the 'ends of man'. One consequences is that, as Lyotard says, 'In matters of social justice and scientific truth alike, the legitimation of that power (the power to ...) is based on its optimizing the system's performance – efficiency' (PMC: xxiv). When applied to all the different 'language games' that circumscribe the diverse aspects/elements of sociality – pedagogical, medical, economic, cultural, technological, developmental – the criterion of efficiency-as-performativity entails a terror: be operational or disappear. This other sense of the postmodern means that the project of modernity 'has not been abandoned, forgotten, but destroyed, "liquidated"' (1988: 32).

This elimination of the ethico-political ideals of modernity is completed in the new world order of neo-liberalism. The latter is progressively colonizing all other 'language games' in the name of a rational efficiency that is itself far from rational since it rests on a quasi-religious faith in capitalism. (Is this why so many upholders of neo-liberalism appear to subscribe to religious fundamentalism?) The instrumental objectification of human beings in the biopolitics of postmodern governance, the latter's reduction of the human to facticity, to zoë (objective being), as opposed to bios (way of living, implying an ethos), sits uncomfortably with religious doctrine (except, as I have indicated in the book, when the latter too is instrumentalized in terms of a theological form of insurance). The extreme individualism of the post-modern condition – society does not exist, there are but individuals making choices – is consistent with these mutations in the narrative of being.

Check out: Lyotard ([1976] 1984), D. Harvey (1989), Walter Benjamin (1999), the Surrealist or the Futurist manifestoes; examine the Bauhaus and their aims. There is obviously a massive literature and an ongoing polemic about the postmodern.

Poststructuralism

A misleading term. What is the problem at the basis of the disputes and confusions? And, what is at stake? Clearly it is meant to mark a break with structuralism. It is worth starting with the original problem here, which is about different frameworks for explanations for social phenomena, and thus about the search in the social sciences for the determination or the causes of such phenomena. There is a whole range of types of explanation, from reference to the action of autonomous individuals, say, the great leader who shapes the course of history, to socio-biological accounts of why we do the things we do: it's all in the genes, and there's nothing much we can do about it. Among the types of explanatory theory are those (outside socio-biology) that recognize regularities and patterns in human behaviour and social action, and the implication that they indicate certain kinds of underlying regularities in the way social forces work. One type of explana-tion has looked for structures and structural relations, following a line of thought long established in the natural sciences, for example, regarding molecular structure, or the structure of the atom. Indeed, finding such structural forces and regularities in the social and human sciences repre-sented a sign of scientific maturity for a field. Early examples are structural linguistics and classical Marxism, that is to say, accounts of language that explain particular utterances in terms of underlying linguistic structures then generate them according to specific conditions (as in Chomsky's struc-tural linguistics and from a different perspective in de Saussure's work), and explanations of society and its development by reference to the model of base and superstructure. In the 1920s and 1930s structuralism achieved impressive success in mathematics (the work of the Bourbaki group in France), and in Piaget's theory of cognitive development. In the 1950s and 1960s, the work of Barthes and Lévi-Strauss extended the application of the conceptual framework of structuralism to the analysis of culture.

Poststructuralism emerged because structuralist accounts were criticized for their weakness in accounting for change, for agency, for indeterminacy in historical process, for mobility in meaning, for neglecting categories such as gender; equally, at a time of suspicion towards positivism, functionalism and scientism, the appeal of structuralism waned. Out went invariable laws of development and neat models of social and semiotic processes. But poststructuralism is a mixed bag, addressing this whole range of issues in different ways depending on the particular author or problem.

Foucault, for example, proposes a search for genealogical explanations, that is, lines of descent from a present state of affairs that we may reconstruct by looking for traces in the conditions that the searcher assumes make for the particular configurations today. His approach owes much to work done in the history of the natural sciences by people like Bachelard, and particularly Canguilhem (see Venn, 1982), so that it is not a matter of flying in the face of 'proper objectivity', as some people may claim about poststructuralist approaches, but of a reconceptualization of the process of producing and authorising knowledge, and of establishing the effects of power, and other factors, in this process.

So, generalizations about structuralism and poststructuralism detract from what they address as problems and from what may be gained from a scholarly approach to the positions they elaborate. Poststructuralism does not claim that anything goes, or that one cannot predict or propose relations of determination, but turns to a series of other terms to explain effects and conditions: over-determination, correlation, co-articulation, genealogy, archaeology, rhizome, indeterminacy, structuration, the processual, that is to say, concepts that draw attention to the dynamic and complex character of historical and social and natural processes, recognising that they are open to plural outcomes.

Power/knowledge

This is a term introduced by Foucault in his studies of discourse and the process of production of knowledge (see Foucault, 1976). It refers to the effects of power in the field of knowledge and indicates the fact that if one is to understand why particular knowledges have emerged at particular times and become authoritative, we cannot separate out the effects of power on not just the process of production but on the statements or content of the knowledge. Foucault's concept is not the same as the claim that knowledge is power or that power confers knowledge, which is an older view and at times seen as common sense. An example will clarify the Foucault's problematic of power/knowledge. A history, or genealogy, of the development of tests of intelligence that have come to be known as IQ tests shows that specific governmental concerns about military and industrial performance incited the need to find reliable means of measuring 'intelligence' and distributing populations for schooling and training according to abilities so that the level of numeracy, literacy and general educational attainment could be improved.

Experts – psychologists like Binet in France, Burt in England, Pearson in the USA, and others – were given the task of developing adequate discourses and tests to constitute norms and produce measures of abilities so that populations could be established and appropriate technologies of formation devised to pursue the aims of normalization. The history of these developments (see Rose, 1979, for details) shows not only that the knowledge produced, psychological as well as statistical and pedagogical, was conditioned by these goals of governance, but that the claims made within the discourse of psychology inscribe these interests in specific ways. Thus, the content as well as the conditions of production of the psychological and pedagogical sciences were shaped by power. Today we could apply power/ knowledge in the analysis of topics like alternative technology, alternative medicine, genetic research or the emergence of the theory of evolution in relation to the fact of European empires and their interests in, for instance, surveying and categorizing all the species of the world (Venn, 1982).

Sciences and technologies of the social (governmentality, pastoral power, power/knowledge)

These are terms used by Foucault (e.g., 1976) to describe the discourses and the techniques that are put into place from around the period of the Enlightenment to constitute populations and subjects. The latter are taken in charge by the state and become the target of interventions that seek to normalize them according to norms determined by discourses such as the science of 'police' and the social sciences that claim objectivity and truth as part of their legitimating strategy. So, questions relating to the standpoint of power/knowledge are central to the understanding of the terms. Their genealogy takes one through the emergence of the form of power that Foucault calls pastoral power and the form of governance that is tied to the idea of governmentality (see Chapter 2).

Third World ('developing', 'newly industrialized', poor, pauperized, the South, 'underdeveloped')

The term Third World has become a problematic concept in some circles, yet continues to carry a political charge, especially in the former territories occupied by European colonial/imperial powers. It emerged in the wake of the cold war, so that technically it refers to a geo-political third block of countries, a tri-continental alliance, inbetween liberal capitalist Euro-America and the communist block (mainly the former USSR, and China). It also simply denotes the set of post-independence countries. It has come to acquire a range of meanings that tends to locate it by reference to the 'First World' as norm or 'ideal type', for instance, in the idea of the Third World as the third set of countries to industrialize, after Euro-America, then the block made up of Japan, Canada, Argentina, South Africa, Australia, and so on (the unevenness of 'development' or industrialization is clearly visible here). We need also to take account of how 'third world' is discursively and technologically constituted through the operation of laws, say, about immigration, through economic strategies, say, as agreed among the economically more powerful countries at WTO meetings, in other words, through practices of constitution that enact and thus confirm the assumptions in the discourses about development. The term developing has increasingly replaced 'third world' and 'underdeveloped', though here too there is the assumption that the model or ideal type is characterized by advanced industrialization, now post-industrial (service, finance, and knowledge-based economies), and the idea that the direction of development is necessarily towards the 'advanced' type. Other measures, principally of GDP (correlated to levels of literacy, longevity, and per capita indices of all kinds: about service provision like telephone or Internet access), locate the divide in terms of North and South. Again this is a very rough categorization, continuing the stereotype way of thinking about development. It is, on the whole, a rich and poor dichotomy, relaying a variety of discourses to account for the disparity among nations, and recognising that the poorest nations are those once colonized, and whose economies were transformed to service the needs of imperialism, many becoming monocultures, for example, the 'banana republics' (see Robert Young, 2003). Interestingly, Cuba is one of the few 'Third World' countries in which measures of longevity, health, education compare favourably with the rich countries, exceeding those for the USA.

Bibliography

Adam, Ian and Tiffin, Helen (1993) *Past the Last Post: Theorizing Post-Colonialism and Post-Modernism*. London: Harvester Wheatsheaf.

Adlam, Diana, Henriques, Julian, Rose, Nikolas, Salfield, Angie, Venn, Couze and Walkerdine, Valerie (1977) 'Psychology, ideology and the human subject', *Ideology & Consciousness*, 1: 5–61.

Adorno, Theodore and Horkheimer, Max (1979) *Dialectic of Enlightenment*. London: Verso.

Agamben, Giorgio (1998) *Homo Sacer: Sovereign Power and Bare Life*, trans. Daniel Heller-Roasen, Stanford, CA: Stanford University Press.

Agamben, Giorgio (1999) *Remnants of Auschwitz: The Witness and the Archive*, trans. Daniel Heller-Roazen. New York: Zone Books.

Ahmed, Sara (2000) *Strange Encounters: Embodied Others in Postcoloniality*. London: Routledge.

Ahmed, Sara (ed.) (2003) *Uprootings/Regroupings: Questions of Home and Migration*. London: Routledge.

Alcoff, Linda Martin (2000) 'Phenomenology, post-structuralism, and feminist theory on the concept of experience', in Linda Fisher and Lester Embree (eds) *Feminist Phenomenology*. Dordrecht: Kluwer.

Althusser, Louis ([1971] 1991) *Lenin and Philosophy and Other Essays*, trans. Ben Brewster. London: New Left Books.

Amin, Samir (1974) *Accumulation on a World Scale: A Critique of the Theory of Underdevelopment*, trans. Brian Pearce. New York: Monthly Review Press.

Amin, Samir (1976) *Imperialism and Unequal Development*. Hassocks: Harvester Press.

Amin, Samir (1997) *Capitalism in the Age of Globalisation: The Management of Contemporary Society*. London: Zed Books.

Amin, Samir (2004) 'For struggles, global and local', in Jai Sen et al. *World Social Forum: Challenging Empires*. New Delhi: Viveka Foundation.

Anthias, Floya and Yuval-Davis, Nira (1989) *Woman–Nation–State*. London: Routledge.

Anzaldúa, Gloria (1987) *Borderlands: La Frontera*. San Francisco: Spinsters/Aunt Lute.

Appadurai, Arjun (ed.) (1986) *The Social Life of Things: Commodities in Cultural Perspective*. New York: Cambridge University Press.

Appadurai, Arjun (1993) 'Disjuncture and difference in the global cultural economy', in Patrick Williams and Laura Chrisman (eds) *Colonial Discourse and Post-Colonial Theory: A Reader*. Hemel Hempstead: Harvester Wheatsheaf.

Appadurai, Arjun (1995) *Modernity at Large*. Minneapolis, MN. University of Minnesota Press.

Appiah, K.A. (1992) *In My Father's House: Africa in the Philosophy of Culture*. London: Methuen.

Arendt, Hannah (1959) *The Human Condition*. New York: Doubleday Anchor Books.

Arendt, Hannah (2000) 'The social question', in *The Portable Hannah Arendt*, ed. Peter Baehr. Harmondsworth: Penguin.

Arghiri, Emmanuel (1972) *Unequal Exchange: A Study of the Imperialism of Trade*. New York: Monthly Review Press.

Arghiri, Emmanuel (1994) *The Long Twentieth Century: Money, Power, and the Origins of Our Times*. London: Verso.

Arnoldi, Jacob (2004) 'Derivatives: virtual values and real risks', *Theory, Culture & Society*, 21(6): 23–42.

Ashcroft, Bill, Griffiths, Gareth and Tiffin, Helen (1998) *Key Concepts in Post-Colonial Studies*. London: Routledge.

Bachelard, Gaston ([1938] 1972) *La Formation de l'esprit scientifique*. Paris: Vrin.

Bachelard, Gaston (1949) *Le Rationalisme appliqué*. Paris: Presses Universitaires de France.

Bachelard, Gaston (1951) *L'Activitée rationaliste de la physique contemporaine*. Paris: Presses Universitaires de France.

Bakhtin, Mikhail (1981) *The Dialogic Imagination*, trans. Caryl Emerson and Michael Holquist. Austin, TX: University of Texas Press.

Baran, Paul (1959) *The Political Economy of Growth*. New York: Monthly Review Press.

Barker, Francis (ed.) (1983) *The Politics of Theory*. Colchester: University of Essex Press.

Barker, Francis et al. (eds) (1985) *Europe and its Others*, 2 vols. Colchester: University of Essex Press.

Barwa, S. and Rai, S. (2002) 'Gender matters: intellectual property rights under globalisation', in P. Newell, S. Rai and A. Scott (eds) *Development and Challenge of Globalisation*. London: IT Publishers.

Bateson, Gregory (1980) *Mind and Nature*. London: Collins.

Bayly, C.A. (1989) *Imperial Meridian: The British Empire and the World 1780–1830*. Cambridge: Cambridge University Press.

Beck, Ulrich (1992) *Risk Society: Towards a New Modernity*. London: Sage.

Beck, Ulrich, Giddens, Anthony and Lash, Scott (1994) *Reflexive Modernization: Politics, Tradition and Aesthetics in the Modern Social Order*. Cambridge: Polity.

Beneria, Lourdes (ed.) (1985) *Women and Development: The Sexual Division of Labour in Rural Societies*. New York: Praeger.

Bergson, Henri (1988) *Matter and Memory*, trans. Nancy M. Paul and W. Scott Palmer. New York: Zone Books.

Berman, M. (1984) *All That Is Solid Melts into Air*. London: Verso.

Best, Jacqueline (2003) 'From the top down: the new financial architecture and the re-embedding of global finance', *New Political Economy*, 8(3): 363–384

Beveridge, W. (1942) *Social Insurance and Allied Services (The Beveridge Report)*. London: HMSO.

Bhabha, Homi (1983) 'The other question: the stereotype and colonial discourse', *Screen*, 24(6): 18–36.

Bhabha, Homi (1984) 'Of mimicry and man', *October*, 28: 125–33.

Bhabha, Homi (1985) 'Signs taken for wonders: questions of ambivalence and authority under a tree outside Delhi, May 1817', in F. Barker (ed.) *Europe and its Others*, vol. 1. Colchester: University of Essex Press, pp. 89–127.

Bhabha, Homi (ed.) (1990) *Nation and Narration*. London: Routledge.

Bhabha, Homi (1994) *Location of Culture*. London: Routledge.

Bhatt, Chetan (2001) *Hindu Nationalism: Origins, Ideologies and Modern Myths*. New York: Berg.

Bishop, Ryan and Phillips, John (2002) 'Manufacturing emergencies', *Theory, Culture & Society*, 19(4): 91–102.

Bishop, Ryan and Phillips, John (2003) 'The Curious Logic of the Hinge', *Body & Society*, 9(4): 69–88.

Bishop, Ryan, Phillips, John, Yeo, W. (eds) (2003) *Postcolonial Urbanism*, New York: Routledge.

Bishop, Ryan and Robinson, Lilian (1998) *Night Market: Sexual Cultures and the Thai Economic Miracle*. New York: Routledge.

Boltanski, Luc and Chiapello, Eve (2000) *Le Nouvel esprit du capitalisme*. Paris: Denoël.

Boltanski, Luc and Thevenot, Laurent (1991) *De la justification: Les économies de la grandeur*. Paris: Gallimard.

Bordo, Susan (1986) 'The Cartesian masculinization of thought', *Signs*, 11(3): 439–56.

Bourdieu, Pierre (1984) *Distinctions: A Social Critique of the Judgement of Taste*, trans. Richard Nice. Cambridge, MA: Harvard University Press.

Bourdieu, Pierre (1991) *Language and Symbolic Power*, trans. Gino Raymond and Matthew Adamson. Cambridge, MA: Harvard University Press.

Bowie, Andrew (1990) *Aesthetics and Subjectivity: From Kant to Nietzsche*. Manchester: Manchester University Press.

Brah, Avtar (1996) *Cartographies of Diaspora*. London: Routledge.

Brah, Avtar and Coombes, Annie (eds) (2000) *Hybridity and its Discontents: Politics, Science, Culture*. London: Routledge.

Braudel, Fernand (1977) *Afterthoughts on Material Civilization and Capitalism*, trans. Patricia Ranum. Baltimore, MD: Johns Hopkins University Press.

Braudel, Fernand (1981–4) *Civilization and Capitalism*, 3 vols. New York: Harper and Row.

Brown, Wendy (1995) *States of Injury: Power and Freedom in Late Modernity*. Princeton, NJ: Princeton University Press.

Butler, Judith (1993) *Bodies that Matter*. New York: Routledge.

Butler, Judith (1997) *The Psychic Life of Power*. Stanford, CA: Stanford University Press.

Cabral, Amilcar (1973) *Return to the Source: Selected Speeches*. New York: Monthly Review Press.

Calhoun, Craig (1995a) *Critical Social Theory*. Cambridge, MA: MIT Press.

Calhoun, Craig (1995b) 'The politics of identity and recognition' in Craig Calhoun *Critical Social Theory*. Cambridge, MA: MIT Press.

Cameron, Angus and Palan, Ronen (2003) *The Imagined Economies of Globalization*. London: Sage.

Canclini, Nestor Garcia (1995) *Hybrid Cultures: Strategies for Entering and Leaving Modernity*. Minneapolis: University of Minnesota Press.

Canclini, Nestor Garcia (1998) *The Future of the Privatization of Culture*, trans. George Yudice. http://www.nyu.edu/projects/privculture/papers/future.htm

Canclini, Nestor Garcia (2001) *Consumers and Citizens: Global and Multicultural Conflicts*, trans. George Yudice. Minneapolis: University of Minnesota Press.

Canguilhem, Georges (1965) *La Connaisssance de la vie*. Paris: Vrin.

Canguilhem, Georges (1966) *Le normal et le pathologique*. Paris: Presses Universitaires de France.

Canguilhem, Georges (1975) *Etudes d'histoire et de philosophie des sciences*. Paris: Vrin.

Cao, Lanh (1998) *Monkey Bridge*. New York: Penguin.

Castells, Manuel (1996) *The Information Age*. Oxford: Blackwell.

Castells, Manuel (1998) *The Information Age*, vol. 3: *End of Millennium*. Oxford: Blackwell.

Castells, Manuel (2000) *The Information Age*, vol. 1: *The Rise of the Network Society*, 2nd edn. Malden, MA: Blackwell.

Castoriadis, Cornelius (1987) *The Imaginary Institution of Society*, trans. Kathleen Blaney. Cambridge: Polity Press.

Césaire, A. ([1955] 1972) *Discourse on Colonialism*, trans. Joan Pinkham. New York: Monthly Review Press.

Chakrabarty, Dipesh (1988) 'Conditions for knowledge of working-class conditions', in Ranajit Guha and Gayatri Spivak (eds) *Selected Subaltern Studies*. Delhi: Oxford University Press.

Chakrabarty, Dipesh (2000) *Provincialising Europe: Postcolonial Thought and Historical Difference*. Princeton, NJ: Princeton University Press.

Chambers, Iain and Curti, Lidia (eds) (1996) *The Post-Colonial Question*. London: Routledge.

Chatterjee, Partha (1986) *Nationalist Thought and the Colonial World: A Derivative Discourse*. London: Zed Books.

Chatterjee, Partha (1989) 'The nationalist resolution of the women's question', in P. Chatterjee (1993) *The Nation and its Fragments: Colonial and Postcolonial Histories*. Princeton, NJ: Princeton University Press.

Childs, Peter and Williams, Patrick (1997) *An Introduction to Post-Colonial Theory*. London: Prentice Hall.

Chomsky, Noam (2000) *Rogue States: The Rule of Force in World Affairs*. London: Pluto.

Chossudovsky, Michel (1996) 'Dismantling Yugoslavia, colonising Bosnia', *Covert Action*, 56.

Chua, Amy (2004) *World on Fire*. London: Heinemann.

Clausewitz, Carl von ([1832] 1968) *On War*, ed. Anatol Rapoport. Harmondsworth: Penguin.

Clavelin, Maurice (1974) *The Natural Philosophy of Galileo*, trans. A.J. Pomerans. Cambridge, MA: MIT Press.

Clifford, James (1994) 'Diaspora', *Cultural Anthropology*, 9(3): 302–28.

Clifford, James (1997) *Routes*. Cambridge, MA: Harvard University Press.

Cohen, Robin (1997) *Global Diasporas: An Introduction*. London: University of London Press.

Columbus, Christopher ([1492] 1988) *The Four Voyages of Christopher Columbus*, ed. J.M. Cohen. London: Century Hutchinson.

Connolly, E. William (2002) *Neuropolitics: Thinking, Culture, Speed*. Minneapolis: University of Minnesota Press.

Cox, R. (2000) 'Political economy and world order: problems of power and knowledge at the turn of the Millennium', in Richard Stubbs and Geoffrey Underhill (eds) *Political Economy and the Changing Global Order*. Oxford: Oxford University Press.

Cox, Robert W. (1987) *Production, Power, and World Order: Social Forces in the Making of History*. New York: Columbia University Press.

Cox, Robert W. and Schechter, Michael G. (2002) *The Political Economy of a Plural World: Critical Reflections on Power, Morals and Civilization*. London: Routledge.

Crombie, A.C. (1961) *Augustine to Galileo*, vol. 1. London: Mercury Books.

Curtis, Neal (2001) *Against Autonomy: Lyotard, Judgement and Action*. Aldershot: Ashgate.

Curtis, Neal (2005) *War and Social Theory*. Basingstoke: Palgrave.

Dabydeen, David (ed.) (1985) *The Black Presence in English Literature*. Manchester: Manchester University Press.

Dangarembga, Tsitsi (1988) *Nervous Conditions*. London: The Women's Press.

de Certeau, Michel (1988) *The Practice of Everyday Life*, trans. Steven Rendall. Berkeley, CA: University of California Press.

de Grieff, Pablo and Cronin, Ciaran (2002) *Global Justice and Transnational Politics*. Cambridge, MA: MIT Press.

DeLanda, Manuel (2002) *Intensive Science and Virtual Philosophy*. London: Continuum.

Deleuze, Gilles and Guattari, Félix (1976) *Rhizome*. Paris: Editions de Minuit.

Deleuze, Gilles and Guattari, Félix (1981) 'Rhizome', *Ideology & Consciousness*, 8: 49–72.

Deleuze, Gilles and Guattari, Félix (1985) *Anti-Oedipus: Capitalism and Schizophrenia*, trans. H.R. Lane and Robert Hurley. Minneapolis: University of Minnesota Press.

Deleuze, Gilles and Guattari, Félix (1988) *A Thousand Plateaux*, trans. Brian Massumi. London: Athlone Press.

Derrida, Jacques (1967) *De la Grammatologie*. Paris: Editions de Minuit.

Derrida, Jacques (1978) *Writing and Difference*, trans. Alan Bass. London: Routledge.

Derrida, Jacques (1982) *Margins of Philosophy*, trans. Alan Bass. Chicago: University of Chicago Press.

Derrida, Jacques (1985) *The Ear of the Other*, ed. Christie McDonald, trans. Peggy Kamuf. Lincoln, NE: Bison Books.

Derrida, Jacques (1987) *The Postcard*, trans. Alan Bass. Chicago: University of Chicago Press.

Derrida, Jacques (1994) *Spectres of Marx: The State of Debt, the Work of Mourning and the New International*, trans. Peggy Kamuf. London: Routledge.

Derrida, Jacques (1995) *The Gift of Death*, trans. David Wills. Chicago: Chicago University Press.

Derrida, Jacques (1997a) *Le droit à la philosophie du point de vue cosmopolitique*. Paris: Editions UNESCO Verdier.

Derrida, Jacques (1997b) *Cosmopolites de tous les pays, encore un effort!* Paris: Galilee.

Derrida, Jacques (1998) *Monolingualism of the Other or The Prosthesis of Origin*, trans. Patrick Mensah. Stanford, CA: Stanford University Press.

Derrida, Jacques (2002) *Acts of Religion*, ed. Gil Anidjar. London: Routledge.

Derrida, Jacques and Stiegler, Bernard (2002) *Echographies of Television*, trans. Jennifer Bajorek. Cambridge: Polity.

Descartes, René ([1637] 1968) *Discourse on Method and Other Writings*, trans. F.E. Sutcliffe. Harmondsworth: Penguin.

Diop, Cheikh Anta (1974) *The African Origin of Civilization: Myth or Reality?* trans. M. Cook. Westport, CT: L. Hill.

Dirlik, Arif (1994) 'The postcolonial aura: Third World criticism in the age of global capitalism', *Critical Inquiry*, 20: 328–56.

Dirlik, Arif (1997) *The Postcolonial Aura: Third World Criticism in the Age of Global Capitalism*. Boulder, CO: Westview Press.

Donald, J. and Rattansi, A. (eds) (1992) *'Race', Culture, Difference*. London: Sage.

Dreyfus, Richard and Rabinow, Paul (1982) *Michel Foucault: Beyond Structuralism and Hermeneutics*. Brighton: Harvester Press.

du Bois, W.E.B. ([1903] 1989) *The Souls of Black Folk*. Harmondsworth: Penguin Books.

du Gay, P. and Pryke, M. (eds) (2003) *Cultural Economy*. London: Sage.

Easlea, Brian (1980) *Witch-Hunting, Magic and the New Philosophy*. Brighton: Harvester Press.

Eisenstadt, S.N. (2000) 'Multiple modernities', *Daedalus*, 129(1): 1–29.

Elias, N. (1982) *The Civilizing Process: State Formation and Civilization*, trans. Edmund Jephcott. Oxford: Blackwell.

Emmanuel, A. (1972) *Unequal Exchange: A Study of the Imperialist Trade*, trans. Brian Peace. New York: Monthly Review Press.

Enwezor, Okwui et al. (eds) (2002a) *Democracy Unrealised (Documenta 11–1)*. Hatje Cantz: Ostfildern-Ruit.

Enwezor, Okwui et al. (eds) (2002b) *Under Siege: Four African Cities: Freetown, Johannesburg, Kinshasa, Lagos (Documenta 11–4)*. Hatje Cantz: Ostfildern-Ruit.

Enwezor, Okwui et al. (eds) (2003) *Créolité and Creolization (Documenta 11–3)*. Hatje-Cantz: Ostfildern-Ruit.

Ettinger, Bracha (1995) *The Matrixial Gaze*. Leeds: University of Leeds, Feminist Arts and Histories Network.

Fabian, Johannes (1983) *Time and the Other: How Anthropology Makes its Object*. New York: Columbia University Press.

Fanon, Frantz (1967) *Wretched of the Earth*. Harmondsworth: Penguin.

Fanon, Frantz (1970) *Black Skin White Masks*, trans. Charles L. Markmann. London: Paladin.

Fanon, Frantz (1989) *Studies in a Dying Colonialism*, trans. Haakon Chevalier. London: Earthscan Publications.

Faye, Jean-Pierre (1972) *Théorie du récit*. Paris: Herman.

Featherstone, Mike (1991) *Consumer Culture and Postmodernism*. London: Sage.

Featherstone, Mike (1995) *Undoing Culture*. London: Sage.

Featherstone, Mike, Lash, Scott and Robertson, Roland (eds) (1995) *Global Modernities*. London: Sage.

Fisher, F. William and Ponniah, Thomas (2003) *Another World is Possible: Popular Alternatives to Globalization at the World Social Forum*. London: Zed Books.

Fitzpatrick, Peter and Tuitt, Patricia (eds) (2004) *Critical Beings: Law, Nation and the Global Subject*. Aldershot: Ashgate.

Foucault, Michel (1970) *The Order of Things: An Archaeology of the Human Sciences*. London: Tavistock.

Foucault, Michel (1972) *The Archaeology of Knowledge*, trans. Alan Sheridan Smith. London: Tavistock.

Foucault, Michel (1975) *Discipline and Punish: The Birth of the Prison*, trans. Alan Sheridan. London: Allen Lane.

Foucault, Michel (1976) *The History of Sexuality*, vol 1: *An Introduction*, trans. Robert Hurley. London: Allen Lane.

Foucault, Michel (1979) 'On governmentality', *Ideology & Consciousness*, 6: 5–21.

Foucault, Michel (1982) 'The subject and power', in Richard Dreyfus and Paul Rabinow (eds) *Michel Foucault: Beyond Structuralism and Hermeneutics*. Brighton: Harvester Press.

Foucault, Michel (1984) 'What is Enlightenment?', in Paul Rabinow (ed.) *The Foucault Reader*. Harmondsworth: Penguin.

Frank, Andre Gunther (1967) *Capitalism and Underdevelopment in Latin America*. New York: Monthly Review Press.

Fraser, Nancy (1997) *Justice Interruptus: Critical Reflections on the 'Postsocialist Condition'*. New York: Routledge.

Fraser, Nancy and Honneth, Axel (2003) *Redistribution or Recognition*. London: Verso.

Friedman, Milton (1962) *Capitalism and Freedom*. Chicago: Chicago University Press.

Fryer, Peter (1984) *Staying Power*. London: Pluto.

Fukuyama, Francis (1992) *The End of History and the Last Man*. London: Hamish Hamilton.

Fukuzawa, Yukichi ([1866] 1973) *An Outline of a Theory of Civilization*. Tokyo: Sophia University Press.

Gates, H.L. (ed.) (1986) *'Race', Writing and Difference*. Chicago: University of Chicago Press.

Geertz, Clifford (1973) *The Interpretation of Cultures*. New York: Basic Books.

George, Susan (1988) *A Fate Worse than Debt*. London: Penguin.

Ghandi, Leela (1998) *Postcolonial Theory: A Critical Introduction*. Edinburgh: Edinburgh University Press.

Gilroy, Paul (1993a) *Small Acts*. London: Serpent's Tail.

Gilroy, Paul (1993b) *The Black Atlantic: Modernity and Double Consciousness*. London: Verso.

Gilson, Etienne (1930) *Etudes sur le rôle de la pensée médiévale dans la formation du système cartésien*. Paris: Vrin.

Goldberg, D.T. and Quayson, A. (2002) *Relocating Postcolonialism*. Oxford: Blackwell.

Goonatilake, Susantha (1984) *Aborted Discovery: Science and Creativity in the Third World*. London: Zed Books.

Goonatilake, Susantha (1998) *Toward a Global Science: Mining Civilizational Knowledge*. Bloomington, IN: Indiana University Press.

Gorz, A. (1989) *Critique of Economic Reason*. London: Verso.

Gramsci, Antonio (1971) *Selections from the Prison Notebooks*, trans. and ed. Quentin Hoare and Geoffrey Nowell-Smith. London: Lawrence and Wishart.

Gray, John (1998) *False Dawn*. London: Granta Books.

Grosz, Elizabeth (1990) *Jacques Lacan: A Feminist Introduction*. London: Routledge.

Grosz, Elizabeth (1994) *Volatile Bodies: Towards a Corporeal Feminism*. Bloomington, IN: Indiana University Press.

Guha, Ranajit and Spivak, Gayatri (eds) (1988) *Selected Subaltern Studies*. Delhi: Oxford University Press.

Habermas, Jürgen (1983) 'Modernity: an incomplete project', in Hal Foster (ed.) *Postmodern Culture*. London: Pluto Press, pp. 3–15.

Habermas, Jürgen (1987) *The Philosophical Discourse of Modernity: Twelve Lectures*, trans. Frederick Lawrence. Cambridge: Polity Press.

Habermas, Jürgen (1996) *Between Facts and Norms: Contributions to a Discourse Theory of Law and Democracy*, trans. William Rehg. Cambridge, MA: MIT Press.

Hall, Catherine (2002) *Civilizing Subjects*. London: Polity Press.

Hall, Stuart (1992) 'New ethnicities', in J. Donald and A. Rattansi (eds) *'Race', Culture and Difference*. London: Sage.

Hall, Stuart (1996a) 'When was the "postcolonial"? Thinking at the limit', in Iain Chambers and Lidia Curti (eds) *The Post-Colonial Question*. London: Routledge.

Hall, Stuart (1996b) 'Introduction: who needs identity', in Stuart Hall and Paul du Gay (eds) *Questions of Cultural Identity*. London: Sage.

Hall, Stuart (1999) 'Thinking the diaspora: home-thoughts from abroad', *Small Axe*, 6: 1–18.

Hall, Stuart (2003) 'Creolization, diaspora, and hybridity in the context of globalization', in Okwui Enwezor et al. (eds) *Créolité and Creolization* (*Documenta* 11–3). Hatje-Cantz: Ostfildern-Ruit.

Hall, Stuart and du Gay, Paul (1996) *Questions of Cultural Identity*. London: Sage.

Hall, Stuart and Gieben, B. (1992) *Formations of Modernity*. Cambridge: Polity Press.

Hannerz, Ulf (1996) *Transnational Connections*. London: Routledge.

Hansen, Anders (2003) 'Dialogue in conflict. Jewish–Palestinian educational projects in Israel', unpublished PhD thesis, Nottingham Trent University.

Haraway, Donna (1991) *Simians, Cyborgs, and Women: The Reinvention of Nature*. New York: Routledge.

Harding, Sandra (1998) *Is Science Multicultural? Postcolonialism, Feminism, and Epistemology*. Bloomington, IN: Indiana University Press.

Hardt, M. and Negri, A. (2000) *Empire*. Cambridge, MA: Harvard University Press.

Hardt, M. and Negri, A. (2003) 'Foreword', in William Fisher and Thomas Ponniah (eds) *Another World is Possible: Popular Alternatives to Globalization at the World Social Forum*. London: Zed Books.

Harootunian, Harry (2000) *Overcome by Modernity: History, Culture and Community in Interwar Japan*. Princeton, NJ: Princeton University Press.

Harvey, David (1989) *The Condition of Postmodernity: An Enquiry into the Origins of Cultural Change*. Oxford: Blackwell.

Harvey, David (2003) *The New Imperialism*. Oxford: Oxford University Press.

Hear, V.N. (1998) *New Diasporas: Dispersal and Regroupings of Migrant Communities*. London: UCL Press.

Heidegger, Martin (1962) *Being and Time*, trans. John Macquarrie and Edward Robinson. Oxford: Blackwell.

Heidegger, Martin (1977) *The Question Concerning Technology, and Other Essays*, trans. William Lovitt. New York: Harper and Row.

Held, David and McGrew, Anthony (eds) (2000) *The Global Transformation Reader: An Introduction to the Globalization Debate*. Malden, MA: Polity Press.

Henriques, Julian (2003) 'Sonic dominance and reggae sound system sessions', in M. Bull and L. Back (eds) *Auditory Culture*. London: Berg, pp, 451–80.

Henriques, Julian, Hollway, Wendy, Urwin, Cathy, Venn, Couze and Walkerdine, Valerie (1984) *Changing the Subject: Psychology, Social Regulation and Subjectivity*. London: Methuen.

Henriques, Julian, Hollway, Wendy, Urwin, Cathy, Walkerdine, Valerie and Venn, Couze (1998) *Changing the Subject: Psychology, Social Regulation and Subjectivity*. 2nd edn. London: Routledge.

Herder, Johann Gottfried ([1800] 1997) *On World History*, ed. H. Adler and E.A. Menze, trans. E.A. Menze and B. Palma. New York: M.E. Sharpe.

Hobsbawm, Eric (1962) *The Age of Revolution*. London: Weidenfeld and Nicolson.

Hobsbawm, Eric (1987) *The Age of Empire, 1875–1914*. London: Weidenfeld and Nicolson.

Hochschild, Adam (1999) *King Leopold's Ghost*. London: Mariner Books.

Hodgson, Godfrey (2004) *More Equal than Others*. Princeton, NJ: Princeton University Press.

Hourani, Albert (1991) *A History of the Arab Peoples*. London: Faber and Faber.

Hulme, P. (1985) 'Polytropic man: tropes of sexuality and mobility in early colonial discourse', in F. Barker (ed.) *Europe and its Others*, vol. 1. Colchester: University of Essex Press.

Jackson, Cecile and Pearson, Ruth (1998) *Feminist Visions of Development*. London: Routledge.

Jalée, Pierre (1981) *Le Pillage du tiers monde*. Paris: Maspero.

Jameson, F. (1984) 'Post-modernism, or the cultural logic of late capitalism', *New Left Review* 146.

Jameson, F. (1991) *Postmodernism or the Cultural Logic of Late Capitalism*. London: Verso.

JanMohamed, A. (1986) 'The economy of Manichean allegory', in H.L. Gates (ed.) *'Race', Writing and Difference*. Chicago: University of Chicago Press.

Jansen, Marius (1984) 'Imperialism: Late Meiji perspectives', in Ramon H. Myers and R. Peattie (eds) *The Japanese Colonial Empire, 1885–1945*. Princeton, NJ: Princeton University Press.

Johnson, Richard (2004) 'Muscle, masculinities and nations at war: the frontier rhetorics of Bush and Blair', seminar paper, Cultural Studies Research Seminar, Nottingham Trent University, 31 March 2004.

Joxe, Alain (2002) *Empire of Disorder*. Los Angeles: Semiotext(e).

Julien, Isaac (2003) 'Creolizing vision', in Okwui Enwezor et al. (eds) *Créolité and Creolization* (*Documenta* 11–3). Hatje-Cantz: Ostfildern-Ruit, pp. 149–56.

Kamen, Henry (2002) *Spain's Road to Empire*. New York: HarperCollins.

Kandiyoti, Deniz (ed.) (1991) *Women, Islam and the State*. Basingstoke: Macmillan.

Kant, Immanuel ([1784] 1992) 'An answer to the question: What is Enlightenment?', in Patricia Waugh (ed.) *A Reader in Postmodernism*. London: Routledge.

Khatibi, Abdelkebir (1971) *La Mémoire tatouée*. Paris: Denoël.

Khatibi, Abdelkebir (1990) *Love in Two Languages*, trans. Richard Howard. Minneapolis: University of Minnesota Press.

Klein, Naomi (2000) *No Logo*. London: HarperCollins.

Klein, Naomi (2002) *Fences and Windows*. London: HarperCollins.`

Knorr-Cetina, Karin (1981) *The Manufacture of Knowledge: An Essay on the Constructivist and Contextual Nature of Science*. Oxford: Pergamon.

Knorr-Cetina, Karin and Bruegger, Urs (2002) 'Traders' engagements with markets: a post-social relationship', *Theory, Culture & Society*, 19(5/6): 161–86.

Koyre, Alexandre (1971) 'Paracelsus', in Stephen Ozment (ed.) *The Reformation in Medieval Perspective*. Chicago: Quadrangle Books.

Koyre, Alexandre (1978) *Galileo Studies*, trans. John Mepham. Hassocks: Harvester Press.

Kraniauskas, John (2000) 'Hybridity in a transnational frame: Latin-Americanist and post-colonial perspectives on cultural studies', in Avtar Brah and Annie Coombes (eds) *Hybridity and its Discontents: Politics, Science, Culture*. London: Routledge.

Kristeva, Julia (1982) *Powers of Horror*, trans. L. Roudiez. New York: Columbia University Press.

Kuhn, Thomas (1962) *The Structure of Scientific Revolutions*. Chicago: University of Chicago Press.

Lacan, Jacques (1966) *Ecrits I*. Paris: Editions du Seuil.

Lacan, Jacques (1977) *Ecrits: A Selection*, trans. Alan Sheridan. London: Tavistock.

Lacan, Jacques (1979) *The Four Fundamental Concepts of Psychoanalysis*. Harmondsworth: Penguin.

Lahiri, Jhumpa (2003) *The Namesake*. Boston: Houghton Mifflin.

Lakoff, George and Johnson, Mark (1999) *Philosophy in the Flesh: The Embodied Mind and its Challenges to Western Thought*. New York: Basic Books.

Laplanche, Jean (1989) *New Foundations for Psychoanalysis*, trans. David Macey. Oxford: Blackwell.

Laplanche, Jean and Pontalis, J.-B. (1980) *The Language of Psychoanalysis*. London: Hogarth Press.

Lash, Scott (1994) *Reflexive Modernization*. Cambridge: Polity Press.

Lash, Scott and Urry, John (1994) *Economies of Signs and Space*. London: Sage.

Latour, Bruno (1987) *Science in Action*. Cambridge, MA: Harvard University Press.

Latour, Bruno (1991) 'Technology is society made durable', in John Law (ed.) *A Sociology of Monsters: Essays on Power, Technology and Domination*. London: Routledge.

Latour, Bruno (1993) *We Have Never Been Modern*. trans. Catherine Porter. Cambridge, MA: Harvard University Press.

Latour, Bruno (1997) 'The trouble with actor-network theory', *Philosophia*, 25(3–4: 47–64.

Latour, Bruno (1999) *Pandora's Hope: Essays on the Reality of Science Studies*. Cambridge, MA: Harvard University Press.

Latour, Bruno (2002) 'Morality and technology: the end of the means', trans. Couze Venn, *Theory, Culture & Society*, 19(5/6): 247–60.

Law, John and Hassard, John (eds) (1999) *Actor Network Theory and After*. Oxford: Blackwell.

Lee, B. and LiPuma, E. (2002) 'Cultures of circulation: the imaginations of modernity', *Public Culture*, 14(1): 191–213.

Lefort, Claude (1986) *The Political Forms of Modern Society: Bureaucracy, Democracy, Totalitarianism*, trans. John B. Thompson. Cambridge: Polity Press.

Lefort, Claude (1988) *Democracy and Political Theory*, trans. David Macey. Minneapolis: Minnesota University Press.

Le Roy Ladurie, Emmanuel (1978) *Montaillou*, trans. Barbara Bray. London: Scolar Press.

Levinas, Emmanuel (1969) *Totality and Infinity*, trans. Alfonso Lingis. Pittsburgh, PA: Duquesne University Press.

Levinas, Emmanuel (2001) *Is It Righteous To Be? Interviews with Emmanuel Levinas*, ed. Jill Robbins. Stanford, CA: Stanford University Press.

Lévi-Strauss, C. (1962) *The Savage Mind*. London: Weidenfeld and Nicolson.

Litvin, Daniel (2003) *Empires of Profit: Commerce, Conquest and Corporate Responsibility*. Oxford: Oxford University Press.

Locke, John ([1690] 1963) *Two Treatises of Government*. Cambridge: Cambridge University Press.

Loomba, A. (1991) 'Overworlding the "Third World"', *Oxford Literary Review*, 13(1, 2): 62–94.

Loomba, A. (1998) *Colonialism/Postcolonialism*. London: Routledge.

Luther, Martin ([1517] 1971) 'Disputations against scholastic theology', in Steven Ozment (ed.) *The Reformation in Medieval Perspectives*. Chicago: Quadrangle Books..

Lyotard, Jean-François (1983) *Le Différend*. Paris: Editions de Minuit.

Lyotard, Jean-François ([1976] 1984) *The Postmodern Condition: A Report on Knowledge*, trans. Geoff Bennington and Brian Massumi. Manchester: Manchester University Press.

Lyotard, Jean-François (1986) 'Defining the postmodern', *ICA Documents*, No. 4. ???.

Lyotard, Jean-François (1988) *Le Postmoderne expliqué aux enfants*. Paris: Editions Galilée.

Lyotard, Jean-François (1994) *Lessons on the Analytic of the Sublime*, trans. Elizabeth Rottenberg. Stanford, CA: Stanford University Press.

Macey, D. (2000) *The Penguin Dictionary of Critical Theory*. London: Penguin.

MacIntyre, Stuart (2003) *The History Wars*. Melbourne: Melbourne University Press.

Madsen, Deborah (ed.) (2003) *Beyond the Borders: American Literature and Post-Colonial Theory*. London: Pluto Press.

Magas, Branka (1993) *The Destruction of Yugoslavia: Tracking the Break-Up, 1980-1992*. London: Verso.

Mann, Michael (2003) *Incoherent Empire*. London: Verso.

Marchand, Marianne and Runyan, Anne (eds) (2000) *Gender and Global Restructuring*. London: Routledge.

Matar, Dina (2004) 'Narrative and news consumption: the Palestinian diaspora in Britain', Centre for Narrative Research lecture, 7 December, London School of Economics.

Mattelart, Armand (1994) *Advertising International: The Privatisation of Public Space*, trans. Michael Chanan. London: Routledge.

Mattelart, Armand (2000) *Networking the World, 1794–2000*, trans. Liz Carey-Libbrecht and James A. Cohen. Minneapolis: University of Minnesota Press.

Mattelart, Armand, Delcourt, X. and Mattelart, M. (1984) *La Culture contre la démocratie*. Paris: La Découverte.

Maturana, Hector and Varela, Francisco (1980) *Autopoiesis and Cognition: The Realisation of the Living*. Dordrecht: D. Reidel.

Mbembe, Achille (2001) *On the Postcolony*. Berkeley, CA: University of California Press.

McClintock, Anne (1995) *Imperial Leather: Race, Gender and Sexuality in the Colonial World*. New York: Routledge.

McClintock, Anne, Mufti, Aamir and Shohat, Ella (eds) (1997) *Dangerous Liaisons: Gender, Nation, and Postcolonial Predicaments*. Minneapolis: University of Minnesota Press.

Merefield, Matthew (2004) 'The fortress, the siege, and the haven: the British politics of mobility control within colonial-capitalism and globalization', unpublished PhD thesis, Nottingham Trent University.

Merleau-Ponty, Maurice (1945) *Phénoménologie de la perception*. Paris: Gallimard.

Merleau-Ponty, Maurice (1964) *L'œil et l'esprit*. Paris: Gallimard.

Merleau-Ponty, Maurice (1968) *The Visible and the Invisible*, ed. Claude Lefort, trans. Alfonso Lingis. Evanston, IL: Northwestern University Press.

Miller, D. (2003) 'The unintended political economy', in P. du Gay, and M. Pryke (eds) *Cultural Economy*. London: Sage.

Mohanty, Chandra Talpade et al. (eds) (1991) *Third World Women and the Politics of Feminism*. Bloomington, IN: Indiana University Press.

Mohanty, Chandra Talpate (1993) 'Under western eyes: feminist scholarship and colonial discourse', in Patrick Williams and Laura Chrisman *Colonial Discourse and Post-Colonial Theory*. Hemel Hempstead: Harvester Wheatsheaf.

Monbiot, George (2003) 'Don't cry for Clare', *Guardian*, 13 May 2003.

Moore-Gilbert, Bart (1997) *Postcolonial Theory: Contexts, Practices, Politics*. London: Verso.

Morley, D. and Robbins, K. (1995) *Spaces of Identity: Global Media, Electronic Landscapes and Cultural Boundaries*. London: Routledge.

Morrison, Toni (1987) *Beloved*. New York: Plume.

Morrison, Toni (1992) *Playing in the Dark: Whiteness and the Literary Imagination*. New York: Vintage Books.

Mulvey, Laura (1975) 'Visual pleasure and narrative cinema', *Screen*, 6(3): 6–18.

Myers, Ramon H. and Peattie, R. (eds) (1984) *The Japanese Colonial Empire, 1885–1945*. Princeton, NJ: Princeton University Press.

Nandy, Ashis (1990) *Science, Hegemony and Violence: A Requiem for Modernity*. New Delhi: Oxford University Press.

Needham, Joseph (1969) *The Grand Titration: Science and Society in East and West*. London: George Allen and Unwin.

Neocleous, Mark (2004) 'Heads of cabbage and mouths full of water: on corporate slaughter', *Radical Philosophy*, 122: 2–6.

Ngugi, Wa Thiong'o (1981) *Decolonising the Mind*. London: James Currey.

Nora, Pierre (ed.) (1984–93) *Les Lieux de mémoire*, 7 vols. Paris: Gallimard.

Nordstrom, Carolyn (2000) 'Shadows and sovereigns', *Theory, Culture & Society*, 17(4): 35–54.

Nozick, Robert (1975) *Anarchy, State and Utopia*. Oxford: Blackwell.

Nussbaum, Martha (1995) 'Human capabilities, female human beings', in Martha Nussbaum and Jonathan Glover (eds) *Women, Culture and Development*. Oxford: Clarendon Press, pp. 61–104.

Nussbaum, Martha (2000) *Women and Human Development: The Capabilities Approach*. New York: Cambridge University Press.

Nussbaum, Martha (2002) *Beyond the Social Contract: Toward Global Justice*. Cambridge, MA: Harvard University Press.

Nussbaum, Martha and Glover, Jonathan (eds) (1995) *Women, Culture and Development*. Oxford: Clarendon Press.

Ondaatje, Michael (2000) *Anil's Ghost*. London: Bloomsbury.

Ong, Aihwa (2000) 'Graduated sovereignty in South-East Asia', *Theory, Culture & Society*, 17(4): 55–76.

Ong, Aihwa (2003) *Buddha is Hiding: Refugees, Citizenship, the New America*. Berkeley, CA. University of California Press.

Ong, Aihwa and Collier, Stephen (2004) *Global Assemblages*. Oxford: Blackwell.

Osborne, Peter (1995) *The Politics of Time*. London: Verso.

Osborne, Peter and Sandford, Stella (eds) (2002) *Philosophies of Race and Ethnicity*. London: Continuum.

Oxfam Report (2002) *Rigged Rules and Double Standards*. Oxford: Oxfam.

Ozment, Steven (ed.) (1971) *The Reformation in Medieval Perspectives*. Chicago: Quadrangle Books.

Pagden, A. (1993) *European Encounters with the New World*. New Haven, CT: Yale University Press.

Pahuja, Sundhya (2004) 'IMF conditionality and the South as legal subject', in Peter Fitzpatrick and Patricia Tuitt (eds) *Critical Beings: Law, Nation and the Global Subject*. Aldershot: Ashgate, pp. 161–79.

Panday, G. (1988) 'Peasant revolt and Indian nationalism', in Ranajit Guha and Gayatri Spivak (eds) *Selected Subaltern Studies*. Delhi: Oxford University Press.

Papoulias, Tina (2002) 'The uses of memory in social constructionism: how culture enters the psyche', unpublished PhD thesis, University of East London.

Parreras, Rhacel Salazar (2001) *Servants of Globalisation: Women, Migration, and Domestic Work*. Stanford, CA: Stanford University Press.

Parry, Benita (1997) 'The postcolonial: conceptual category or chimera?', *Yearbook of English Studies* 27: 3–21.

Pasquino, Pasquale (1978) 'Theatrum politicum: the genealogy of capital – police and the state of prosperity', trans. Colin Gordon, *Ideology & Consciousness*, 4: 41–54.

Patterson, Wendy (2002) *Strategic Narrative: New Perspectives on the Power of Personal and Cultural Stories*. New York: Lexington Books.

Patton, Paul (2000) *Deleuze and the Political*. London: Routledge.

Pheng Cheah (2004) *Spectral Nationality. Passages of Freedom from Kant to Postcolonial Literatures of Liberation*. New York: Columbia University Press.

Prakash, Gyan (1992) 'Postcolonial criticism and Indian historiography', in *Social Text*, 31/32: 8–19.

Pratt, Mary Louise (1992) *Imperial Eyes: Travel Writing and Transculturation*. London: Routledge.

Prigogine, Ilya and Stengers, Isabelle (1984) *Order Out of Chaos: Man's Dialogue with Nature*. London: Heinemann.

Procacci, Giovanna (1978) 'Social economy and the government of poverty', in *Ideology & Consciousness*, 4: 55–72.

Quayson, Ato (2000) *Postcolonialism: Theory, Practice or Process?* Cambridge: Polity.

Radstone, Susannah and Hodgkin, Katharine (eds) (2003) *Regimes of Memory*. London: Routledge.

Rai, S.M. (2002) *Gender and the Political Economy of Development*. Cambridge: Polity.

Rawls, John (1971) *A Theory of Justice*. Oxford: Oxford University Press.

Ricoeur, Paul (1984) 'The creativity of language', in Richard Kearney (ed.) *Dialogues with Contemporary Continental Thinkers*. Manchester: Manchester University Press.

Ricoeur, Paul (1988) *Time and Narrative*, vol. 3, trans. Kathleen Blamey and David Pellauer. Chicago: University of Chicago Press.

Ricoeur, Paul (1991) 'Discussion: Ricoeur on narrative' and 'Narrative identity', in David Wood (ed.) *On Paul Ricoeur*. London: Routledge.

Ricoeur, Paul (1992) *Oneself as Another*, trans. Kathleen Blamey. Chicago. University of Chicago Press.

Ricoeur, Paul (1996) 'A new ethos for Europe', in Paul Ricoeur *The Hermeneutics of Action*, ed. Richard Kearney. London: Sage.

Roberts, Gwyneth (1996) 'Under the hatches', in Bill Schwarz (ed.) *The Expansion of England: Race, Ethnicity and Cultural History*. London: Routledge.

Robertson, Roland (1994) *Globalization: Social Theory and Global Culture*. London: Sage.

Rodney, Walter ([1972] 1989) *How Europe Underdeveloped Africa*. Nairobi: Heinemann Kenya.

Rose, Kalima (1997) 'SEWA: women in movement', in Nalini Viswanathan et al. (eds) *The Women, Gender and Development Reader*. London: Zed Books, pp. 382–6.

Rose, Nikolas (1979) 'The psychological complex: mental measurement and social administration', *Ideology & Consciousness*, 5: 5–70.

Rose, Nikolas (1985) *The Psychological Complex*. London: Routledge.

Rose, Nikolas (1989) *Governing the Soul*. London: Routledge.

Rose, Nikolas (1996) 'Identity, genealogy, history', in Stuart Hall and Paul du Gay (eds) *Questions of Cultural Identity*. London: Sage.

Roy, Arundhati (2002) *The Algebra of Infinite Justice*. London: HarperCollins.

Ryan, Alan (1987) *Property*. Minneapolis: Open University Press/University of Minnesota Press.

Safran, William (1991) 'Diasporas in modern societies: myths of homeland and return', *Diaspora*, 1: 83–99.

Said, Edward (1978) *Orientalism*. London: Routledge.

Said, Edward (1993) *Culture and Imperialism*. London: Chatto and Windus.

Sakai, Naoki (1997) *Translation and Subjectivity*. Minneapolis: University of Minnesota Press.

Sakai, Naoki (2001) 'Dislocations of the West and the status of the humanities', *Traces*, 1: 71–94.

Sangari, Kumkum and Vaid, Sudesh (eds) (1993) *Recasting Women: Essays in Indian Colonial History*. New Delhi: Kali for Women.

Santner, Eric (2002) *On the Psychotheology of Everyday Life: Reflections on Freud and Rosenzweig*. Chicago: University of Chicago Press.

Sassen, Saskia (1999) *Globalization and its Discontents: Essays on the New Mobility of People and Money*. New York: New Press.

Sassen, Saskia (2000) *Cities in the World Economy*. Thousands Oaks, CA: Sage.

Sassen, Saskia (2001) *The Global City: New York, London, Tokyo*, new edn. Princeton, NJ: Princeton University Press.

Sassen, Saskia (2002) *Global Networks/Linked Cities*. New York: Routledge.
Sayyid, Bobby (1997) *A Fundamental Fear. Eurocentrism and the Emergence of Islamism*. London: Zed Books.
Sayyid, S. (2005) 'Mirror, mirror. Western democrats, oriental despots?', *Ethnicities* 5(1): 30–50.
Schwarz, Bill (ed.) (1996) *The Expansion of England: Race, Ethnicity and Cultural History*. London: Routledge.
Sen, Amartya (1985) *Commodities and Capabilities*. Amsterdam: Elsevier.
Sen, Amartya (1990) 'Gender and cooperative conflicts', in Irene Tinker (ed.) *Persistent Inequalities: Women and World Development*. New York: Oxford University Press.
Sen, Amartya and Nussbaum, Martha (1993) *The Quality of Life*. Oxford: Clarendon Press.
Sen, Jai, Anand, Anita, Escobar, Arturo and Waterman, Peter (2004) *World Social Forum: Challenging Empires*. New Delhi: Viveka Foundation.
Sennett, Richard (1976) *The Fall of Public Man*. Cambridge: Cambridge University Press.
Shapiro, Ian (1999) *Democratic Justice*. New Haven, CT: Yale University Press.
Sherman, Alexie (1998) *Smoke Signals*. New York: Miramax Books.
Shiva Vandana (1989) *Staying Alive: Women, Ecology, and Development*. London: Zed Books.
Shohat, Ella and Stam, Robert (1994) *Unthinking Eurocentrism: Multiculturalism and the Media*. London: Routledge.
Silverman, Kaja (1988) *The Acoustic Mirror: The Female Voice in Psychoanalysis and Cinema*. Bloomington, IN: Indiana University Press.
Silverman, Kaja (2000) *World Spectators*. Stanford: Stanford University Press.
Simone, Abdou Maliq (2001) 'The worldling of African cities', *African Studies Review*, 44.
Smith, Adam ([1776] 1812) *The Wealth of Nations*. London.
Sousa Santos, B. de (2004) 'The WSF: toward a counter-hegemonic globalization', in Jai Sen, Anita Anand, Arturo Escobar and Peter Waterman *World Social Forum: Challenging Empires*. New Delhi: Viveka Foundation, pp. 235–45.
Spivak, Gayatri Chakravorty (1985) 'The Rani of Sirmur', in F. Barker (ed.) *Europe and its Others*, vol. 1. Colchester: University of Essex Press.
Spivak, Gayatri Chakravorty (1988) *In Other Worlds*. London: Routledge.
Stengers, Isabelle (1997) *Power and Invention: Situating Science*. Minneapolis: University of Minnesota Press.
Stiglitz, J. (2002) *Globalization and its Discontents*. London: Penguin.
Strange, Susan (1998) *Mad Money*. Manchester: Manchester University Press.
Stubbs, Richard and Underhill, Geoffrey (eds) (2000) *Political Economy and the Changing Global Order*. Oxford: Oxford University Press.
Suleri, S. (1992) *The Rhetoric of English India*. Chicago: University of Chicago Press.
Tagore, Rabindranath (1922) *Creative Unity*. London: Macmillan.
Tamari, Tomoko (2002) 'The socio-cultural role of department stores and the formation of gender identity in Japan', unpublished PhD thesis, Nottingham Trent University.
Tarde, Gabriel (1999) *Monadologie et sociologie*. Paris: Les Empêcheurs de penser en rond.
Taussig, Michael (1993a) *Shamanism, Colonialism and the Wild Man: A Study in Terror and Healing*. Chicago: University of Chicago Press.
Taussig, Michael (1993b) *Mimesis and Alterity* London: Routledge.
Taylor, Charles (1989) *Sources of the Self: The Making of the Modern Identity*. Cambridge: Cambridge University Press.
Taylor, Charles (1994) 'The politics of recognition', in *Multiculturalism: Examining the Politics of Recognition*, ed. Amy Gutmann. Princeton, NJ: Princeton University Press, pp. 25–74.
Teivainen, Teivo and Wallerstein, Immanuel (2002) *Enter Economism, Exit Politics: Experts, Economic Policy and the Political*. London: Zed Books..
Todorov, Tzvetan ([1982] 1992) *The Conquest of America*, trans. Richard Howard. New York: Harper Perennial.
Tomlinson, John (1991) *Cultural Imperialism*. Baltimore, MD: Johns Hopkins University Press.
Tomlinson, John (1999) *Globalization and Culture*. Cambridge: Polity Press.
Touraine, Alain (2000) *Can We Live Together: Equality and Difference*, trans. David Macey. London: Polity Press.

Trinh Minh-ha (1989) *Woman, Native, Other*. Bloomington: Indiana University Press.

Trinh Minh-ha (1996) 'The undone interval', in I. Chambers and L. Curti (eds) *The Post-Colonial Question*. London: Routledge.

Vattimo, Gianni (1988) *The End of Modernity*, trans. Jon Snyder. Cambridge: Polity Press.

Venn, Couze (1982) 'Beyond the science–ideology relation', unpublished PhD thesis, University of Essex.

Venn, Couze (1998) 'Algeria and Occidentalism', *Parallax* 7: 79–88.

Venn, Couze (1993) *Occidentalism and its Discontents*, monograph. London: University of East London.

Venn, Couze (2000) *Occidentalism: Modernity and Subjectivity*. London: Sage.

Venn, Couze (2002a) 'Altered states: post-enlightenment cosmopolitanism and transmodern socialities', *Theory, Culture & Society*, 19(1/2): 65–80.

Venn, Couze (2002b) 'Refiguring subjectivity after modernity', in Valerie Walkerdine (ed.) *Challenging Subjects*. Basingstoke: Palgrave.

Venn, Couze (2004) 'Post-Lacanian affective economy, being-in-the-world, and the critique of the present', *Theory, Culture & Society*, 21(1): 149–58.

Venn, Couze (2005) 'The city as assemblage', paper delivered at the 'Negotiating Urban Conflicts' Conference, April, Darmstadt.

Venn, Couze (2005) 'The Repetition of Violence: Dialogue, the Exchange of Memory, and the Question of Convivial Socialities', *Social Identities* 11(3): 283–298.

Verges, Françoise (1996) 'Chains of madness, chains of colonialism: Fanon and freedom', in Alan Read (ed.) *The Fact of Blackness*. London: Institute for Contemporary Arts, pp. 46–75.

Virilio, Paul (1986) *Speed and Politics: An Essay on Dromology*. New York: Semiotext(e).

Visvanathan, N., Duggan, L., Nisonoff, L. and Wiegersma, N. (eds) (1997). *The Women, Gender and Development Reader*. London: Zed Books.

Viswanathan, Gauri (1989) *Masks of Conquest*. London: Faber and Faber.

Vološinov, V.N. (1973) *Marxism and the Philosophy of Language*, trans. Ladislav Matejka and I.R. Titunik. New York: Seminar Press.

Waddingham, Sally (2004) 'The question of corporate social responsibility in the age of neo-liberal capitalism', unpublished seminar paper (PhD research), Nottingham Trent University.

Wallerstein, Immanuel (1974, 1980, 1989) 3 vols. *The Modern World System*. New York: Academic Press.

Wallerstein, Immanuel (1991) *Geopolitics and Geocultures: The Changing World-System*. Cambridge: Cambridge University Press.

Watt, Ian (1957) *The Rise of the Novel*. Berkeley, CA: University of California Press.

Waugh, Patricia (ed.) (1992) *Postmodernism: A Reader*. London: Edward Arnold.

Wild, Anthony (2004) *Coffee: A Dark History*. London: Fourth Estate.

Wilden, A. ([1968] 1981) *Speech and Language in Psychoanalysis*. Baltimore, MD: Johns Hopkins University Press.

Williams, Eric (1964) *Capitalism and Slavery*. London: Andre Deutsch.

Williams, Patrick and Chrisman, Laura (eds) (1993) *Colonial Discourse and Post-Colonial Theory: A Reader*. Hemel Hempstead: Harvester Wheatsheaf.

Yates, Frances (1964) *Giordano Bruno and the Hermetic Tradition*. London: Vintage.

Yates, Frances (1983) *The Occult Philosophy in the Elizabethan Age*. London: Ark Paperbacks.

Young, Iris Marion (1990) 'Throwing like a girl and other essays', in *Feminist Philosophy and Social Theory*. Bloomington: Indiana University Press.

Young, Iris Marion (2000) *Inclusion and Democracy*. Oxford: Oxford University Press.

Young, R. (1990) *White Mythologies*. London: Routledge.

Young, Robert (1998) 'Ideologies of the postcolonial', *Interventions*, 1(1): 4–8.

Young, Robert J.C. (2001) *Postcolonialism: An Historical Introduction*. Oxford: Blackwell.

Young, Robert J.C. (2003) *Postcolonialism: A Very Short Introduction*. Oxford: Oxford University Press.

Index

Transitional space, 86, 99
Transcolonial and transmodern, 126
Transculturation, 81, 85, 117, 162
Translation, 84, 88
Translation as trope, 162, ff.
Transmodern, 1
Triangular Trade, 27
Trinh, Minh-ha, 26, 61, 100
Turner, 86

Unequal exchange, 138
Uneven development, 123, 153
Unita, 156
Universal rights, 158 (Glossary)
Universal tax rate, 167
Universalism, 72, 166, 170
Universalism and particularism, 2
Utility, 125

Vani tradition, 158
Veil as trope, 33
'Veil of ignorance', 166
Venn, C., 3, 7, 12, 16, 81, 103, 104, 114,
   142, 145, 168, 174, fn. 12,
Verges, F., 100
Vernacular cosmopolitanism, 16, 128
Vietnam, 33, 34
Violence, epistemic, ontological and
   symbolic, 11
Virtualization, 146

Viswanathan, G., 28, 75, 76, fn. 13
Viswanathan, N., et al., 159

Waddingham, S., 144, 172, fn. 5
Wallerstein, I., 123,
Walsh, R., 18
War machine, 125
Watt, I., 61
Weak nationalism, 69
Wealth and property, 129, 140, 144
Wealth of nation and colony, 63
Welfarism, 132
Westernization, 46, 67, 83, 85, 87, 88
Wild, A., 134
Williams, E., 171, fn. 1
Williams and Chrisman, 38, fn. 2
Working through, 114
World Bank, 135, 138, 139, 152, 154
   and sex tourism, 173, fn. 10
Worlding, 77, 124
World governance, 128
'World order', 161
WTO and IMF, 161, 164
World poverty, 151
World, Social Forum, 127
World systems theory, 123

Yates, F., 51, 52
Young, I.M., 166
Young, R., 2, 4, 34, 35, 38, fn. 2

Lightning Source UK Ltd.
Milton Keynes UK
UKHW022033051021
391692UK00003B/127